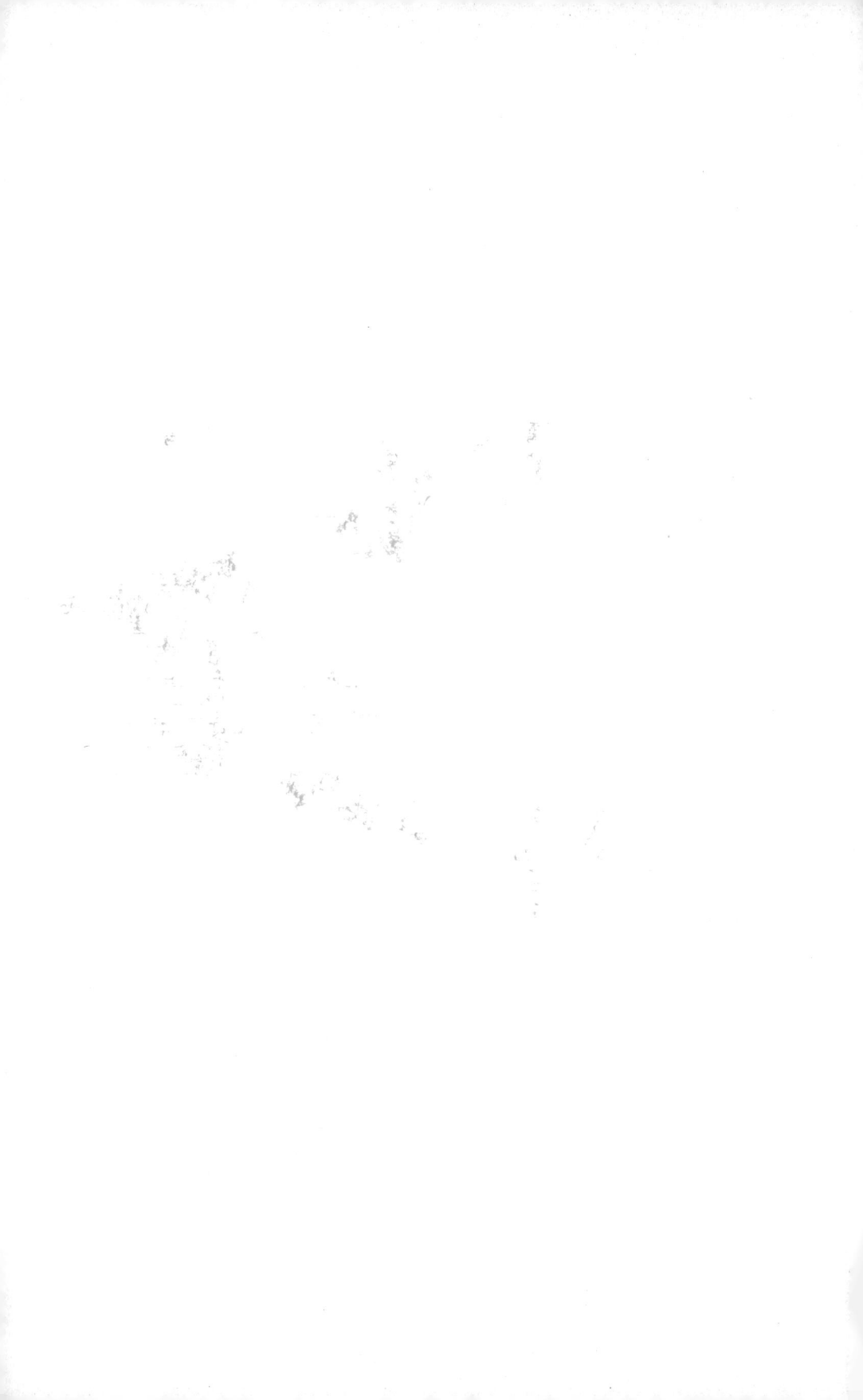

LANDSCAPE AND SOCIETY IN CONTEMPORARY IRELAND

Brendan McGrath

LANDSCAPE AND SOCIETY IN CONTEMPORARY IRELAND

CORK **cup** UNIVERSITY PRESS

First published in 2013 by
Cork University Press
Youngline Industrial Estate
Pouladuff Road, Togher
Cork, Ireland

British Library Cataloguing in Publication data.
A CIP catalogue record for this book is available from the Library of Congress.

ISBN: 978-1-909005-71-6

Printed by Graphy Cems, Navarra, Spain.
Designed and typeset by Anú Design, Tara.

Maps reproduced by kind permission of Ordnance Survey Ireland
Ordnance Survey Ireland Permit No. 8881
© Ordnance Survey Ireland/Government of Ireland

National Mapping Agency
www.osi.ie

CONTENTS

For Nelleke and Karina

ACKNOWLEDGMENTS

This book would not have been possible without generous financial help from family and friends; Pauline and Andy Smith, Patricia Buesnel, Janet and Graham Webb, Camilla Beglan and John O'Connell. I also wish to thank Dennis Latimer and Biddy White Lennon for their encouragement and advice when I first got the idea of the book. Later on Paul Caprani reviewed a manuscript and his enthusiastic response gave me the confidence to submit for publication. The final chapters deal with on-going landscape initiatives. In this regard I am grateful to Dr Brendan Dunford of the Burren Farming for Conservation Programme for his views on current progress in the Burren, to Susanne Forslund and her colleague Ann Moreau in Kalmar County, Sweden for their observations about Southern Öland and to Dr Mary Tubridy and Deborah Tiernan for bringing me up to date on the Howth Special Amenity Area Order. I also wish to acknowledge the contribution of the anonymous reviewers of Cork University Press. Needless to say, while the book benefits from these different viewpoints, its contents are entirely my responsibility.

Chapter 1

INTRODUCTION

———————

In 1999 Clare County Council put up signs beside the access roads to my neighbourhood that welcomed motorists to 'the Burren Protected Landscape'. The message on the signs surprised me because the Burren is not a 'protected landscape' in any generally accepted sense of the term. I used to pass one of the signs on my way to work and was able to monitor the landscape change around the sign on a daily basis. Shortly after the sign went up the old dry-stone wall beside it was replaced by a concrete post-and-rail fence. This was part of an EU-funded road improvement scheme being implemented by the council.

Nearby, over several days, a landowner, with the help of a JCB, razed level a limestone outcrop and its hazel thicket to make way for a brand new field that was topped off with truck-loads of imported soil. Meanwhile, on the other side of the Burren an ugly array of signage, most of it unauthorised, became the backdrop for another 'welcome' sign (see Figs. 1.1 and 1.2). These various bits of new development in the last dozen years are unexceptional in themselves. But they drew my attention because of their proximity to that simple and unequivocal declaration of landscape protection. The contrast between the public message and what was happening around the signs is just one illustration of the unsatisfactory relationship that exists between contemporary Irish society and the places that it inhabits.

This book is an examination of that relationship. The book is about both special places like the Burren and the everyday landscape experience. My aim is to give an account of contemporary Irish landscape and to describe and to explain how and why it has changed over the last forty years. These tasks are undertaken in four stages. In this introduction and the next two chapters I consider what landscape is and I outline the distinctive character of the Irish landscape heritage. Chapters 3 and 4 then describe landscape change and conflict over the last four decades, a period of turbulence and transformation that stands out from the decades of relative calm that came before. If there is no doubt about the wealth of our heritage there is equally no doubt about the problematic relationship that exists between Irish society and its heritage. That legacy is explored in the third section of the book under the headings property and commodity; history, memory and dreams; and beauty. In 1994 Fintan O'Toole suggested that 'Irish society has skipped the evolutionary stage when a society rediscovers the sacred'. Ireland, according to O'Toole, 'has become a post-modern society in which landscape is viewed only as a commodity'.[1] The engagement of contemporary Irish society with the physical world it inhabits is at least as distinctive and striking as the landscape heritage of the island. Having tried to achieve some degree of understanding of that engagement, the final chapters examine specific types of landscape change and the landscape heritage of our generation.

The landscape concept

Sometimes, beguiled by the apparent simplicity of landscape as a concept, we make the mistake of assuming that when we look at a hill or a lake, family members and neighbours see the same thing and feel the same about it. We assume a shared response that does not exist. Discussions about landscape have the capacity to be thoroughly disconcerting because they can reveal differences

Figs 1.1 and **1.2.** Road signs erected beside approach roads to the Burren in 1999 and photographed in 2007. They carry an unequivocal message that is belied by landscape changes in their immediate vicinity. An ugly array of signage, most of it unauthorised, forms the backdrop to the sign in the top photograph, while, in the bottom image, soon after the sign was put up, a concrete post-and-rail fence replaced the dry-stone wall that had formed the road boundary.

of perspective that challenge our comprehension of other people. Some years ago when I worked as a planner in Clare County Council I learnt a painful lesson when I promised a local woman to check on her son's planning application. He had wanted to build a house on the family farm. I was not long in Clare at the time, arriving when the Mullaghmore Visitor Centre saga was drawing to a conclusion. The issue had split the north Clare community in two, the majority of farmers and other locals strongly supporting the Office of Public Works (OPW) proposal to build a visitor centre at the foot of Mullaghmore at the southern end of the Burren. However, I knew that members of this family had supported the Burren Action Group, an ad hoc grouping that had successfully campaigned against the development. I made enquiries about the planning application, as requested, and found out that it was going to be refused permission. The family had chosen a site that was unsuitable for a house for several reasons that included landscape, public health and environmental considerations. This, of course, was unwelcome news but I was confident that a new application could succeed on another, less sensitive site within the large farm holding and I would offer my help in selecting the new site. I decided to drop in to the farm with my wife one Sunday evening. We were warmly welcomed, as I had expected, and we were shown into the kitchen where the family was gathered. Tea was poured and home-made scones produced. However, when they heard my news the convivial atmosphere evaporated. I was bluntly told that the treatment of their brother and son was intolerable. I can still recall the physical sensation of that torrent of verbal abuse. We sat speechless and helpless, hemmed in by bodies and furniture. I had foolishly and very naively assumed that people whom I had taken a liking to on the briefest of acquaintances and who had supported an environment campaign, with which I had sympathy, would be persuaded by a technically competent appraisal of a proposed development on their own land. I had assumed that the problem with the planning application was a lack of information that could be remedied by professional advice rather than one of fundamentally different perspectives about development on their farm.

Landscape matters to us in different ways. At its simplest, landscape is what we see when we look out a window. Views from windows, from roads and streets, are part of everyday experience and contribute to the quality of our lives. Our encounter with a landscape may last a few minutes or it may stretch over a lifetime. Even the briefest of encounters has value and quality. As a tourist we may be moved by a glimpse of a green valley in the shadow of a high mountain. We see what is in front of our eyes and interpret it according to preferences and expectations formed in other places. An inhabitant of that valley, who has lived there all his life, may derive no enjoyment from that same view but may ponder on how the valley has changed over the course of his lifetime. These are two very

Fig 1.3. Housing jostling for position on the shores of Lough Derg in 2007. This high-cost residential area of Cullenagh, Ballina in County Tipperary has developed in a piecemeal fashion over the years. The housing area lacks basic infrastructure such as a reliable water supply and footpaths and managed open spaces but the houses all have their views of the lake.

different but equally valid responses to a physical landscape – one a snapshot, the other fashioned by a life in a place.

Our response to landscape is affected by how we experience it. J.W. O'Connell prefaces an anecdote about the Burren by recalling how William Wordsworth in 1844 objected to the building of a railway to the Lake District.[2] Wordsworth's view was that the Lake District should be approached slowly and carefully as befitted a special place. O'Connell tells the story of a Dubliner who, having driven through the Burren to Lisdoonvarna, was overheard asking a shop assistant in Lisdoonvarna where the Burren was, a question which probably would not have arisen had he walked or cycled there. The best way to appreciate the Erne–Shannon waterway is on a slow boat. Glimpses of the river and its lakes from nearby roads are usually a poor substitute for the views from the water. The watery labyrinth that is Upper Lough Erne, one of Ireland's hidden jewels, the strong character of the Shannonside villages and towns and the majestic site of Clonmacnoise are all best appreciated from the water. But driving also has its pleasures. The motorway building programme of the last decade has restored to Irish motorists the opportunity to glide through an unfolding landscape with vistas undisturbed by roadside clutter.

We give rein to our senses in the physical landscape. Sight is dominant but all the senses play their part. The most ephemeral of sensations can be memorable – a sudden burst of sunlight illuminating a hillside, the sound of a church bell across a still lake, a glimpse of a fox on an empty street. Poets bring these experiences to life by meticulous observation and description. At the level of the individual all these interactions, ranging from a moment in time to a guiding vision, from delight in a view seen for the first time to a proprietary sense of place, contribute to our connectedness with landscape and our wellbeing.

It is this appreciation of landscape as an important component of the quality of everyday living that is spurring a concerted effort to make landscape

Fig. 1.4. Larne Lough, County Antrim in 2003, viewed from Muldersleigh Hill. For a brief time early morning mist bequeaths an ethereal quality to this degraded industrial landscape.

conservation a serious political issue in Europe. Ireland is a signatory to the European Landscape Convention that was adopted in Florence in 2000 and thirty of the forty-seven member states of the Council of Europe are now signatories. The preamble to the convention states that 'landscape is an important quality of life for people everywhere; in urban areas and the countryside, in degraded areas as well as in areas of high quality, in areas recognised as being of outstanding beauty as well as everyday areas . . . is a key element of individual and social well-being and . . . its protection, management and planning entail rights and responsibilities for everyone'.[3]

The word 'landscape' appeared in the English language in the sixteenth century, derived from the Middle Dutch word *lantscap*, with the very limited meaning of 'denoting a picture of natural scenery'. At that time Flemish painters developed a specialisation in painting topography. Some of these artists moved to Italy, where landscape painting became an established genre and where the Flemish painters also worked on the landscape backgrounds of other artists' paintings. A Flemish painter, William Van der Hagen, who probably arrived in Ireland in the 1720s began the Irish tradition of landscape painting. Michelangelo commented that 'in Flanders they paint with a view to external exactness or such things as may cheer you and on which you cannot speak ill, as for example saints and prophets. They paint stuffs and masonry, the green grass of fields, the shadow of trees and rivers and bridges, which they call landscape, with many figures on this side and many on that. [They paint] without reason or art, without symmetry or proportion, without skilful choice or boldness'.[4] There is no trace of a conscious appreciation of landscape in the 1,000 years of Gaelic literary tradition that stretches from the early monasteries to the eighteenth century. While there is much evidence of a love of nature, it is not until the end of the eighteenth century that landscape begins to be consciously celebrated, such as in Brian Merriman's 'The Midnight Court' composed in 1780.[5]

In most European languages, including Irish (*tirdhreach*, comprising *tir* (land) and *dhreach* (appearance, aspect or look) a single word embraces both the physical description of an area of topography and the emotional experience of that topography. Only Russian, borrowing words from other European languages, has different words for different aspects of landscape. In Russian *landshaft* is the objective landscape and *peyzazh* is landscape in emotional and artistic terms. A Russian landscape architect is a *landshafniki* while a landscape painter is a *peyzazhist*.[6]

'Landscape' generally means much the same as 'scenery' in everyday use in Ireland today. This use of the word is hardly different to its meaning in the sixteenth century other than referring directly to the physical world rather than a painted impression of it. Used in this manner, landscape is something physical that is separate from the viewer and can be viewed with a detached and

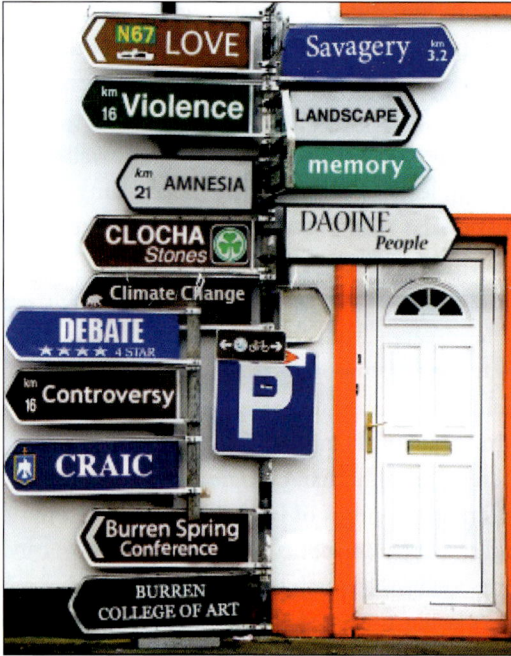

Fig. 1.6.
Programme cover for a 2009 conference on the landscape of the Burren. The illustration is a 'photoshopped' version of a much photographed signpost in Ballyvaughan. The signpost was once used as part of a Fáilte Ireland promotion with the catch-line 'and this is what our Irish friends planned for us before lunch'.[10]

sense of place is often regarded as a defining characteristic of Irish culture, certainly of its literature and poetry. Seamus Heaney has compared the poetry of Patrick Kavanagh, whose sense of place was part of his birthright, with the work of John Montague whose connection to the landscape of Tyrone was forged through knowledge and experience.[12] Most of us are in John Montague's position. As society has become more urban and more transient, a sense of place is no longer automatically part of birthright but something that is consciously acquired in life. I suggest that in Irish society sense of place and knowledge of local landscape are becoming increasingly conscious aspirations.

If 'landscape' is problematical, 'landscape heritage' is even more so. Landscapes and seascapes are part of the brief of the Heritage Council that was set up as a statutory advisory body to help safeguard the country's heritage. However, the majority of people do not recognise landscape as being part of that heritage. Neolithic tombs and medieval churches and tower houses are seen as heritage but their landscape settings are not. This situation contrasts strongly with other countries. At an international landscape symposium some years ago a British artist proclaimed that 'More than their poets, or their architecture, the English love their landscape, and woe betide any who would threaten it.'[13] It is difficult to imagine a similar statement being uttered in Ireland and, if it were, it is inconceivable that anyone would take it seriously. In a 2006 national survey of attitudes to heritage, landscape was given the lowest priority for protection behind virtually every other heritage category.[14]

Table 1.1. summarises a contemporary definition of landscape and its diverse components.

Table 1.1 A Definition of Landscape

LANDSCAPE =	Nature	PLUS	People
LANDSCAPE =	The Past	PLUS	The Present
LANDSCAPE =	Physical attributes (scenery, nature, historic heritage)	PLUS	Associative values (social and cultural)

Source: *Management Guidelines for IUCN Category v Protected Areas* (Gland, Switzerland: International Union for the Conservation of Nature and Natural Resources (IUCN), 2002), p. 5.

Fig. 1.7. Parknabinnia wedge tomb at Roughan Hill in the Burren, photographed in 2009. There is a general acknowledgement that monuments like this tomb are part of our national heritage but there is much less appreciation that the surrounding landscapes are also part of that heritage. At this location the tomb is just one element of an extensive Late Neolithic/Early Bronze Age landscape of homesteads, fields and tombs, part of a larger cultural landscape that has been settled for millennia.

Fig. 1.8. A NAMA controlled landscape in the winter of 2010, on the northern outskirts of Ennis. NAMA (National Assets Management Agency) controls this housing estate in which half the houses are vacant. There is a possibility that some of the housing will be demolished. Part of the skyline is the cliff face of Whelan's limestone quarry, closed down as a result of legal action by NAMA in 2010.

The aim of this book is to describe contemporary landscape in Ireland and to analyse how it has changed and is changing. In order to do this honestly and effectively I need to set out my own background. I am a town planning consultant who grew up in England but who has spent most of his working life in Ireland. I have worked in a number of Irish local authorities and I have also worked in several developing countries in Africa and Australasia. This broad experience has taught me to be wary of simple explanations of landscape and, if at all possible, to avoid describing and trying to explain places that I do not know reasonably well. We humans seem to have an irresistible urge to extract meaning from landscape, regardless of our competency in a given situation. Therefore, while my objective is a comprehensive review, I have tried to do this by reference only to the places that I know. The choice of place is therefore idiosyncratic because I have mined my own direct experience, the main exception being Erris in Mayo where I have relied on a number of separate accounts of the ongoing Ballinaboy terminal and pipeline saga. County Clare gets disproportionate attention for no better reason than I live there, although I believe that the Burren offers an exceptional case study of contemporary Irish landscape in all its guises.

I have written the book from the perspective of a planning practitioner.

For all its shortcomings, the statutory planning system is a forum in which landscape issues and conflicts are exposed and confronted on a regular basis. There is probably no better way than working in the system to gain insight about landscape in contemporary Irish society. The landscape role is highly distinctive, a distinctiveness that has been heightened by the physical consequences of the property market collapse in Ireland in 2008. The extent of 'ghost villages' and 'ghost estates' may have been exaggerated in the media but they are graphic manifestations of a dysfunctional landscape relationship. More so than the other environmental professions, striving for balance between competing social, economic and environmental objectives is a core element of the planning ethos. That holistic outlook equips the planner better than most to view landscape in all its complexity.

The book itself, a consequence of my own engagement with the world, to use the wider definition of 'landscape' offered by Conor Newman, is just one representation of contemporary Irish landscape. On the basis of how thinking about landscape has changed so much over the last half century, I have little doubt that, even in a few short years, much of what I offer here will eventually come to appear dated and short-sighted but will nevertheless retain value as a perspective of Irish landscape at the turn of the century.

Chapter 2

CULTURE

———

When my wife and I moved to this rural area of north Clare in 1999 we got to know the farmers around us. With two exceptions they are full-time farmers who have lived here all their lives. One of them drops in for a chat from time to time. He once told us about a farmer who had lived a few miles to the north of our home. This man had owned an extraordinary cow that could produce an endless supply of milk until the day it was killed by a neighbour. The cow's fantastic talent was the only clue that we were listening to an account of something 'out of the ordinary'.

Fig. 2.1. Winter grazing in 2004 at Slievenaglasha, the home place of the legendary Lon the Smith (Lon Mac Liomhta).

I subsequently found out that we had heard an ancient Burren tale about a smith called Lon Mac Liomhta and his cow Glas Ghaibhneach. The smith had stolen the fabulous animal in Spain and brought her back to his fortress home in the Burren. There the cow had filled any vessel placed beneath her, until the day she had tried to fill a sieve that was presented to her by a jealous neighbour. The milk that had flowed from the sieve turned into the seven streams of Taosca, which can still be seen, flowing over the rim of an otherwise waterless plateau. What made the story so memorable was that it was not possible to distinguish the quality of its telling from the humdrum gossip in the rest of the conversation. I later heard the story recounted with more finesse at a folk night in a pub in Ennis but that telling had none of the impact of the tale told at our kitchen table.

That experience has been the extent of my direct contact with what is a dying tradition of a magical and spiritual interpretation of landscape. Others have been more fortunate. Seamus Heaney, writing in 1980, acknowledged the good fortune of his own birthright in Derry.

The landscape was sacramental, instinct with signs, implying a system of reality beyond the visible realities. Only thirty years ago and thirty miles from Belfast, I think I experienced this kind of world vestigially and as a result may have retained some vestigial sense of place as it was experienced in the older dispensation. As I walked to school, I saw Lough

Beg from Mulholland's Brae, and the spire of Church Island rose out of the trees. On Church Island Sunday in September, there was a pilgrimage out to the island, because St. Patrick was supposed to have prayed there, and prayed with such intensity that he branded the shape of his knee into a stone in the old churchyard. The rainwater that collected in that stone, of course, has healing powers, and the thorn bush beside it was pennanted with the rags used by those who rubbed their warts and sores in the water. Then on a clear day, out in the Antrim hills beyond Lough Beg, I could see the unmistakable hump of Slemish, the mountain where the youthful Patrick had tended sheep.

He describes the rest of his walk to school through a landscape replete with spiritual and mythical references and says that 'There if you like, was the foundation for a marvellous or a magical view of the world . . .'[1]

Fig. 2.2. Walking to school each day, Seamus Heaney could see and appreciate all manner of wonderful things including, in the far distance, 'the unmistakable hump of Slemish, the mountain where the youthful Patrick had tended sheep'.

An ancient magical connection with the land had already been seriously damaged in the previous century. The historian Roy Foster records that contemporaries had noticed the abandonment of magical practices in rural life from the late 1840s as new devotional practices such as the rosary, benediction, shrines and retreats started replacing holy wells, bonfires and patterns.[2] He suggests that the trauma of the Famine played its part in undermining a trust in magic to control the natural world and put things right.

There was sometimes an acute awareness that the old connection was dying. There is a poignant description by Séamus Ó Duilearga, written in 1945, of the last years of Seán Ó Conaill of Cill Rialaigh in Kerry. Ó Conaill, who could not speak English and was illiterate in both Irish and English, was one of the great seanchaí of his generation.

> *Finally, there came a time when it was but rarely that he had opportunity himself of practising his art in public. So, lest he should lose command over the tales he loved, he used to repeat them aloud when he thought no one was near, using the gesticulations and the emphasis, and all the other tricks of narration, as if he were once again the centre of a fireside storytelling. His son Pats told me that he had seen his father thus engaged, telling his tales to an unresponsive stone wall, while herding the grazing cattle.*[3]

Our need for magical interpretation of the world is probably as strong as it ever was but nowadays that need is satisfied by story books, television, DVDs, cinema and the other products of a mass culture. My 7-year-old daughter spends a great part of her day inhabiting imaginary worlds of her own making and I do my best to follow her lead. However, I am self-conscious about retelling the legends of the local landscape even though they are as rich as any created or recycled by Disney or Pixar. I imagine, had I been born here and heard the stories from my own parents, I would feel differently. But I am not from here, nor have I any recollection of my own parents, who emigrated to England before I was born, telling me the old stories. I have recounted one local tale to my daughter. We live close to Lake Inchiquin, where the O'Quins used to have a castle, and there is a story of how the O'Quins came to be supplanted by the O'Briens and to disappear from history. In summary, a young chieftain of the O'Quins fell in love with a beautiful maiden who was part human and part swan. She agreed to marry him on two conditions; he had to keep their union secret and he was never to allow a member of the O'Brien clan into their home. If he broke the promise she would become a swan again and the O'Quin clan would come to an end. Of course, in the story, after many happy years together and the birth of two children, the chief forgets his promise. The story that was told at the end of the nineteenth century to local antiquarian Dr George U. Macnamara ends as follows. Too late that night, the O'Quin remembered his oath and rushed to his bedroom, only to find it empty. Out of the window 'he beheld a lone swan with two cygnets swimming towards the shore. For a moment she turned on her wretched husband one lingering glance of love and sorrow and disappearing into the grey mists of the lake, was seen no more'.[4]

I told the tale to my daughter as well as I could. She enjoyed it but it did not capture her imagination in the way that other stories do. At the time she was particularly taken with C.S. Lewis', *The Lion, The Witch and the Wardrobe* as realised in the Walt Disney film version starring Tilda Swinton as the White Witch. Although we walk most days to Lake Inchiquin and there are always swans there and we can see where the young chieftain had his castle and where he first saw the swan maiden, this direct physical link is not as potent as the computer-generated imagery rendered by the film studio.

Our popular culture has virtually lost a direct emotional connection with the world that surrounds us, a connection that probably grew in richness over the millennia of settlement and has now atrophied. There are still individuals in our midst who can summon up the magic and mystery but these experiences are no longer woven into ordinary life. It is now impossible to understand the mindset of Irish people in the sixteenth century and earlier when, according to Roy Foster, 'the literal representation of the country was less important than its poetic dimensions. In traditional bardic culture, the terrain was studied, discussed: every place had its legend and its own identity'.[5] That careful scrutiny has now become largely an esoteric exercise practised by a few scholars and poets like Tim Robinson, Seamus Heaney and Michael Longley. For the first 3,000 years of settlement in Ireland, before farming began, the connection was probably even more profound. The anthropologist Hugh Brody believes that among hunter-gatherers the ties to a place and its resources are often stronger than ties of history, community or even family.[6]

Three thousand years ago, according to legend, the sons of Mil sailed from Spain to Ireland. They made landfall in Kerry before going on to defeat the Tuatha Dé Danann and to conquer Ireland. Stepping from his boat in Ballinskelligs Bay, Allergin, one of the sons, laid claim to the land by a powerful incantation of landscape. The 'Song of Allergin' is part of the legend which was recorded by scholars in the middle ages and was part of the repertoire of local seanchaí Seán Ó Conaill in the last century. Now Paddy Bushe has reinterpreted the landscape of Ballinskelligs Bay in terms of the Milesian legend.[7] Such an imaginative response remains accessible because today's landscape is not totally different to the landscape that existed before the industrial revolution, unlike in many other places in Western Europe where industrialisation and urbanisation have obliterated the old landmarks. Nor have we lost all the knowledge of how the generations that preceded us interpreted the landscape. A pre-industrial, agrarian society survived in Ireland into the twentieth century, in time for its stories, songs and rituals to be recorded for posterity. The preservation of this legacy was a priority of the newly established state. Under Séamus Ó Duilearga, the Irish Folklore Institute, founded in 1930 and its successor, the Irish Folklore Commission, gathered an enormous collection of material. The establishment of these bodies reflected the important role given to folklore in defining the new state. There continued to be an academic focus on traditional Irish life throughout the last century, an emphasis that can in large part be explained by an urge to concentrate on those aspects of Ireland which most distinguished it from the neighbouring island of Great Britain. This led to an emphasis on relict and dying traditions sometimes at the expense of studying contemporary social upheaval. The influential *Irish Folk Ways* by Estyn Evans, published in 1957, is a case in point. In those times people had to look beyond academia, to literature, theatre and poetry, for an understanding and interpretation of contemporary rural life.[8]

The greatest scholarly landscape work of the nineteenth century was the survey of the whole island between 1833 and 1846 by the Ordnance Survey, at a scale of 6 inches to the mile. This was an imperial project with the primary purpose of mapping townlands to calculate acreages for taxation purposes. However, the surveyors went far beyond their basic brief, eventually leading to an order for the Ordnance Survey 'to revert immediately to its original object under the Valuation Acts'.[9] The maps and the surveyors' notes of the Ordnance Survey are an unparalleled historical snapshot of the Irish landscape, sometimes providing invaluable clues to assist its interpretation in the twenty-first century.

The naming of places is a basic response to living in a place, of comprehending it and taking possession of it. Place names therefore are an insight into landscape and our relationship with landscape over the centuries. It is a telling metaphor of our times that there is ambiguity and confusion about how we spell the places where we now live. We are probably the only family in Corrofin which spells the village in the official way, which is the spelling of the first edition of the Ordnance Survey. Everybody else spells the village with one 'r'. Most of the villages and towns in our area have two or more spellings of the English name; the official one and one or two unofficial versions. Many of the Ordnance Survey spellings have never 'caught on' so that throughout Ireland visitors and tourists are directed to villages and towns by road signs that have the official English spelling only to arrive at a place that spells itself differently.

Ireland has an enormous wealth of place names. To take just one county, the recently completed Kerry place names archive contains 80,000 names.[10] The maps of the Ordnance Survey only capture a fraction of the names of places that were once in everyday use. It was inevitable that the strong link between people and the land would weaken during the course of the twentieth century as Ireland became an urban society and the countryside ceased to be the place where the majority of people lived and worked. There is an astonishing wealth of place names in the countryside now lost or being lost. For instance, below the village of Inistioge in County Kilkenny, there is a graceful meander of the River Nore, 300 metres in length (see Fig. 2.3). The modern Discovery Series OS sheet names the river and Inistioge village and Woodstock Park to the south and the townlands of Coolshanvogh, Oldcourt and Clonamery that border the river. The 1839 first edition 6-inch map also names the bridge at Inistioge, two islands in the river, three quays and four dwellings on or near the meander. It shows the salmon weir downstream of Inistioge Bridge and it names the promontory of land on the inside of the meander. This amounts to eighteen named topographical references. The meander was part of a productive river fishery during the nineteenth and early twentieth centuries. The fishermen accumulated a detailed knowledge of the river which translated into a comprehensive nomenclature of the river and its banks. Interviews with the last generation of traditional cotmen revealed forty-six named features on the river meander which are either additional features to

Fig. 2.3. The meander of the River Nore downstream from Inistioge, County Kilkenny in 2005. The river is now a quiet backwater. A century ago it was a busy thoroughfare and important local fishery.

those named on the Ordnance Survey map or more elaborate versions of the Ordnance Survey names.[11] The names are diverse and colourful, for example Ettie Dalton Stocks (a cut in the bank where Ettie Dalton's boat had been moored), the Brew House, Mick's Lub (Mick's Bend), Queen Bess Salmon Weir, The Cat's Ladder and The Bolg (the pouch, deep pool).

The toponymic expert Breandán Ó Ciobhain attributes the explosion of naming in the eighteenth and nineteenth centuries to a need to differentiate an increasingly fragmented ownership of land and 'consequent exploitation of the total landscape' but, as was the case on the Nore, it is not unreasonable to surmise that the comprehensive naming of places also reflected a more general sense of proprietorship of the landscape than we share today.[12]

Many names have an older lineage, some are so old that it is only possible to speculate about their meaning. The older names offer invaluable insights into how landscape has changed over the last two millennia. Breandán Ó Ciobhain's analysis of the place names of the Iveragh peninsula in Kerry includes a study of the distribution of toponmyic elements relating to oak woods, doire (oak wood), and doirín (little oak wood).[13] On the basis that most townland names on the peninsula are about a 1,000 years old and that it takes up to 400 years for oak to mature, Ó Ciobhain concludes that the distribution of the place names reflects the distribution of oak woods in the Early Christian period. According to the place names, they were to be found across the peninsula with concentrations in

Fig. 2.4. Tomies Wood in the Killarney National Park in 2011. The wood comprises a sessile oak canopy with an open under-storey of holly. There is also birch and rowan. Such a view would have been commonplace in south-west Ireland 2,000 years ago.

and around what is now the Killarney National Park, south of the Macgillycuddy's Reeks around Sneem and in the Caragh River basin. The extensive distribution of oak woods at that time is in marked contrast to the limited distribution today.

In the last fifty years place-naming has continued at a furious pace as new residential suburbs have been built, but whereas the traditional naming of places generally derived from some characteristic of a locality or the inhabitants of the locality, much of the new naming is deliberately unrelated to local character. Many names are anodyne confections that once graced glossy sales brochures, for example The Elms, The Oaks, The Rise, The Bramblings, or they were part of the sales pitch itself, such as Georgian Village, Georgian Hamlet and Park View. The naming has been done by developers and auctioneers whose only interest in locality has been the sale of property. The modern place names are therefore often informative about place only in so far as emphasising the dislocation between society and its landscape. Only in the last decade have planning authorities started to tighten up on the choice of names and to insist on names with a local rationale, for example by using the townland name.

More often than not townland names have a straightforward meaning, but sometimes a name can be extraordinarily interesting. Two such examples are 'Anneville' in north Clare and 'Garraunbaun' in Connemara. Anneville, a small

Fig. 2.5. The townland of Anneville, otherwise Eanach an Bhile, 'the marsh of the sacred tree', viewed through the enclosure of a holy well with its 'blessed tree', dedicated to Saint Inawee. The saint is the Christian incarnation of a goddess that was worshipped by a tribe which once inhabited this area and is responsible for the modern place name.

townland outside Corrofin on the main road to Killinaboy, sounds like it was named after one of the fine Georgian villas that are to be found in the locality. In fact, as local historian Michael MacMahon has described, Anneville is a corrupt rendering by the nineteenth century map surveyors of *Eanach an Bhile*, which translates as 'the marsh of the sacred tree'.[14] Anneville is a marshy place to this day and there is still a tree there known locally as 'the Blessed Tree'(Fig. 2.5). The tree overhangs a holy well dedicated to Saint Inawee (*Iníon Bhaoith*). There are three holy wells dedicated to this saint in Killinaboy parish and there are others in mid- and north Clare.

We know nothing about Saint Inawee other than that she was worshipped by a particular tribe, Clann Ifernáin, which used to inhabit this area, having migrated into Clare from Limerick. They disappear from the historical record in the middle ages. But in the name Killinaboy (the church of the daughter of Baoth) and the holy wells dedicated to the saint, the tribe has left a faint but enduring imprint of their bardic sensibility to place.

The etymology of the townland of Garraunbaun has been untangled with skill and perseverance by Tim Robinson. The townland is in the Ballynakill area, north of Clifden in Connemara. According to the Ordnance Survey, Garraunbaun is an anglicisation of the Irish 'An Garrán Bán', the white or fallow thicket, garrán, which is a shrubbery or thicket, being a common element in place names. However, Robinson discovered various bits and pieces about Garraunbaun in his researches and travels in Connemara that eventually led him to a different explanation. From an archaeologist he heard about a standing stone of white quartz on a hill. From the field name books in the Ordnance Survey archives, kept by the surveyors who had first mapped the area in 1839, he learnt that the Irish name of the place was 'An Gearrán Bán'. From an old man who had lived in Garraunbaun House he heard the legend of a white horse that had galloped out of Garraunbaun Lake to be ridden by a man before it had plunged back into the lake. In the legend the rider had left the horse's saddle on a rock which still bore its mark but the old man did not know where that rock was. Robinson found the rock one evening, a 5 foot-high creamy-white stone standing just inside the hedge of a meadow overlooking Ballynakill Bay. In the half-light the stone looked exactly like the rump of an old white horse, peacefully grazing (See Fig. 2.6). Robinson is in no doubt that this ancient stone, which for thousands of years would have been the most prominent landmark in the area, is the source of the townland name, which is properly An Gearrán Bán, the white horse. He surmises that the folk tale he had heard from the old man is an impoverished version of an older tale of a white horse that had literally turned to stone. And that tale was a magical explanation of the standing stone, hauled up from the bay below by Bronze Age settlers and carefully sited for a purpose or purposes about which we can now only speculate.[15]

Fig. 2.6. An Gearrán Bán in Connemara with Ballynakill Harbour in the background. Tim Robinson speculates that a Bronze Age group found the large stone on one of the islands in Ballynakill Bay where there is a vein of quartz by the shore, rafted the stone across the bay and then lifted it up the hillside to this prominent position.

Robinson and the archaeological survey team from NUI Galway have discovered in this area of Galway, west of the Corrib, one of the richest concentrations of standing stones in Ireland. An Gearrán Bán is one of eighteen single standing stones in the area. There are also ten stone pairs and five rows of four or more stones. The survey team believe that the stones were erected in the late Bronze Age, which stretches from about 1500 BC to 1000 BC. They are aligned with dips in the horizon into which the sun appears to set on the shortest day and were no doubt associated with important spiritual beliefs and practices. However, Robinson also speculates that they were a highly visible expression of the dominance of a territory by these settlers, an enterprise not so different in character to the work of the imperial map makers, 3,000 years later. Robinson also surmises that the bronze age farmers would have been as mystified as we are by the monuments left behind by the Neolithic farmers a thousand or more years earlier. These people built substantial tombs which are mainly found on valley floors and near the seashore. Thirty-two such tombs have been found in north-west Connemara.

The standing stones, graves and forts, and the castles and towers of more recent times, are landmarks in the landscape, signs that we inhabit an island that has been continuously settled for millennia. This has always been recognised but the extent of the human impact in the wider landscape has not always been appreciated.

woodland area of only 52,000 hectares (less than 1 per cent) at the beginning of the twentieth century. More than 20 per cent of County Wicklow is now wooded and more than 15 per cent of counties Clare, Leitrim and Waterford but in most counties the wooded area remains below 10 per cent.[20] Even in a treeless landscape like the upland Burren, woodland would quickly appear once farming stopped. Sharon Parr of the Burren for Farming Conservation Programme has reported survival rates of 68 to 83 per cent for hazel seedlings after three to four years of seasonal grazing. 'If grazing is relaxed or removed, the seedlings are poised to begin more rapid growth and the seemingly inexorable spread of hazel will continue'.[21]

In summary, the Irish landscape has been shaped by millennia of settlement and this is most strikingly illustrated by the relative scarcity of what would otherwise have been the most common habitats on the island: forest and woodland. The quantity and distribution of woodland and of other so-called natural habitats have been decided by cultural forces.

Even though the forests were depleted, wood was such an important resource in the medieval economy that there would have been a strong tradition of woodland management and woodworking throughout the country. This tradition, which has survived and flourished in other parts of Europe, died out during the land-hungry decades of the seventeenth and eighteenth centuries to be replaced by a more equivocal relationship. Tree planting and new plantations then came to be associated as the preserves of the landed gentry rather than wider

Fig. 2.7. Hazelwood (formerly Annagh) on the shore of Lough Gill, County Sligo. This sylvan setting was created by the Wynne family about 200 years ago, one of many examples of woodlands planted in the eighteenth and nineteenth centuries and now valued for their natural quality.

society. Having lost the tradition of woodland management, Ireland has been slow to find a sustainable role for forestry over the past century, many thousands of hectares of poor-quality conifer woodland having being planted. But there is also an abiding attachment to native broadleaf woodland which comes into view whenever some kind of threat to woodland materialises. There have been successful interventions by individuals and small groups in recent decades: Tomnfinnogue Wood in Wicklow in the 1980s, Ballyseedy near Tralee in Kerry in the early '90s and Charleville Wood near Tullamore in 2000.[22] There was also the highly publicised protest in the Glen of the Downs in County Wicklow in the 1990s, which failed to stop a road-widening scheme through the wooded glen.

Despite such setbacks there is a desire for woodlands to become a more significant element of the landscape. This has led to two current projects: the Native Woodland Scheme and the People's Millennium Forests Project. The Native Woodland Scheme is targeted at 15,000 hectares of existing woodland and the creation of 15,000 hectares of new wood. The €2 million People's Millennium Forests Project was one of the more popular government projects to mark the millennium. Every household in the Republic received a certificate stating that a native tree would be planted on their behalf. The Millennium Forests website tells me that our tree has been planted at Derrygill Wood near the village of Woodford in east Galway. The project was criticised as a cynical political stunt, it being wrong to promise that 1.2 million collected seeds would be grown into forests and that every household would be able to visit a forest to see their growing tree. This is not how forests grow. Because of natural selection and woodland management only a fraction of the seeds planted will survive into maturity. The use of the word 'forests' exaggerated the scope of the project which involved planting at sixteen sites with a combined area of only 607 acres (245 hectares).

This chapter has been an exploration of two layers of the landscape typology described by Lorzing – the man-made landscape and the factual landscape. Contemporary society is creating a physical legacy with probably a greater consciousness than recent generations of the role of that legacy as a heritage for future generations. The legacy includes sprawling suburbs, dispersed rural housing, an impressive intercity motorway network and wind farms. It also includes enlivened town and city centres that showcase a rediscovered confidence in architecture and urban design that appeared at the end of the twentieth century.

A rich cultural imprint fosters what the geographer calls topophilia, a love of place, which includes all the human being's affective ties with the material environment. At a deeper level of the mind lies biophilia, which is a subject for the next chapter.

Chapter 3

NATURE

In 2008 members of an educational trust asked me to find a site for them that was 'full of nature', so that they could build a primary school. I took on the assignment and one day in late spring, the following year, I decided to explore a sloping wooded area within the search zone. It was a beautiful evening as I climbed up from the road through dappled shade and drifts of bluebells. At the top of the wood I found myself gazing over a substantial meadow, divided in two by a line of trees (see Fig. 3.1). A fox and a herd of cattle stared back at me. The moment of stillness was shattered when a small flock of wild duck erupted from a reedy depression in the field.

Fig. 3.1. The attractive site of a future primary school, photographed in 2009. The site is in hummocky terrain, left behind by the last ice advance.

The fox turned on its heels and scampered away and I realised that here was the site I had been searching for, a short scramble from the centre of town but insulated from its hubbub by the steep wooded hillside. In my mind's eye I imagined a graceful school building, facing south towards the line of trees and, beside the school, a small, clear lake. The trust has since bought the field and got outline planning permission to build a school.

The educational trust is dedicated to the promotion of Steiner education in north Clare. Using natural materials and learning through nature are features of the Steiner or Waldorf educational approach, pioneered by Rudolf Steiner in Germany a century ago. In contrast to an emphasis on academic learning that is prevalent in mainstream primary education, Steiner schools, especially in the first two years of schooling, encourage learning through nature and play.[1] There are nearly 1,000 Steiner schools around the world today and there are three in Ireland. The Steiner approach to education is substantiated by recent scientific thinking. In 1984, Edward O. Wilson, a professor of science at Harvard University, published a book in which he advanced the Biophilia Hypothesis, a hypothesis that the human species has a genetic disposition to seek out an intimate connection with the natural world. Wilson believes that 'for human survival and mental health and fulfilment, we need the natural setting in which the human mind almost certainly evolved and in which the human mind has developed over these millions of years of evolution.[2] David Orr, a professor of environmental studies, believes that 'for the Biophilia Hypothesis to take root we must take our children seriously enough to preserve their natural childhood'.[3]

Ireland has an exceptional natural heritage that is frequently taken for granted. As a nation we more readily identify aspects of the built environment as heritage, and landscape is the least acknowledged part of the natural heritage.[4] But even in countries sometimes associated with a more elevated sensibility towards nature such as the United States, with its national park system, and Japan, with its garden and festival traditions, nature is ignored. Surveys of attitudes among the general populations of these countries reveal 'a meagre appreciation of the natural world'.[5] In Ireland, natural heritage is woven into everyday life regardless of the limited attention we give it. We rely on physical topography to help define the places that we inhabit. All of us have a personal geography and we also share a communal sense of place that is shaped by physical geography. While there are other ways to define and to distinguish places, the physical structure of the land is pre-eminent.

The profile of Knocknarea, for instance, dominates lowlands on the south side of Sligo Bay, an area with strong cultural associations. An archaeologist

Fig. 3.2. Beside the Royal Canal in Phibsborough, Dublin, in 1997. There is an increasing acceptance of the notion that human beings have an innate desire to seek out an intimate connection with nature.

could view the area as the home territory of the first inhabitants who left their mark on the landscape. Their territory was centred on the Carrowmore grave complex to the east of Knocknarea, and included Knocknarea and its cairn and the seasonal hunting grounds on the shores of Ballysadare Bay and along the Garavogue and Unshin Rivers.[6] Alternatively, a much more extensive cultural landscape corresponds to the countryside that inspired a young W.B. Yeats more than a century ago, and which has since transmuted into a tourism asset. The core of Yeats Country spans Knocknarea,' the cairn-heaped grassy hill/where passionate Maeve is stony still', extends north to Drumcliff and Rosses, 'choke-full of ghosts', south to the Hawk's Well in the Ox Mountains and west to the Lake Isle of Inisfree.[7]

Tim Robinson's books on the Aran Islands and Connemara represent an unrivalled cultural exploration of landscape. But it must surely be more than coincidence that these places, chosen as places to reside and study, also have an arresting physical presence. That presence is vividly captured in the story he tells about a bus journey from Galway back to his home in Roundstone, one summer's evening.

> *Surely there is point on that road where a sudden lifting of the heart, in defiance of all logics fuzzy or stark, unarguably fixes the beginning of Connemara! The gossiping shoppers and the foreign tourist rhapsodizing over the sky-coloured mountains and mountainous skies fell quiet, and we rolled on in hushed silence, past lakeful after lakeful of sunset, as if through the sequence of a lofty ceremony over which our driver presided with accustomed friendly seriousness . . . On this occasion as we got out of the bus at Roundstone, we said to Michael something about the exceptional splendour of the journey, and he replied: 'I know, that's why I didn't turn on the old radio.[8]*

The landforms that we see today were shaped and refined by glaciation in the last 150,000 years, the Midlandian Cold Stage which started 80,000 years ago and finished just 13,000 years ago, and the earlier cold stage of the Munsterian. The last advance of the ice began 25,000 years ago and the whole country was then probably covered by ice sheets to depths of up to 600 metres. It had been thought that there had been two ice caps with a narrow ice-free zone separating the two. The northern ice cap spread south to a line extending from the Shannon Estuary to south Wicklow and there had been a smaller ice cap in the south-west over the mountains of Cork and Kerry. Now it is believed that there were three ice domes covering the whole island.[9]

Recent glaciation has rendered Ireland a much more characterful place than

Fig. 3.3. The commanding presence of Knocknarea, overlooking Ballysadare and Sligo Bays.

Fig. 3.4. 'Yeats Tavern' at Drumcliff, County Sligo, photographed in 2009.

Fig. 3.5. Corrie above Delphi in the Mweelrea Mountains, County Mayo.

many parts of the world. I was struck by this when I revisited the school site in north Clare. The site is not somewhere with 'outstanding' scenery yet the local topography is intriguing. Beside the row of trees that had first caught my attention there is a deep, rounded, grassy depression. I think it may be a small 'kettle hole', a feature resulting from a melting block of ice being trapped in the gravelly detritus of an ice sheet. The whole hummocky site appears to be part of a large moraine feature moulded some 20,000 years ago.

Glaciation sharpened and accentuated the rugged character of the Irish uplands. Deeply carved, U-shaped valleys, large boulders dumped hapzardly (erratics) and remote corrie lakes are among the signature features of these places. Over the midlands and the other lowland areas glaciation left a legacy of low hills and ridges, bogs and lakes. Michael Viney, Frank Mitchell and Michael Ryan recount how generations of geologists have tried to decipher the conundrums of the lowland landscape.[10] Ireland has bequeathed two features, the esker (*eiscir*) and the drumlin (*droimnín*) to the lexicon of glaciation. Eskers were formed in the ice sheet by discarded meltwater channels that silted up with sand and gravel. When the ice retreated the eskers emerged as low ridges, snaking across the midland countryside. Drumlins are small elongated hills, aligned in the direction of the ice flow, whose formation is still not fully understood. Swarms of drumlins create the 'basket of eggs' topography that characterises parts of the north midlands.

In the broadest terms Ireland is shaped like a shallow bowl. The centre of the bowl is the low-lying grasslands and bogs. Here are glacial deposits overlying a bedrock of soft limestone. The broken rim of the bowl is a series of uplands fashioned in the main out of harder and older rocks. There are a number of isolated hills within the central area, also made of harder rock. But geologists have long puzzled over the courses taken by some Irish rivers. The Shannon in the west and the Nore, Barrow and Slaney in the south-east all make their way to the sea through bands of resistant rock. This calls into question a simple model of landform creation based on differential erosion. Whatever process, or combination of processes, has been at work, in the south-east it has created some of the most beautiful valley scenery in Ireland. It is now generally accepted that the rivers there have maintained their courses in the face of a gradual tectonic uplifting of the island's rim, with valleys then becoming more gorge-like as a result of glaciation.[11] There is other evidence of an upraised rim. Michael Viney refers to the recent (six million years ago) uplifting of the Maumtrasna massif in Mayo and Frank Mitchell and Michael Ryan also explain features of the Wicklow Mountains in terms of recent uplifting.

This summary does not do justice to the regional variety of our landscape, which requires a more detailed geological account. There is a strong relationship between landscape and the underlying geology but the relationship is often not straightforward. Tim Robinson recounts a day spent with a young geologist around Killary Harbour.[12] Robinson was hoping to substantiate Killary as not

Fig. 3.6. A glacial erratic at Rinnamona in the Burren.

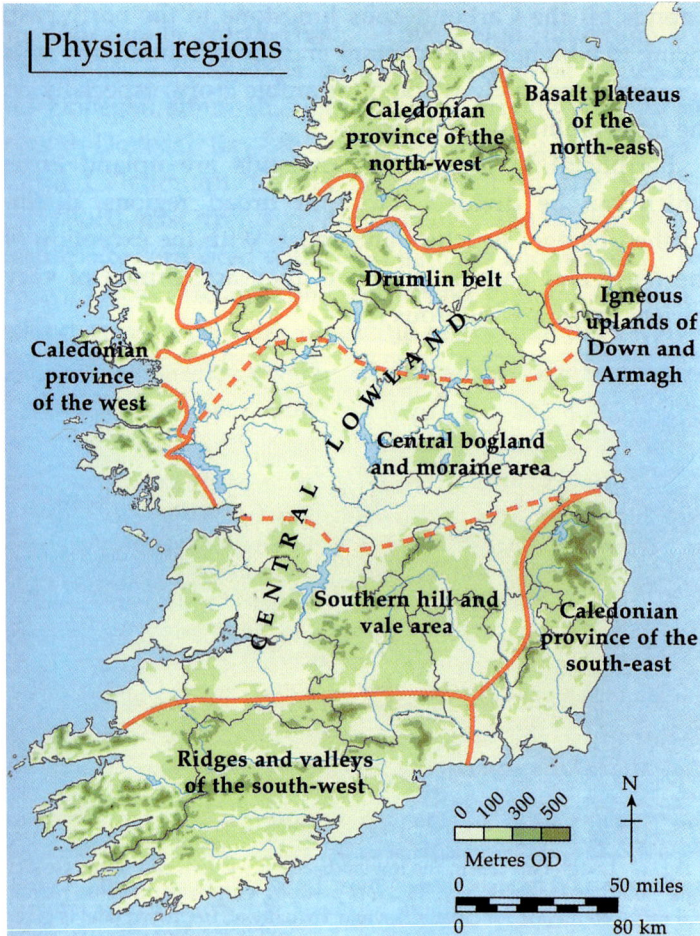

Fig. 3.7.
Physical regions
of Ireland.

only the cultural boundary of Connemara but also a very ancient geological divide. However, he was to learn that the local topography, which mainly took shape between 400 and 500 million years ago, is very complicated. There is a geological division between the ancient folded and faulted metamorphosed rocks of Connemara and the rocks that were subsequently formed (443 to 495 million years ago) from sediments in the nearby ocean basin, the South Mayo Trough. The mountains to the south of Killary Harbour, the Twelve Bens, are the remnants of the ancient Caledonian range that predates the sedimentation in the Trough. Mweelrea, by contrast, on the north side of Killary, is made of upraised sandstones from the Trough. However, after those sandstones were formed, the then ocean (the Iapetus) overflowed the coastal margin and another extensive period of sedimentation occurred, creating mudstones and sandstones that now form the hills on the south side of Killary. A consequence of that sedimentation is that 'somewhere under that pile, which grew to a thickness of a couple of miles, is the join between Connemara and the Mweelrea rocks of the South Mayo Trough' for which Robinson had been searching.[13]

It is worth persevering with a geological exploration of scenery for two reasons. First, geology has a major influence on landform, vegetation cover and land use and, second, geology provides an essential introduction to mining, an activity with a potentially profound landscape impact. Ireland's geological history is summarised in the Table 3.1. There have been three prominent cycles of mountain building, erosion and sedimentation, the first involving the Caledonian orogeny (mountain building), 500 million years ago, and the last, involving volcanic activity in the Irish Sea area, between 65 and 15 million years ago.

Ireland can be sub-divided into several physical landscape regions (see Fig. 3.7). While much of the island is a lowland area, full of the characterful quirks of recent glaciation but lacking a distinctive regional character, there are six more well-defined peripheral regions. Three of the regions owe their rugged character in part to the Caledonian mountain-building episode between 450 and 500 million years ago. Present-day Ireland was then divided in two, forming part of two landmasses either side of a narrowing ocean. As the continents converged this became a turbulent geological zone where chains of volcanoes developed and intense folding and faulting took place. In conditions of extreme heat and pressure, existing rocks were metamorphosed into much harder rocks, sandstones to quartzite and limestones to marble. In places continental plate materials became molten and were intruded into older rocks where they cooled slowly to become granite. Over subsequent era differential erosion has created the mountain scenery that we admire today. Hard quartzite rocks form the mountain summits of the Twelve Bens, Croagh Patrick and Mount Errigal in the west. In the east they form the craggy profiles of Howth and Bray Heads, guarding the entrance to Dublin Bay and, further south, a large granite intrusion constitutes the upland expanse of the Wicklow Mountains.

During the Devonian period, the Caledonian mountains were intensely eroded in hot, arid conditions to eventually become sediments of sandstone, shale and conglomerate, what we collectively call Old Red Sandstone. The land mass was then inundated by a tropical sea that heralded a new phase of rock formation, resulting in the Carboniferous limestones and shales. These Devonian and Carboniferous rocks underlie the south-west as a series of valleys and ridges, folded and faulted on an east–west axis by the Variscan orogeny. The softer rocks have eroded away to leave upstanding the Old Red Sandstone ranges of hills and mountains that include the Comeraghs and Knockmealdowns in Waterford and Tipperary and Macgillycuddy's Reeks in Kerry. The Carboniferous rocks form the lowland of the 'Golden Vale' and the sea inlets of west Cork and Kerry.

Fig. 3.8. Dooaghtry and the Mweelrea Mountains in County Mayo in 2011. In the foreground lies the green sward of the Dooaghtry machair and, to the rear, the brown and green expanse of blanket bog covering the mountains. At first glance, and to the uneducated eye, the machair holds no more interest than a chemically improved pasture or the carefully managed fairway of a golf course. But the whole of the view is part of a large Natura 2000 site (Mweelrea-Sheffry-Erriff Complex) and both machair and blanket bog are designated as priority European habitats within the overall site.

on their hands and knees (with a pocket lens), 'taking it all in'.[19] The machair harbours 'rich and diverse communities' that are dominated by mites or acari. Under the microscope the micro-arthropods, varying in size from the virtually invisible to a few millimeters across, appear as 'lumbering armoured dinosaurs'. Most of them are slow-moving grazers of dead vegetation. There are 111 types in Dooaghtry, two or three of which are found nowhere else in Ireland.[20] It can be safely assumed that this ecosystem, like most natural systems, lies entirely outside the knowledge and interest of the great majority of people.

There is no guarantee therefore that a place of exceptional ecological heritage will command reverence and very often such places are ignored and even reviled. Bogland, perhaps the most characteristic group of Irish habitats, is a prime example. Popularly regarded as wet, featureless wastelands, they are Ireland's most important contribution to European and global biodiversity. According to the Environmental Protection Agency (EPA) Bogland report 'Ireland, together with the UK, represents the heartland of the world blanket bog resource. Therefore Ireland has a clear international responsibility for the conservation of such exceptional biodiversity'.[21]

There are two main types of Irish bog: the raised bogs that are mostly found in the midlands and the blanket bogs in the high rainfall areas of the west. The pollen record shows that around 9,000 years ago sphagnum-dominated raised bog vegetation replaced reedswamp and fen in the midlands.[22] Then about 4,000 years ago there was widespread growth of blanket bog as the Irish climate deteriorated. By 3,000 years ago blanket bog was overwhelming established agricultural landscapes. The Ceide fields in north Mayo were quite suddenly abandoned (within the space of fifty years), though several centuries before the climatic downturn and the expansion of the blanket bog elsewhere.[23] The Irish boglands were substantially intact until the beginning of the nineteenth century but have been seriously depleted over the last 200 years, especially during the last half century. It is now estimated that only 10 per cent of the original raised bogs and 28 per cent of the original blanket bogs remain suitable for conservation, given the extent of degradation that has taken place.[24] Some 35 per cent of the country's raised bogs were lost in the decade 1995 to 2005.[25]

The bogs support 15 per cent of Ireland's native flora and 26 per cent of Irish mammals. Some 49 per cent of all of Ireland's endangered birds rely on peatland and 23 per cent of Ireland's endangered plants are peatland species.[26] Such statistics cut no ice with Irish politicians and decision makers and there has

Fig. 3.9. The degraded surface of a former raised bog outside Kinnegad in County Westmeath in 2012.

Fig. 3.10. A trackway (part of the east Clare Way trail) through the otherwise featureless Glandree Blanket Bog Special Area of Conservation (SAC) in east Clare in 2010.

been a marked reluctance to conserve the bogs.

Bogs mean different things to different people. They may be seen as 'non-places' because of their remoteness and low economic value. John Feehan describes how historically bogs 'were regarded by most people as a wet desert, a tragic waste of land . . .' Yet bogs are also valued as a convenient fuel resource and they can elicit affection and even love, as is evident in John Feehan's evocation:

> *The annual cycle of the peat harvest was more than the laborious round of activities necessary to lay up an adequate supply of turf for the winter. The days on the bog were days of hard work, but they were enjoyed, because there was something more here . . . the time spent on the bog was much more than an economic exercise: contact with the bog was an aesthetic experience, a cultural ritual which added richness and meaning to the fabric of life.*[27]

Our perception of bogs continues to evolve. The scientific community now appreciates their important role in global environmental systems but that appreciation has yet to permeate popular culture. Bogs make a vital contribution to the regulation of world climate by storing carbon and by actively removing carbon from the atmosphere on a large scale. Peatland management is therefore a crucial aspect of an effective climate change policy. Peatlands are the most space-effective carbon stores of all terrestrial systems, including rainforests. Irish peatlands are storing more than 75 per cent of national soil organic carbon and it is estimated that near-intact bogs in Ireland remove (sequester) more than 57,000 tonnes of carbon a year from the atmosphere.[28] Bogs therefore deserve star treatment, receiving at least as much respect and attention as their exotic cousins, the rain forests and coral reefs. But this is far from the case at the present time. The sequestering capability of the 227,000 hectares of the near intact bogs, cited above, pales into insignificance when compared to the more than 1.2 million tonnes of carbon that is lost every year from cutover bogs (468,000 hectare) and the extraction of peat from the 100,000 hectares of industrial peatlands.[29] In 2002 Irish environmental non- governmental organisations declared that 'Ireland has typically disregarded the conservation importance of peatlands . . .'[30] A 2007 official assessment of Irish habitats concluded that the conservation status of both active raised and blanket bogs was 'bad', the worst status category available.[31] By continuing to allow turf cutting on protected sites, Ireland is still not in compliance with the Habitats Directive and faces the prospect of serious financial penalties.

Bogs illustrate the difficulty of trying to summarise landscape heritage in a meaningful way. But some summarising and categorisation are necessary prerequisites for effective landscape management. The methodology of Landscape Character Assessment (LCA) seemed to offer a solution when it became available in the last fifteen years. Irish planners initially had high expectations for the tool, which had been developed in Britain during the 1990s.[32] In LCA a surveyed area – it can be a parish, a county or a whole country – is subdivided into distinctive types of landscape that are relatively homogenous in character, for example a river valley, farmland, upland hills, a built up area, etc. These are called *character types*. Several areas will share the same character type and these different areas are called *character areas*. There are, for instance, a number of upland hills in Clare, including Slieve Callan and Slieve Elva. Upland hills is the generic *character type* and Slieve Callan and Slieve Elva are *character areas*. This simple classification system of *types* and *areas* provides the framework for a methodical description of landscape. The methodology, which avoids value judgements, enables places which are valued in very different ways, such as the bogs mentioned above, to be subsumed within a common system of description and classification. Because of the close and complex interaction of nature and

Fig. 3.11. Sand dunes at Lackakeely and beyond them the sand flats at Trawleckachoolia and Carrickwee and the lower slopes of Mweelrea at Doovilra. In the Landscape Appraisal for County Mayo, published by Mayo County Council in 2002, this locality is categorised as part of the South West Mountains Moorland Landscape Unit, one of the 16 landscape units into which the County Mayo is divided. South West Mountains Moorland comprises 'exposed montane moorland with smooth steep slopes, broad valleys and ridge-top plateaux' and is an area 'largely covered by peat bog'. The photograph illustrates the wonderful variety of west of Ireland coastal scenery and a limitation of the application of Landscape Character Assessment methodology. For cost reasons LCA is usually only carried out at a very broad spatial scale, e.g. a whole county utilising data assembled at a scale of 1:50,000. This can lead to generalised descriptions that bear little relationship to the character of many places.

culture there is often a close correspondence between the boundaries of natural and cultural areas. The Burren would be a case in point, the distinctive geology and landform of the area having a decisive effect on contemporary and historical patterns of land use and settlement.

Over the last decade advances in Geographic Information Systems (GIS) and the increasing availability of digital data have greatly assisted the roll out of LCA. There is a comprehensive LCA of Northern Ireland, dividing the territory into 130 landscape character areas.[33] Whether that project has brought any practical benefit, however, is open to question. The messy status of LCA in the South, where draft guidelines have been prepared but shelved and LCA exercises have been carried out on a piecemeal basis, reflects the equivocal status of landscape policy in this country.[34] The draft guidelines, which recommend significant elaboration of the basic LCA model, do justice to the complexity of the Irish landscape experience but fail to appreciate the practical need for a simple, objective methodology that can be widely understood and applied.[35]

Chapter 4

CHANGE

———

Dramatic change in a landscape or the prospect of such a change brings a landscape into focus. Without that catalyst we may never really take note of where we are. Sometimes, unfortunately, to quote the lyric of the Joni Mitchell song, 'you don't know what you got 'til it's gone'. As individuals we persist in regarding the physical landscape as a reassuring constant, subject to seasonal rhythms, but otherwise relatively unchanging. It can therefore be upsetting, traumatic even, when that assumption is shaken by the possibility of change.

When such events affect whole communities they can lead to conflicts which expose deep differences in the way that the surrounding world is viewed. Examining how we perceive and manage change and what happens when conflict breaks out provides the deepest insight of contemporary society's relationship with its landscape.

An auctioneer's 'For sale' sign went up recently at the field gate opposite our house and immediately caught our attention. In the winter part of the half-acre field is a pond rimmed by sedges. In the early summer it produces one of the best displays of yellow flags on our road. A while ago somebody worked their way through the field with a pair of hand shears, lopping the tops of the sedges and the flags so that, for the next few weeks, weather permitting, the field will pass muster as a meadow. It is more than half a mile from a public sewer or a mains water supply, there is an electricity pole in the middle of it from which three power lines radiate. On the face of it, its development potential is negligible but a phone call to the auctioneer revealed an asking price of €60,000 'subject to planning'. I assume that this price has been arrived at because the field's dimensions are such that a house could fit on it, there is road frontage and it is an easy drive from Ennis. The price compares with current local agricultural land values in the area of around €10,000 an acre. I doubt if there will ever be a house in this field but one cannot be certain on the evidence of the recent past. Roadside signs of 'site for sale' have been familiar harbingers of change

Fig. 4.1. New bungalow being built in the Glengish Pass, West Donegal, in 2007.

in rural areas and, like so many townlands across Ireland, this one has seen more development in the past thirty years than in the whole of the previous century. What distinguishes the recent past from earlier decades is that there seems to have been a possibility of dramatic change nearly everywhere, not just in towns and cities and near those places but virtually everywhere. In our townland nine new houses have been built in the past decade while others have been modernised and extended. For a few years the pounding of rock breakers preparing sites, the early-morning traffic of builders' vans and jeeps threading their way to work and a mid-morning queue for bacon and sausage rolls at the hot food counter in the village supermarket were part of the daily rhythm of our neighbourhood. Now things have quietened down and the builders have long departed although there is still a restoration project ongoing at the 'big house'.

House construction is a small component of change in a rural landscape. We are hardly aware of much of what is going on. Sensitivity is blunted by a detachment from the land which is part and parcel of contemporary living. There are no full-time farmers living in our immediate locality, even though we inhabit a landscape fashioned for and by agriculture. One neighbour, whose husband had been a farmer, still keeps a few cattle and another rents out fields for grazing and silage. That is about the extent of the direct economic connection that exists between this settled landscape and its settlers. The absence of a connection through livelihood is partly compensated for by experiencing the countryside through leisure. In my case bird-watching encourages me to look more carefully than I might otherwise do. When I first came here, in 1999, I occasionally saw a hen harrier, one of Europe's rarer birds of prey, on the ridge above our house, but I haven't seen one now for several years. Its presence then and absence now probably reflects a stage in the commercial forestry cycle of planting and harvesting rather than any long-term environmental trend. The maturing conifer stands on the ridge are no longer an attractive hunting ground and the harrier may return when the trees are harvested and the habitat becomes more open again. A more profound environmental change may be signalled by the arrival, last winter, of a little egret. The egret, a dainty snow-white heron, did not even merit an illustration in the bird book that was given to me when I was a schoolboy. Forty years ago it was an uncommon migrant to Ireland from its Mediterranean home. Now it breeds here, one indicator of a changing climate.

I strongly suspect that the quality of my local landscape has declined in living memory and there is not much doubt that there has been widespread deterioration over the last half century. Kingfishers and dippers used to breed on the stretch of river beneath the ridge but they have not bred in recent summers. I hope this is no more than part of a natural pattern of variation but local anglers have been concerned for decades about the river and our local lake,

Lake Inchiquin. There is still good fishing here, brown trout in Inchiquin and in the river, and pike and other course fish in nearby lakes, but the place has lost its once almost mythical status. *An Angler's Paradise*, written nearly a century ago, is a paean to local rivers and lakes. F.D. Barker, the author, who was an expatriate American living in London, changed all the place names in the book. He explained: 'I regret that it is denied me to tell you where Eden is and how it is named on the map. If I were to do so, it would be Eden no longer. You might all be for taking tickets and trying to engage rooms.'[1]

The environmentalist John Feehan grew up near Birr in County Offaly. He remembers three special places from his childhood: a small wood of ancient willows with a sandpit, where bee orchids grew, a raised bog filled with the churring of nightjars on summer nights and where toadstools grew 'to rival any fairy story' and, further away, high up on Slieve Bloom, a mountain bog, haunted by the Spirit of the Well. By 1994 all those places had gone, the mountain bog planted over with conifers and the Spirit fled, the raised bog drained and silent and the wood turned into a barren grassland.[2] Writing in 1997, in an introduction to a new edition of *The Way That I Went* by Robert Lloyd Praeger, Michael Viney was in no doubt that there has been decline in the sixty years since Praeger walked the length and breadth of the country. 'To read him with any knowledge of the modern Irish landscape is constantly to be prodded by irony and regret,' Viney writes.[3] He quotes Praeger on the Central Plain, bemoaning 'the monotony of the scenery [which] is equalled only by the poverty of the flora' but wonders what the naturalist, if he were alive today, would make of the 'wholesale ruin and obliteration of the bogs, and the monotony and floral poverty of endless ryegrass pasture'.[4]

A direct encounter with a destructive act of change can be traumatic, with the potential to permanently affect one's perception of a place, even when the change itself, by most standards of measurement, is inconsequential. At the time it happens – the felling of a tree, the ripping out of a hedgerow or a wrecking ball demolishing an old house – it can feel like unspeakable desecration. In north Clare one of my favourite places is Bishop's Quarter, near Ballyvaughan. The strand there has all the ingredients of a perfect seaside playground. It is never crowded and often we have the place to ourselves. The shallow bay is good for bathing and splashing. We can watch crabs scuttling along the sandy floor and small fish dodging our feet and there are numerous rock pools to explore. The dunes behind the beach provide vantage points and sheltered picnic spots and scope for all manner of chasing games. This is how we enjoy Bishop's Quarter but a friend of ours who lives not far from the beach rarely goes there. It used to be one of her favourite places until the time she watched trucks carrying away sand to build a golf course.

Direct experience has a crucial influence on our relationship with a place and its landscape. It shapes our emotional response and has the potential to enhance our understanding. But, paradoxically, the eye-witness account has to be carefully interpreted, it cannot be taken at face value. In the 1990s I spent many weeks over a four-year period getting to know the Howth peninsula in Dublin while I was working on a landscape project for Fingal County Council (see Chapter 8). I did most of the work on foot, walking from the DART stations in Sutton or Howth or from one of the peninsula's car parks. The peninsula has a network of paths, one of the most attractive of which is a coastal path on the south side connecting Sutton and the Baily (see Figs. 4.2 and 4.3). Part of the charm of the path is its hidden quality. The path is narrow and winding, in places clinging to the cliff top, concealed behind high hedges and fences at the backs of bungalows and houses that were built in the early part of the last century. But in 1937 Praeger, an enthusiastic and insightful observer of Irish landscape, saw the situation quite differently:

> As I first knew Howth almost a half-century ago, it was a delightful old-world place. Even round its rock-bound margin houses were few and one could wander at will along its grassy slopes and over its broad heathery top. Now houses and bungalows, most of them inartistic eyesores quite out of keeping with their setting, encroach more and more on the open spaces; along the southern shore, with its superb view across Dublin Bay, the greed of landowners confines the visitor to a narrow muddy track between high barbed-wire fences.[5]

Fig. 4.2. The narrow cliff walk on the south side of Howth, linking Sutton and the Baily, photographed in 2011. 'Earlscliffe', the warm-temperate garden created by the late David Robinson, is part of the woodland on the skyline.

I believe that Praeger's description, which is uncharacteristically caustic, was coloured by living through a transformation of a place that he loved into part of suburban Dublin. Howth still retains a delightful detached quality but I never knew Howth as the 'old-world place' Praeger first encountered. I got to know that muddy track he refers to quite well and for me it is an enchanting walk, full of interest and with marvellous views of Dublin Bay and the Wicklow coastline beyond. Praeger's response illustrates the deflating effect of drastic landscape change, when that change takes place without the consent of those who enjoy the place, whether they live there or are just visitors. For most of us, most of the time, this is our lot. Where we are responsible for change, generally when we own the land, effecting change can be an enormously energising experience. This is the potent first layer of interaction in Lorzing's typology, 'landscape is what you make'. One of those houses to which Praeger probably took exception, was subsequently bought in 1969 by the horticulturalist, the late David Robinson. He took full advantage of the sheltered south-facing slope of the headland to turn 'Earlscliffe' into a garden of international renown full of warm-temperate plants, thriving in the local microclimate. It was a transformation that did not pass without controversy. Gardener and television presenter Monty Don once visited the garden and took exception to David Robinson's reliance on chemicals to eliminate weed growth, describing the garden as a 'strangely barren and repugnant' place. That judgement understandably irked Robinson, leading him to make an impassioned case for the 'landscape is what you make' perspective. Robinson proclaimed that 'your garden is one of the last places on earth where you can be yourself' and advised his audience to 'Do your own thing and to hell with begrudgers'[6]

Fig. 4.3. View of Dublin Bay and the Wicklow Mountains from Red Rock on Howth in 2011.

The history of Irish woodland is especially difficult to decipher because of the need to make allowance for an array of distorting effects, that is, the deep-seated psychological associations of woodland, the impact on the observer of a visually arresting act of change, such as the clear-felling of a wood, and the practical difficulty of estimating woodland cover from ground level. In earlier centuries descriptions of woodland were infected by cultural preoccupations. In the sixteenth and seventeenth centuries it is likely that the accounts of colonisers exaggerated the extent of forests, which were the hideaways of rebels and criminals, because these fears loomed over-large in their consciousness. And there also may have been a tendency at the time, within a native Irish culture in retreat, to emphasise and amplify the status of the old forests. Valerie Pakenham, citing contemporary accounts, states that at the start of the seventeenth century most of Ireland was still covered with woodland although in the south and east the woods were fast disappearing to fuel the appetites of local ironworks.[7] On the other hand, another historian writes that the woodland cover was already severely depleted by the seventeenth century and that the deforestation was due almost entirely to the rapidly expanding rural population and the spread of farmland. It had little or nothing to do with the demands of industry.[8] Both writers agree that there was rapid and severe deforestation in the seventeenth and eighteenth centuries; only about a tenth of the woodland that was present in 1655 was still there 180 years later.

Every year the Fáilte Ireland survey of visitors to the country reassuringly confirms high levels of visitor satisfaction. In a recent survey 79 per cent of visitors cite scenery and 70 per cent the natural unspoilt environment as the main reasons for choosing Ireland as a destination. The only more popular reason (81 per cent) is the friendliness of the people. For nearly a third of visitors an Irish holiday exceeds expectations and of that third, 42 per cent state that the high level of satisfaction is because of the scenery.[9] These findings are at odds with the pessimistic outlook of many local commentators. In 1992, in an introduction to a book of landscape photography, prose and poetry, the historian and writer Tim Pat Coogan railed against 'the short-sighted avarice of generations that used Irish independence as a means of emulating the exploiters, but with less style'.[10] Roy Foster views, with unrelieved gloom, the physical transformation of Ireland since 1970, with the pace of change accelerating in the Celtic Tiger years. 'The face of the country has changed, first in the 1990s with subsidised afforestation and setting designated land aside; now in place of a field of beasts there are likely to be fields with brand-new houses rained down into them . . .'[11] In 2009, in the aftermath of the Celtic Tiger, Heritage Council chief Executive Michael Starrett stated that he would be shirking his responsibility if he did not admit that the country was 'woefully ill-equipped to deal with the pace of development, and that serious damage has been done to our landscape'.[12] Sarah Poyntz from Wexford retired to the Burren in the mid-1980s and began to write a nature diary for the *Guardian* newspaper. She confided to travel writer Paul Clements in 2011 that Ballyvaughan, where she lives, 'has developed very badly over the years and sometimes I despair but I try not to convey that despair to my readers because I think there is enough doom and gloom around'.[13] Clements, who lives in Belfast but is a frequent visitor to the Burren, has a more sanguine view of recent change, believing that 'few developments blight the Burren. Apart from small clusters of holiday homes and thatched cottages, it has not reached the epic proportions of the bungalow blitz that afflicts large parts of Donegal or Achill Island . . . opportunities for building are limited and the developers are forced to move on elsewhere leaving the Burren largely undesecrated'.[14]

In 2004 the *Irish Letter*, a New York publication for the Irish-American community, wrote that 'In real estate terms, a kind of "perfect storm" is going on in Ireland that combines sudden wealth with a decline in farming, weak zoning laws and a popular architectural style that looks wildly out of place. It's threatening to turn the west of Ireland, in particular, into one of Europe's less attractive suburbs'.[15] However, such a negative observation from an outsider is the exception rather than the rule. Resident commentators will not easily find visitor accounts to substantiate a precipitous decline in landscape quality. Ireland continues to be viewed from afar as a green and pleasant land. A recent edition of the *Rough Guide to Ireland* begins with the statement that 'Many come to Ireland with high expectations of its romantic scenery, a blend of the raw and rugged with mist-covered verdancy, and seldom return home disillusioned'.[16] Readers of the American Frommer's travel guides voted Ireland the world's top tourist destination in 2011.[17]

Ireland's scenery is in a state of permanent flux, buffeted by physical, social and economic forces. Arguably the greatest change in the middle decades of the last century was the destruction of the great midland bogs. Father J.J. Moore of UCD, who pioneered the field of peatland phytosociology in this country, was presented with the European Prize for the Protection of Nature in 1982. In his acceptance speech he recounted that 'when I wandered over the raised bogs of the midlands in the 1950s I enjoyed an experience which it is impossible to have anymore – the experience of being isolated in a vast brown ocean of bog, extending to the horizon on all sides, where the only landmarks were church steeples. One always needed to carry a compass in these vast areas. The experience can no longer be enjoyed since all these larger bogs of up to 10 kilometres diameter have now been cut'.[18] By the time Bord na Móna was set up in 1946 about half the total area of the midland bogs that had existed in 1814 had been cut and by 1969 there was only about 100,000 hectares of raised bog left.[19]

This compares with the more than one million hectares of bog that had existed in Ireland at the start of the nineteenth century, half of it upland bog and the other half lowland bog in the midlands.[20]

There remains a popular misconception that the farming landscape is relatively static. This is perhaps a hangover from the first two-thirds of the twentieth century when an 'impressive stability' reigned.[21] Such is the rapidity of the upheaval now taking place that, in retrospect, other contemporary landscape change may, in time, come to appear trivial. Ireland joined the European Union (then the EEC) in 1973, accelerating the transformation of farming from a way of life to a business. While agriculture is currently enjoying a resurgence, this is against the backdrop of long-term decline. There were 278,500 farms in Ireland in 1960 but by 2004 that number had more than halved, to less than 120,000. In 1991 there were more than 500 census areas or district electoral divisions (DEDs) in the Republic in which more than half the workforce was working in farming, forestry or fishing (see Figs 4.5 and 4.6). By 2002 there were only 53 areas where more than 39 per cent of the workforce was engaged in the sector.[22] It has been estimated that by 2015 this country will have only 25,000 commercial farmers, including 15,000 dairy farmers, 5,000 drystock farmers, 2,000 arable farmers and 500 pig farmers. There will be a further 35,000 part-time farmers reliant on an off-farm income.[23]

Fig. 4.4. A traditional agricultural landscape, a hillside near Annascaul on the Dingle Peninsula in 2011. The 'impressive stability' that we associate with traditional countryside no longer reflects the actual situation.

In 1991 the OPW announced its plan to build a visitor centre at the foot of Mullaghmore, near the southern edge of the Burren. The announcement sparked a bitter conflict which is described in the next chapter. However, the site for the centre is located in an agricultural landscape that is changing anyway. What we regard as the Burren landscape today – a relatively open, rocky place with fields and rough ground grazed by cattle, interspersed with patches of scrub – is a product of a centuries-old pastoral farming system that is now in decline. Geographer Eileen O'Rourke, has described an array of forces at work over the last half century.[24] There has been both a dramatic decline in the number of farmers and an increase in farm productivity, driven by the Common Agricultural Policy. The total number of farmers in Ballyvaughan Rural District, which covers most of the Burren, fell by 42 per cent (562 farms to 325 farms) between 1980 and 1991 but in the period 1960 to 1991 there was a 122 per cent increase in the number of cattle. Farm resources were directed towards maximising productivity. Lands were cleared and improved, resulting in an estimated loss of 30 per cent of the archaeological sites of the area. Continental breeds replaced traditional breeds, stocking densities were increased by introducing supplementary feeding on winterages (the high ground where, traditionally, cattle are overwintered) and by building slatted houses to augment the winterage grazing. These changes amounted to a radical change in farming practice with significant landscape and environmental consequences. Secondary land activities have declined and disappeared, most notably the exploitation of the hazel scrub. The scrub was once a valuable resource that was used for a variety of purposes. It was coppiced and harvested for firewood and to make wicker baskets and 'scallops' for thatching. It provided fodder for goats and other livestock when every farm had its herd of goats. No longer grazed or harvested, the scrub is now starting to obliterate the historic field patterns. Conor Skehan believes that 'across large swathes of the Irish countryside this generation will witness something that hasn't happened for 6,000 years. For the first time since the late stone age the tree canopy will close out the sun and sky from the ancient fields and meadows'.[25] The OPW has contracts with local farmers to maintain grazing levels and to control hazel scrub within the national park, in the interest of conservation and recreational amenity. But all around the park a landscape of fine detail is being overwhelmed. In time the Burren we know, lying outside the small national park, may entirely disappear. But this process, which is already under way, has hardly impinged on public consciousness, in marked contrast to the visitor centre, which, as things have turned out, was never built.

The ruins of former settlement are part of the character of the Burren just as they are of other areas of rural Ireland. Their presence has contributed to the romantic allure of the Irish landscape and substantiate the idyll of a once-

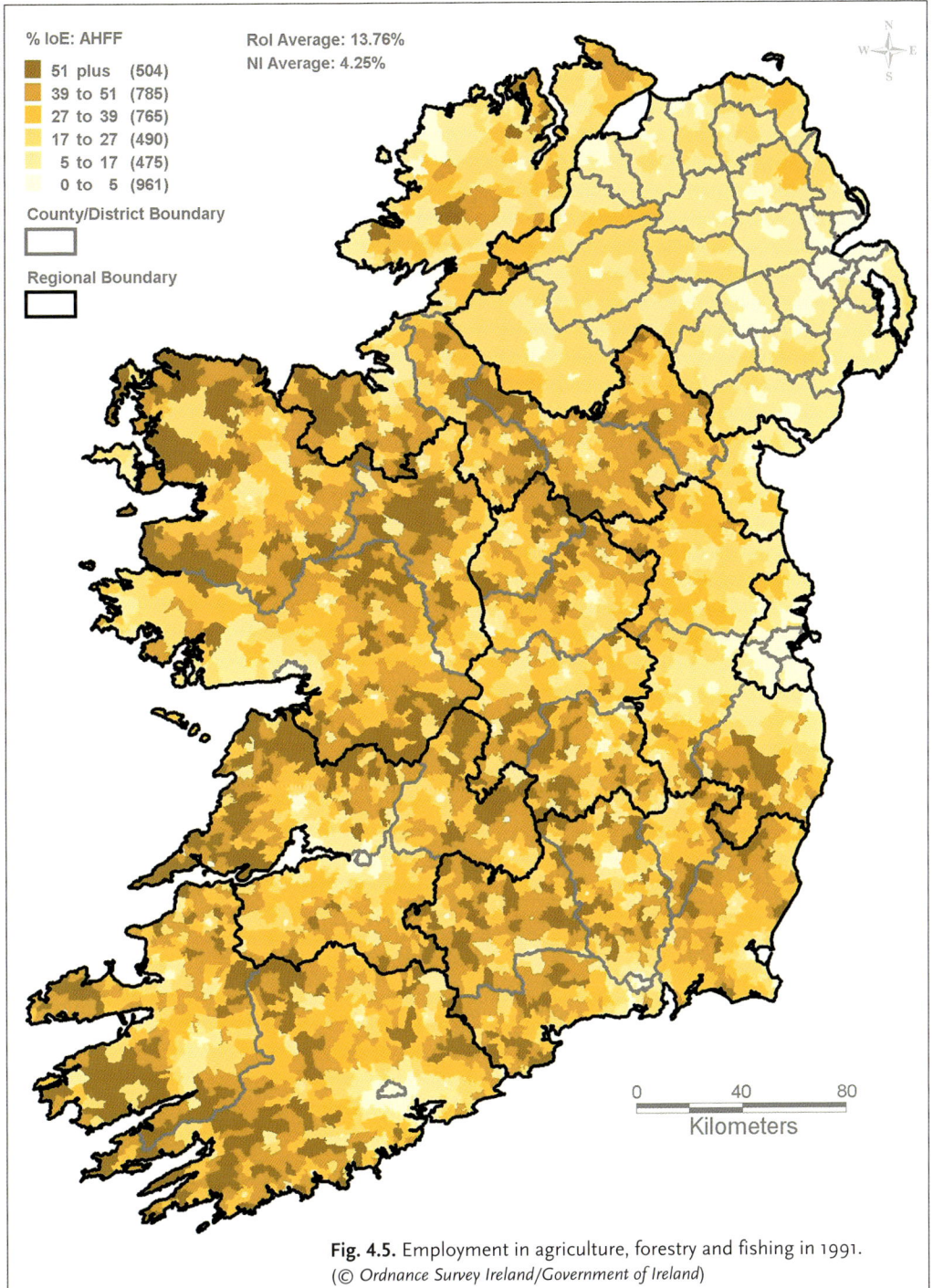

% IoE: AHFF

▮	51 plus (504)
▮	39 to 51 (785)
▮	27 to 39 (765)
▮	17 to 27 (490)
▮	5 to 17 (475)
▯	0 to 5 (961)

County/District Boundary

Regional Boundary

RoI Average: 13.76%
NI Average: 4.25%

Fig. 4.5. Employment in agriculture, forestry and fishing in 1991.
(© *Ordnance Survey Ireland/Government of Ireland*)

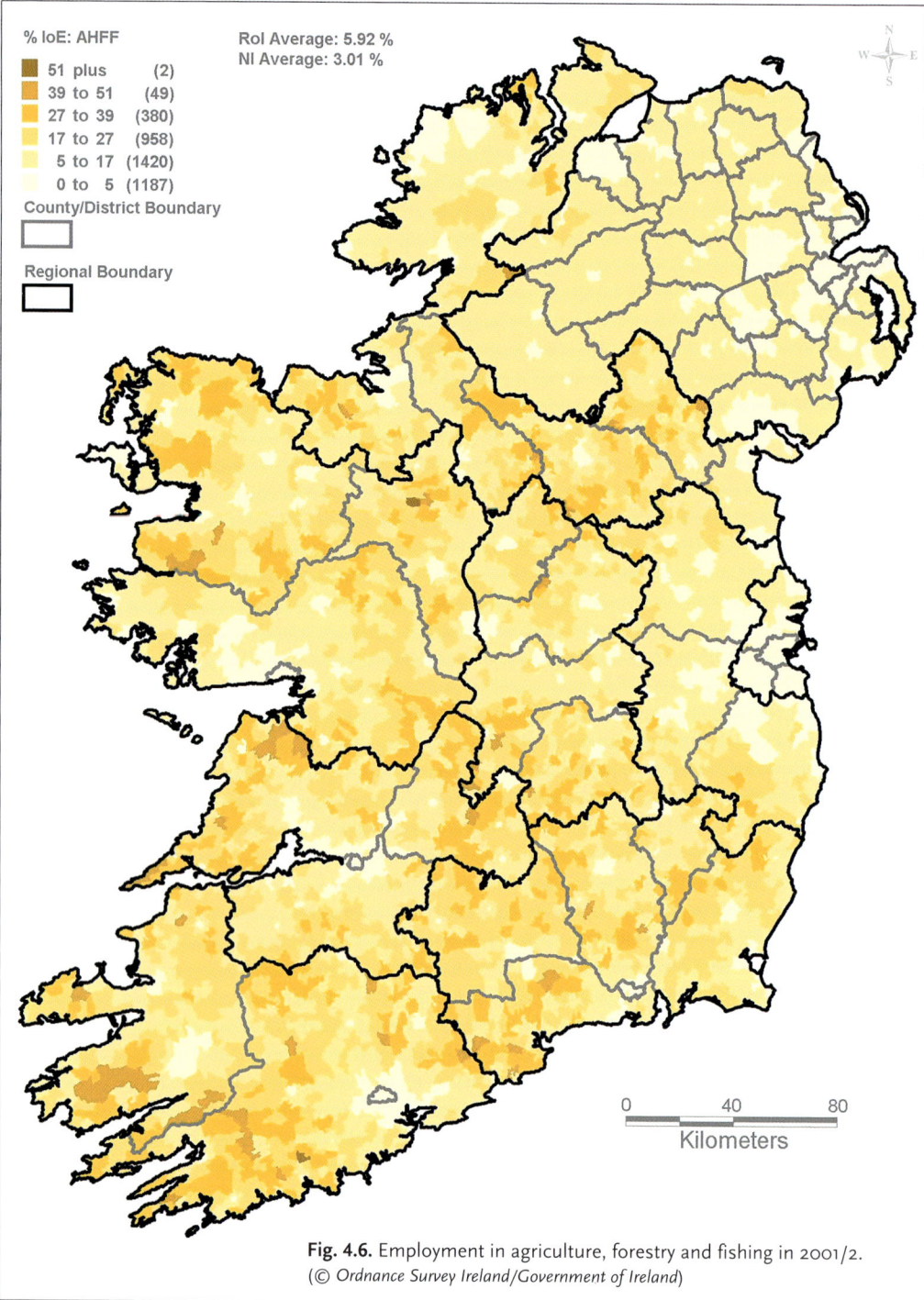

% IoE: AHFF

 RoI Average: 5.92 %
NI Average: 3.01 %

- 51 plus (2)
- 39 to 51 (49)
- 27 to 39 (380)
- 17 to 27 (958)
- 5 to 17 (1420)
- 0 to 5 (1187)

County/District Boundary

Regional Boundary

Fig. 4.6. Employment in agriculture, forestry and fishing in 2001/2.
(© *Ordnance Survey Ireland/Government of Ireland*)

populous countryside. However, new houses rather than old ruins are now a more conspicuous aspect of contemporary landscapes. There has been population growth throughout Ireland in recent decades. In 1961 the population of the Republic was less than three million. By 2011 it exceeded 4.5 million. There were fewer than 700,000 households in 1961 but nearly 1.5 million by 2006, a more than doubling of the households in the period. The first widespread rural growth took place in the 1970s after more than a century of decline.[26] By the turn of the century depopulated areas such as Leitrim and the Dingle and Beara Peninsulas were also experiencing a rapid rise in population (see Fig. 4.10). New growth has manifested itself as low-density suburbs around cities, housing estates tacked on to small towns and villages and a proliferation of single new houses in the open countryside. Dublin has become a striking example of suburban sprawl. One of Europe's fastest-growing cities in the last decades of the century, it is also now renowned as one of the most sprawling, occupying about the same area as Los Angeles but with a quarter of the population.[27] In 2006 the head of the European Environmental Agency's spatial analysis unit told *The Irish Times* that Dublin was being held up for new member states such as Poland as a 'worst case scenario' of urban planning.[28]

Fig. 4.7. New housing on the southern outskirts of Tuam in 2009. Tuam is 32 kilometres north of Galway city, in theory an easy commute were it not for the horrendous traffic jams around Galway city. The population of the town grew by more than a thousand (22 per cent) in the period 1996 to 2006 while the population of the historic core of the town fell by 11 per cent, a typical pattern across the country.

The pattern of new settlement is the strongest physical manifestation of a key feature of present-day Irish society, which is a very high dependency on the private car for everyday life. This dependency has grown very rapidly (see Fig. 4.11). The number of private cars in the Republic increased by 140 per cent between 1970 and 1994.[29] There were over a million private cars by 2000, and nearly two million by 2009.[30] By 2006, seven out of ten workers were private vehicle users.

This pace of change nearly scuppered a small research project that I carried out on travel patterns in north County Dublin in 1995.[33] The study was to test

Figs 4.8 and 4.9. Examples of the Irish car culture in 2011: collecting children from school in An Cheatrú Rua (Carraroe) and a retail park at the Liffey Valley shopping centre in south Dublin. In 1981 nearly half the children in the Republic walked to primary school and only a fifth were driven, but by 2002 the proportions had almost exactly reversed with nearly half of the children being driven to school.[31] James Wickham identifies the development of the Liffey Valley shopping centre as a key event in the emergence of Dublin as a car-based, American-style edge-city. The centre, built in the 1990s at the junction of the M50 and M4 motorways on a site that had not featured in any official strategic development plan before then, has a catchment of 1.45 million car-driving customers.[32]

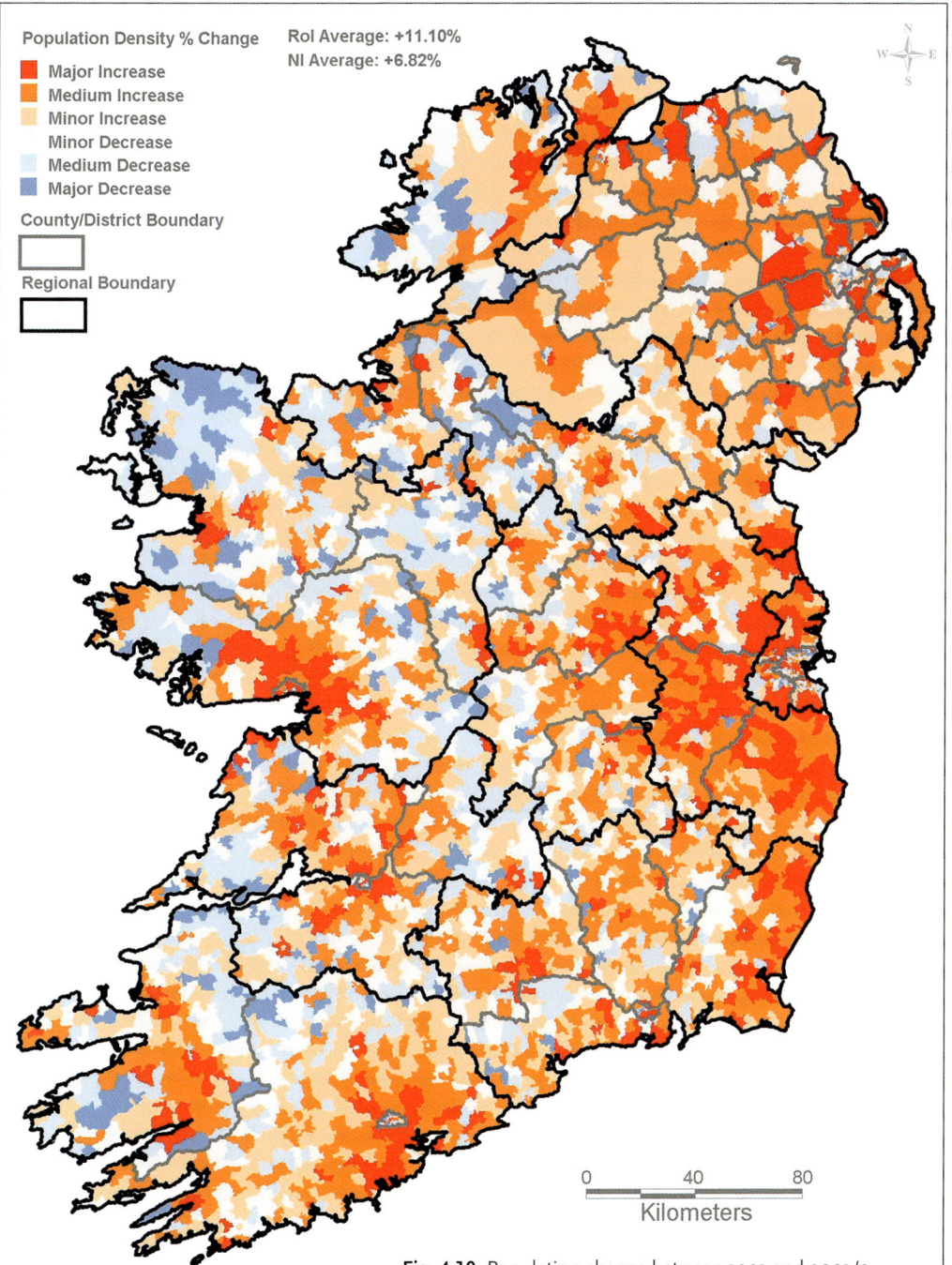

Population Density % Change

- Major Increase
- Medium Increase
- Minor Increase
- Minor Decrease
- Medium Decrease
- Major Decrease

County/District Boundary

Regional Boundary

RoI Average: +11.10%
NI Average: +6.82%

Fig. 4.10. Population change between 1991 and 2001/2. (© *Ordnance Survey Ireland/Government of Ireland*)

the hypothesis that, from a transport perspective, dispersed rural settlement is relatively unsustainable. This required surveying the travel behaviour of a group of households that were similar in every respect other than where they lived. The household type that I chose to survey was a middle-class family owning a car. The sample had two subsets: a group of families living in Skerries (commuter town) and another group in the Hollywood and Garristown DEDs (dispersed rural settlement). For the purpose of making meaningful statistical comparisons I needed a minimum of thirty households in each subgroup. However, when I came to compile the sample I found it extremely difficult to locate thirty families in the rural area, the problem being that nearly all the households contacted had at least two cars. I had to discount two families because they had bought a second car during the survey period and, out of desperation, included another family because, although they had bought a second car, they had not taxed and put the car on the road. The need for a second car in the rural area was very clear. When I did my research the only public transport consisted of school buses and a daily return bus service between Garristown, the largest village, and Dublin. Figure 4.11 shows the rapid growth of 'two-car and more' households at the time and it can be seen that north County Dublin had one of the fastest rates of change.

As part of that research I was also interested in exploring the health effects of commuting but the only research I could find about 'long-distance commuting' defined it as journey times of 45 minutes or longer.[34] In 1995 that research did not seem to have much relevance to Ireland. However, analysis of census data reveals that by 2002 broad arcs of commuter land had formed around the main urban centres, in particular Dublin and Galway, within which more than a third of workers were travelling between 15 and 30 miles to work. There is an area around Dublin, extending north to Louth, south to Wexford and west into Westmeath, within which, by 2002, 20 per cent or more of workers were travelling more than 30 miles to work (see Fig. 4.12). It is clear that the last four decades, an era of universal car ownership and cheap fuel seemingly liberating Irish society from the tyranny of physical distance, have spawned a settlement pattern that has profound consequences for the future.

The one-off housing phenomenon has affected the whole of rural Ireland, from the 'humble scene in a backward place, where no one important ever looked' to quote Patrick Kavanagh, to the iconic landscapes of Kerry and Connemara. John McGahern, like Patrick Kavanagh, also lived in that unregarded drumlin landscape that stretches across the northern middle of the island. In his memoir, McGahern evokes the quiet beauty of that landscape, imagining being with his beloved mother again and 'If we could walk together through these summer lanes, with their banks of wild flowers that "cast a spell", we probably would not be able to speak, though I would want to tell her all the local news'.[35] Through

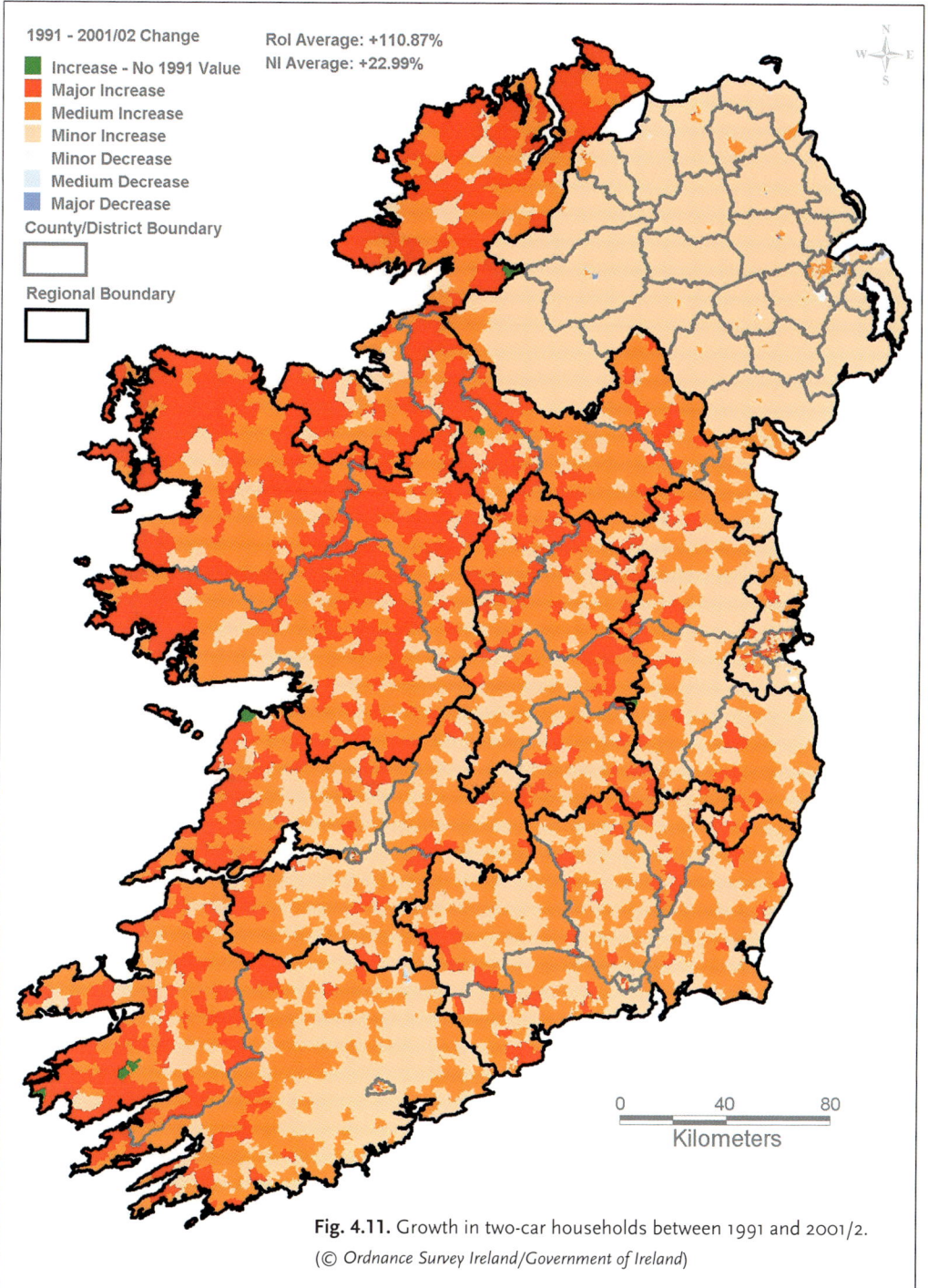

1991 - 2001/02 Change

RoI Average: +110.87%
NI Average: +22.99%

- Increase - No 1991 Value
- Major Increase
- Medium Increase
- Minor Increase
- Minor Decrease
- Medium Decrease
- Major Decrease

County/District Boundary

Regional Boundary

Fig. 4.11. Growth in two-car households between 1991 and 2001/2.
(© *Ordnance Survey Ireland/Government of Ireland*)

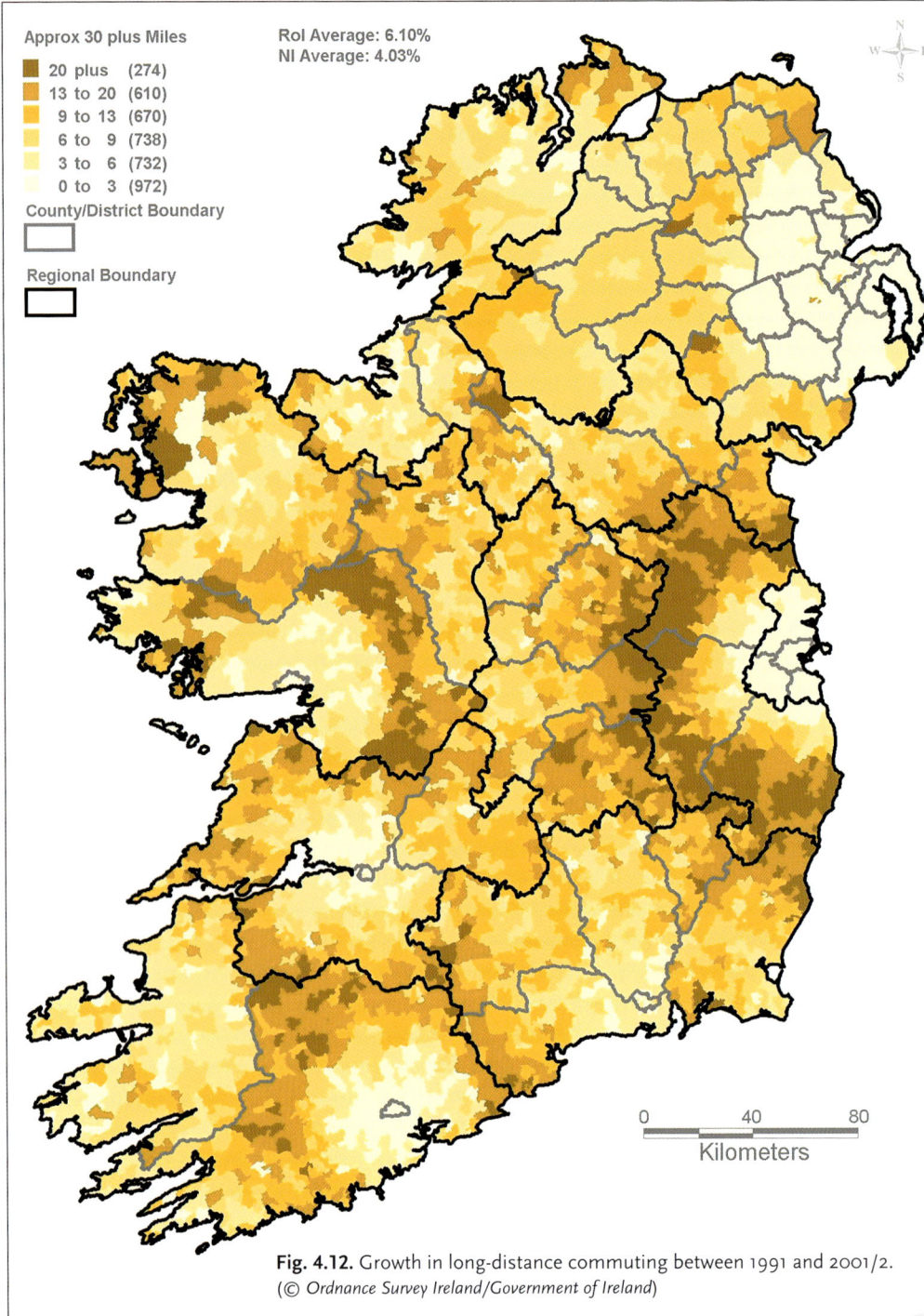

Approx 30 plus Miles

RoI Average: 6.10%
NI Average: 4.03%

- 20 plus   (274)
- 13 to 20 (610)
- 9 to 13 (670)
- 6 to   9 (738)
- 3 to   6 (732)
- 0 to   3 (972)

County/District Boundary

Regional Boundary

0   40   80
Kilometers

Fig. 4.12. Growth in long-distance commuting between 1991 and 2001/2.
(© *Ordnance Survey Ireland/Government of Ireland*)

Figs 4.13 and 4.14. Further examples of Irish car culture in 2010. Above, informal parking at Junction 14 on the M1 in Northern Ireland and, below, a car park in Dublin city centre Workers from the countryside around the M1 car-pool for the daily commute into Belfast at the other end of the motorway. Dublin is the only city in the Republic with a half-decent public transport system but still about 70 per cent of workers in Greater Dublin travel to work by car.[35]

the length and breadth of the country many of those summer lanes are no more, their banks, ditches and hedges broken open to accommodate the driveways and garden walls of new houses. Brendan O'Sullivan, an academic and professional planner, casts a benevolent eye on the transformation, suggesting that 'one must unravel and appreciate the experience of the many hundreds of individual stories that help to make up the planning narrative emerging each year'. O'Sullivan, who was writing about change in the Iveragh Peninsula, argues that 'managing change is never easy. It is a continuous political, economic and environmental struggle, but with some care and understanding we certainly have the capacity to ensure that it rests easily in our landscape'.[36] Paul Stack, the senior planner in Kerry County Council, is less sanguine about what has happened. He describes the 'incredible damage' done by the proliferation of housing (see, for example, Figs 4.15 and 4.16). After an absence from the county of fourteen years, he 'couldn't believe what I came back to, planning went out of control'.[37] In a report to a meeting of Kerry County Council in March 2011, he stated that between 2002 and 2007, 600 one-off houses had been built, representing 43 per cent of the new housing stock in the county.[38]

Fig. 4.15. Rural housing at Reenard Point, near Cahirciveen, in Kerry. The base map shows a very low density of settlement at the beginning of the twentieth century. The overlay of red dots, one dot per dwelling, shows the pattern of housing in 2007.

Fig. 4.16. This photograph, taken in 2011, shows the east–west boreen at the south side of the map area.

Changes in lifestyle and technology are now happening with such rapidity that we cannot help but be aware of the ephemeral character of our culture. This awareness has practical consequences for landscape management. It has become standard practice, for instance, for planning permissions for phone masts and wind turbines to be accompanied by conditions requiring their removal and site restoration when the structures become obsolete. But that sensitivity to the ephemeral is not matched by a sensitivity to more profound change. Bill McKibben proclaimed the end of nature more than two decades ago.[39] However, for all the talk about global warming, the omnipotence of human culture as an environmental force has yet to fully register in the conduct of our affairs.

Marek Kohn has speculated about the future of landscapes of Britain and Ireland.[40] Based on current knowledge of climate change, he expects that the two islands, especially the smaller one, will not change that much in the near future (to the end of the century). Along with a few other places in the world, such as New Zealand, we will temporarily escape the calamitous consequences of global warming and we may even enjoy a better climate from a human comfort perspective than the one we now have. A little hard to credit, given the run of recent wet summers, Kohn suggests that 'visitors to Ireland in the future are not going to complain that it isn't constantly raining, and with the advent of reliably fine summer weather, Ireland's tourist industry will gain the one advantage it now significantly lacks'.[41]

Chapter 5

CONFLICT

———

Conflict crystallises out the different ways that we look at landscape, differences that might otherwise remain hidden in the ebb and flow of everyday life. Development or planned development in a landscape can be so contentious that the resulting conflict throws lives out of balance and communities into disarray. One recent conflict, for instance, has been reported as being 'more divisive than the Civil War'.[1] These situations draw the interest of anthropologists, who have developed the concept of 'the contested space', which concerns the dynamics of conflict centred on geographical areas.

These conflicts reveal cultural differences and ideological divisions in a community that would otherwise remain hidden. It is the nature of contested spaces, according to anthropologist Adrian Peace, that 'they expose the fragility and frailty of social life by contrast with the constancy and solidity of the physical order'.[2] The conflicts have the potential to precipitate significant change in the wider society. Recent and current controversies include the gas pipeline project in Erris, County Mayo, the North-South electricity connector through Meath, Cavan and Monaghan and the Galway city and Slane village bypass routes. Major conflicts in the recent past have included the route of the M3 motorway past the Hill of Tara, proposed visitor centres at Mullaghmore and the Cliffs of Moher in Clare and at Luggala in the Wicklow Mountains, golf courses at the Old Head of Kinsale in Cork and at Doonbeg in County Clare, construction of the M50 at Carrickmines in County Dublin and of the N11 road through the Glen of the Downs in Wicklow. The frequency and wide distribution of conflict has prompted Peace to describe the Irish countryside as 'a perennial site of struggle'.[3] The conflicts in Erris, the Burren and at the Old Head of Kinsale are examined in this chapter and the next. This chapter also explores the ideological conflict that underlies the planning system and contributes to the distinctive character of Irish planning and of the Irish countryside.

Contested spaces are difficult to decipher. Layers of ideological conflict accrete around a space to such a degree that the physical reality of a place may be entirely obscured. Contemporary Erris in County Mayo is a case in point. In 2000 Enterprise Energy Ireland finalised the design of a terminal on an inland site to process gas from the newly discovered Corrib gas field. Enterprise Energy got planning permission from Mayo County Council but the decision was appealed. An Bord Pleanála eventually granted permission in 2004 to what was now Shell, the multinational having taken over Enterprise Energy. However, opposition to the project gained momentum, spearheaded by the 'Shell to Sea' campaign group. The gas terminal has been built but the focus of the opposition has shifted to the on-shore pipeline connecting the gas field to the terminal. Father Kevin Hegarty of Kilmore Erris parish, a supporter of the project, has depicted the opposition as a motley crew. There are those 'utterly caught in a vision of thatched cottages and small farms and seemingly happy times' and there are those who believe that the state has sold the gas resource too cheaply. There are 'extreme environmentalists' who include 'eco warriors who, committed as they are to the environment, find the harsh environment of Erris too difficult in winter. They usually disappear for winter and return in April like the swallows.' And there are also the extreme nationalists who 'have a vision of Ireland almost like the Aryan vision that Hitler had, that above all Ireland must be pure, even of course if it ends up poor'.[4] Father Hegarty's disparaging description portrays opponents driven by ideological fervour and largely detached from the realities of Erris. Some credibility is lent to his portrayal by the subsequent unmasking of a protester as an undercover London Metropolitan Police officer who, while in Mayo, argued that it 'was really important for campaigns not only in Ireland, in Mayo or in Iceland but also campaigns in Spain, in Italy [to] work together'.[5] PC Mark Kennedy has since said that he has been at five major protests and that he has received a commendation from Prime Minister Tony Blair for his intelligence work in relation to the G8 summit in Scotland in 2005.

However, an entirely different perspective emerges from the account written by journalist Lorna Siggins and from *The Pipe*, a film documentary directed by Risteard Ó Domhnaill who had been a local resident.[6] Reading Siggins and watching *The Pipe*, it is clear that there is a core group of objectors who are not bent on an ideological crusade of any kind. It is a small group of local families who are motivated by fear and anger. The fear is the fear of living beside a potentially dangerous high-pressure gas pipeline. The anger is a response to the approach taken by the developer and the state agencies. That approach exemplifies the 'DAD' project management model, Design, Announce and Defend, that has been described by geographer Eileen O'Rourke and which she regards as a mindset inherited from the colonial era.[7] As Willie Corduff, one of the local residents, explained to journalist Ed Vulliamy 'It was a Scottish fellow came one morning. And you know, it was the arrogance that triggered me off. There was no asking. He told me what was going to happen, taking me for a fool'.[8]

Fig. 5.1. Graffiti, photographed in 2011 on the pier at Rossport, at the entrance of Sruwaddacon Bay, looking out into Broadhaven Bay. The gas pipeline has been laid on the floor of the two bays.

Vulliamy cannot avoid giving his report about Erris a romantic flourish. 'If the sea is calm, you can hear the traffic in New York, goes the local introduction to the breathtaking beauty of Erris in the north of County Mayo, where the coastline winds its way through little coves beneath the cliffs of the wild seaboard at Europe's edge.' But in truth the role of landscape in Erris is subtle and low key, primarily an aspect of the attachment to place that is strengthening the resolve of the small group facing the advancing pipeline. One of the group, Micheál Ó Seighin, has an especially refined sense of Erris, which he sees as a complex place, its cultural history reflected in a mosaic of place names and distinctive local dialects.[9] It may be that in Erris landscape conservation has been a convenient rallying point standing in for reasons and emotions that are more difficult to articulate. A senior inspector in An Bord Pleanála has observed how 'landscape' is often a prominent issue at the start of oral hearings but disappears into the background as 'real reasons' come to the fore.[10]

If in Erris the role of landscape has become relatively peripheral, in other places landscape is centre stage. One such place is Mullaghmore in County Clare. Adrian Peace and geographer Eileen O'Rourke have studied this contested space, where, in the early 1970s, the Office of Public Works was authorised to investigate as a potential Burren National Park.[11] W.A. Watts, Professor of Botany at Trinity College in Dublin, advised the OPW to make Mullaghmore the nucleus of the park, due to the range and quality of habitats on and beside the hill. The OPW began to buy land there in 1976 and the establishment of the park, covering an area of just over 1,100 hectares, was announced in 1991. The OPW also unveiled plans to build a visitor centre at the same time. As the law stood in 1991, the OPW did not need planning permission for its scheme; it could do pretty well what it liked. The project was presented to the public as a fait accompli, but it quickly ran into serious opposition, led by the Burren Action Group (BAG), an ad hoc collection of individuals. In a matter of weeks Mullaghmore became a bitter dispute with long-term consequences. It was a David and Goliath contest. On the one side was the state, supported by the local establishment, including local branches of the IFA, GAA and Fianna Fáil. This group saw Mullaghmore as 'just a piece of old crag' that could be exploited to create jobs and to boost the local economy. Local farmers, according to O'Rourke, 'interpreted the landscape essentially in terms of its production values' and got angry with people who ascribed other values to it.[12] On the other side of the dispute was BAG, a diverse group, most of whom were well educated and, although from the local area, had lived elsewhere and were not so well connected locally. This group regarded Mullaghmore as a fragile and exceptional place, even a sacred place, which had to be protected at all costs, individuals putting their homes and livelihoods on the line to fund a court action. At a meeting of the pro-development group, a local

Fianna Fáil councillor labelled them as 'blowins, hippies, homosexuals, drug-smokers, intellectuals, and non-meat eaters'.[13] Two local farmers in BAG told O'Rourke how 'they were not welcome in local pubs and shops and they were ignored at local football matches'.[14] They were cut adrift from their community and, as one of them put it, 'we saved the hay on our own that year'.[15]

Following unsuccessful lobbying of the EU, which was the main funder of the project, BAG secured an injunction to stop further work on the visitor centre site on the grounds of the unconstitutionality of the OPW actions. The courts, including the Supreme Court, found in favour of BAG. This meant that the OPW had to apply for planning permission, just like any other individual or body in the state. It duly applied for a scaled-down development, now called an 'entry point', in 1996. Permission was initially refused by Clare County Council and that decision was appealed by the Minister for Arts, Heritage, Gaeltacht and the Islands to An Bord Pleanála. The board held an oral hearing in Ennis in July

Fig. 5.2. Sod-turning ceremony in November 1992 at the site of the proposed Mullaghmore Interpretative Centre.

1999 and decided to refuse permission in March 2000. BAG then got a High Court order to have the site restored to its original condition and the restatement works were completed in 2001. Since then nature has taken a hand and it is now not that easy to see where the visitor centre site had been (see Figs 5.2 and 5.3). The National Parks and Wildlife Service has laid out an attractive walking trail through the site, and seasonal grazing by a herd of Belted Galloway cattle has helped to restore the quality of the species-rich grassland. The lepidopterist Jesmond Harding now describes the land as part of the best butterfly site in Ireland.[16]

Fig. 5.3. Lepidopterist Jesmond Harding leading a field trip to the former interpretative centre site in June 2010 (Mullaghmore in the background). The flower-rich meadows are seasonally grazed to maintain their biodiversity. Harding regards the area as the best place in Ireland for butterflies.

Simon Bourke has identified three contemporary ideologies which, at different times, dominate the heritage discourse. They can be summarised as: heritage is a valuable commodity which can be conserved and exploited; heritage has an intrinsic value and is part of national identity; and heritage is abundant and dispensable.[17] The Mullaghmore conflict illustrated the interplay of these perspectives in the arena of a contested space. The developer, the OPW, decided to build a visitor centre to exploit the tourism potential of the site and the availability of generous EU funding for visitor centres. With only a few exceptions, local businesses, landowners and politicians, who shared the perspective of the OPW, enthusiastically supported the project. Their attitudes illustrate the 'landscape as commodity' viewpoint, focused on tangible material benefits such as an enhanced local economy and new jobs. For the landowners, 'in their entirely pragmatic mode of thinking, land was not so much a thing as a complex relation entailing a remorseless struggle to extract maximum economic return'.[18]

By contrast, the concerns of the leaders of the Burren Action Group were centred on the 'aesthetic, intangible and sensuous qualities' of Mullagmore. 'It was Mullaghmore's magic and mystery which [they] returned to in public meetings, fundraising events, Xeroxed pamphlets and innumerable encounters with media'.[19] They regarded the landscape as 'priceless' and unique. They valued the mountain for 'itself' rather than for the potential economic benefits that could be extracted from it.

The antithesis of that BAG perspective is the view that, by virtue of its ubiquity, landscape heritage is worthless. There were a good many people in north Clare in 1991 who could not see what all the fuss was about at Mullaghmore. For them, the mountain, as Peace and O'Rourke have described, was no more than 'just a bit of old crag'. O'Rourke tells how the local IFA had to bring in 'experts' to explain to its members what is was that was special about the Burren.[20] Indeed, before 1991, Mullaghmore hardly registered in the national consciousness even within 'high culture' circles. In the well-regarded 1967 cultural guide by Lord Killanin and Michael Duignan, the only reference to Mullaghmore is the Mullaghmore in County Sligo.[21]

Simon Bourke describes a depressing trajectory over recent times in which 'heritage possessing an intrinsic value' has been replaced as the dominant ideology by 'heritage as commodity' during the 1970s, only in turn to be displaced by the notion that 'heritage is dispensable' in the '90s. This chronology does not tally with my own experience in the Irish planning system over that period. As far as I am concerned the contrasting perspectives have always been present. Landscape as a marketable asset enters the thinking of every farmer and auctioneer who has ever advertised a site with a view of the sea, a lake or a mountain. The economic parameters nearly always dominate the discourse about more contentious planning applications. There has always been scepticism about landscape having an intrinsic heritage value. In public attitude surveys carried out on behalf of the Heritage Council, landscape and flora are the categories least recognised as heritage by the general public. Historic sites and buildings are the most valued and recognised heritage, followed by memorabilia and historical artefacts, culture and sport, fauna and nature reserves.[22] If the

centuries, leading to 'a situation in which the acquisition of property became a disproportionately important goal in Irish society'.[29]

Clientelism is a strong component of political life in this country and, as land and property are such important aspects of Irish society, it is no surprise to find clientelism at the heart of the planning system.[30] The informal clientelist structures support, and are exploited by, democratically elected politicians and senior bureaucrats. The local tier of government is especially weak, James Wickham believing that 'local authorities have so few resources and effective strategic powers . . . that they are always likely to attract politicians whose vision of politics is limited to doing favours for their friends (or even finding friends for whom they can do favours)'.[31]

The movers and shakers in the planning system have often expressed little time for a heritage agenda. The oft-quoted phrase by Fianna Fáil minister Kevin Boland denouncing conservationists in 1971 as a 'consortium of belted earls and their ladies and left-wing intellectuals' continues to resonate. The dysfunctional character of local planning authorities occasionally comes to light. Kerry County Council is frequently in the spotlight, the outstanding landscape heritage of the county presenting a perennial challenge for the planning system. In 2001, then councillor and TD, Jackie Healy-Rae, in a debate in the council chamber about rural planning, warned then county manager Martin Nolan that 'there are places in this county thou dare not . . . you or other officials'.[32] The state of planning in Kerry at the time prompted Professor Frank Convery of University College Dublin (UCD) to wonder how 'the tourism industry in Kerry has been so passive in the context of the collapse of the planning system there'.[33]

Clientelism, although rooted in local affairs, is conspicuously blind to the heritage of place. A clientelist culture can be profoundly corrupt but this would misrepresent its nature in Ireland, with the notable exception of the poisonous climate surrounding land dealings in County Dublin in the 1980s and '90s, that has been unmasked by the Flood and Mahon Tribunal.[34] Both the inherent humanity and inequity of the Irish culture is best illustrated by a specific example. Frank McDonald and James Nix, in *Chaos at the Crossroads*, tell the story of an illegal quarry near Athleague in County Roscommon.[35] Local residents complained to the council about the major disturbance they were suffering from rock blasting and from the trucks using the quarry. The local council began enforcement proceedings against the brothers who owned the quarry. However, one of them was a secretary of the local Fianna Fail cumann and another lived in Bertie Ahern's Dublin constituency (when he was taoiseach). That brother called to the taoiseach's clinic for help. Within a month the council received a letter from Bertie asking it to defer action against the quarry. Senator Cyprian Brady, who ran the constituency office, explained that the intervention was a

Fig. 5.4. Croagh Patrick viewed from outside Westport. In 2002, councillors adopted a blanket ban on mining activity in the area but in 2003 they also zoned all the low-lying land in this photograph for residential development.

'humanitarian gesture' because one of the brothers was undergoing treatment for cancer. Here then were well-intentioned politicians deploying the influence at their disposal for the benefit of a client. It is an example of clientelism at work, made somewhat unusual only by the involvement of a serving taoiseach. In 2009, Roscommon County Council granted planning permission for the quarry, a decision that was subsequently upheld on appeal by An Bord Pleanála by a majority of two to one.

There is only one example in recent decades of a landscape conservation issue that was vigorously promoted by local politicians. This is the landscape setting of Croagh Patrick, Ireland's sacred mountain. In 1992, prompted by gold prospecting activity near the mountain, Mayo County Council voted by twenty-two to eight, and against the advice of the Department of Energy, to declare a blanket prohibition on the extraction of minerals over a 300-square-mile area, including Croagh Patrick.[36] At that time mining operations did not require

the low-rise suburbs north and south of the city built by private developers. In the case of England and the Netherlands, the 'new town' label is a more-or-less accurate description of new settlements with distinctive identities. I was at a planning conference in Dublin in 2008 where a Dublin planner invited Richard Forman, one of the conference speakers, to compare the designated green belts in north Dublin with green belts around other cities. Forman, Professor of Landscape Ecology at Harvard University, has applied an ecological approach, incorporating the green belt concept, to a masterplan for the Barcelona city region. The Barcelona green belt contains great swathes of protected natural habitat and expanses of cultivated farmland. The areas of natural habitat are connected by vegetated corridors to form an 'emerald network'.[42] These areas perform an array of important social, ecological and economic functions and are assets that, in Forman's view, can underpin a sustainable city region. The green belts in north Dublin in some places are no more than two or three fields in width. Forman, who had had the opportunity to look around North Dublin before the conference, politely informed his questioner that the only feature shared by the Dublin and Barcelona green belts was the 'green belt' label (Fig. 5.5).

There is a sharp distinction between planning at the local authority level where most planning is done and the regulatory role performed by An Bord Pleanála at national level. The board, which took over the appeal responsibility from a government minister in 1976, is insulated from clientelism by an array of legal and administrative barriers. In recent years the board has been assiduous in its efforts not only to be above the fray but also to be seen to be above reproach. In a speech made shortly before his retirement in 2011, the board's chairman made a point of stating that 'while some will disagree with the Board's decisions, the independence or impartiality of the Board has never been seriously questioned. Despite all of the controversies about property and planning, I can truthfully say that nobody from any quarter ever made an improper approach to me'.[43] Although appointed by a minister, board members are well qualified individuals (not necessarily planners), who are nominated to panels by independent bodies.

The decision making of the board provides a gauge of decision making in local planning authorities. When it assesses a planning decision, the board takes account of the same plans and policies as the local planning authority. The board is advised by professional planners with the same education and professional background as their local authority counterparts. The board does not have to accept the recommendations of its inspectors but it has to give reasons for not doing so, based on planning grounds. It might reasonably be expected therefore that An Bord Pleanála would endorse the great majority of decisions by local authorities. In fact it overturns about a third of all decisions and makes significant changes to the majority of others. In a handful of counties, a high proportion of planning decisions are overturned. In the period 2005 to 2010, the board reversed more than 40 per cent of the decisions of Wexford, Roscommon and Cavan County Councils and more than 50 per cent of Donegal County Council's.[44] In County Louth, Gerry Crilly, a member of An Taisce's national council, has appealed all the grants of permission by the council for large housing projects in Dunleer, his home town, over the past decade. The current population of the town is under 2,000 but councillors had envisaged the town growing to between 40 and 50,000 people. Simply by restating local and national planning policies, as they relate to Dunleer, Crilly has won all his appeals.[45]

There are two explanations for this discrepancy between council and board decisions. It illustrates the absence of a consensus about the nature of common good, the principle that lies at the heart of the planning system. It is quite possible that different groups of well-qualified, well-intentioned individuals will arrive at quite different conclusions, based on the same information, about potential development. However, this factor cannot explain the enormous discrepancy between the performances of different local authorities in relation to appeal decisions and the very high percentages of overturned decisions that there are in some areas. That suggests a very different modus operandi in the two tiers of the regulatory planning system; that is, a system influenced by clientelism at local authority level in contrast to a technocratic decision-making system at board level.

At national level the decisions of An Bord Pleanála are often criticised but the fact that criticism comes from a range of opinion would suggest that the board is performing its function in an impartial manner. The board is a critical component of an increasingly complex system. Decision making in planning is more transparent than in most branches of government. In 2008, local planning authorities in the Republic made decisions on 62,000 planning applications and An Bord Pleanála considered appeals against 5,000 of those decisions.[46] Very few of the decisions were challenged in the courts, which have given a strong message over the years that planning should be left to the planning authorities. Despite a permanent clamour of opposition from grassroots politicians, the Irish planning system has retained checks and balances that rein in the worst excesses of clientelism. The status of An Bord Pleanála is secure, the right of third-party appeal is entrenched and other bodies, most notably An Taisce, have retained a controversial statutory role.

As the appeal figures above illustrate, only a very small proportion of development decisions are appealed, so that An Bord Pleanála's influence on landscape change has a serendipitous quality. It may be safely assumed, based on the appeal decisions that are made, that a significant proportion of development

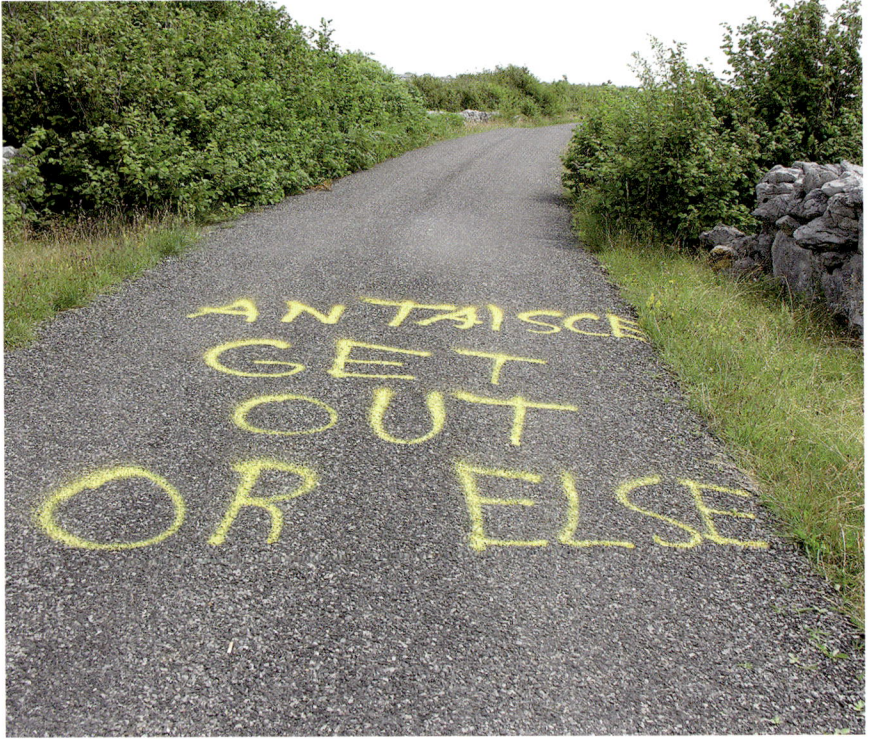

Fig. 5.6. Road graffiti in the Burren National Park in 2007. An Taisce owns 15 hectares of land in the national park at Mullaghmore but the sentiment of the sign carries a wider message (Source: Deirdre O'Mahony, An Taisce Get Out, Inkjet print on Diebond, 21.7 x 16.5 cm 2007. Copyright the artist)

that does take place would not withstand the scrutiny of the board. If the performance of the planning system falls seriously short, measured against the stated objective of 'proper planning and sustainable development', it does play an invaluable role in mediating and mitigating the conflicts that are an inevitable consequence of development in settled landscapes.

Mullaghmore illustrates how a reformed planning system successfully mediated the development process at one contested space, though Mullaghmore cannot be portrayed as an unalloyed success. The planning system ensured that a visitor centre was not built in the wrong place but did not result in it being built at a more appropriate site in one of the nearby villages. The conflict seems to have resulted in the state temporarily abrogating responsibility for visitor management in this national park. The Erris story exposes the limitations of the statutory system and signals a need for new approaches to scoping the location of major infrastructure projects in the settled landscapes of Ireland. In Erris, a common refrain of the five local men, who comprise the Rossport Five, has been the inability of the developer, the contractors, lawyers or politicians involved in the conflict to give credence to anything other than the financial aspects of the project.[47, 48] Landscape, viewed through the prism of property and commodity, is the dominant perspective. This perspective is examined in the next chapter.

Chapter 6

PROPERTY AND COMMODITY

———

I grew up about as far away from the sea as it is possible to be on these islands. When I was a child, a trip to the seaside was a rare treat. This may help to explain why, when I got a job in Dublin in 1978, I wanted to live by the sea. When I first arrived in the city I spent part of every weekend exploring the suburbs and villages on the coastal rail line for somewhere to live, and eventually I found an attractive Victorian terraced house for rent in Skerries, the dormitory town that lies to the north of the city. The house had a garden that backed onto the beach. I led an uncomfortable and, in many respects, unsatisfactory existence in Skerries.

I could only afford the rent by taking in a lodger with whom, it turned out, I had little in common. The house had never been modernised so that living conditions were primitive. I still have a memory of coming home from work and the icy draught of air from the inside of the house which used to hit me when I opened the front door. This was in the days when the only CIÉ suburban trains were clapped-out old diesels and I had an uncomfortable commute to Dublin. I had a poor social life as Skerries was a settled place of families with children. What life there was for a single person revolved around the rugby and sailing clubs, neither of which interested me. All in all, in retrospect, it was a fairly miserable existence but at the time I considered myself fortunate. My Dublin friends and colleagues had bought houses on new housing estates without, it seemed to me, redeeming features. Their houses had back gardens facing other back gardens and the backs of other houses. They were surrounded by ugly houses and roads. I lived in an attractive house even if it lacked mod cons. There was a beach at the end of my garden where I could watch breaking waves and the sunrise. I rented my house; they had bought theirs with the help of a mortgage. My priority was to live somewhere that I liked, theirs seemed to be to live somewhere that they could eventually own.

Surveys carried out around that time reveal how out of step my own priorities were. A review of Irish housing in 1979 concluded that for 'an overwhelming majority of residents the system works rather well'.[1] Most people owned their homes and high levels of satisfaction were recorded in attitude surveys. In one survey, 55 per cent of householder respondents were 'very satisfied' and 37 per cent 'fairly satisfied'.[2] The survey found that the most important physical factors which explained satisfaction were to do with the quality of house construction, such as good heating and freedom from damp and draughts. The researchers found that aesthetic and locational factors were not influential. A sustained consumer demand, for what most urban designers would regard as a seriously inadequate form of urban development, is one of the more perplexing aspects of Irish suburbia. The findings lend support to that often-expressed opinion that, as a society, Ireland is not as interested in visual beauty as it is in other manifestations of beauty such as literature, the theatre and music. In the last fifteen years, suburbia has leapfrogged the outer suburbs of our cities and large housing estates have sprouted around most towns and many villages. The dormitory suburbs of Dublin now extend from Louth in the north to Wexford in the south and Westmeath in the west. In 2009 *Irish Times* journalists re-interviewed families they had first interviewed in 2003, shortly after they had moved to their new homes in the outer reaches of the region. Despite a daily grind of ninety-minute and longer commutes and the deficiencies of local services and facilities, the interviewees, with few exceptions, reported an improved quality of life and an intention to remain where they were.³ However, I view those responses with suspicion. I believe they are as likely to reflect a natural inclination to make the best of circumstances and to justify the biggest investment most people ever make, as to represent a reliable picture of the quality of life in these relatively remote new places.

The importance we place on the ownership of property is a crucial aspect of our culture, not just in terms of our actions as individuals but also its effect on the well-being and distinctive character of our society. Property choices largely explain the genesis of the contested spaces that were described in the last chapter. The idea of a visitor centre at Mullaghmore became a concrete proposal because the prospective developer, in this case the state, owned land at Mullaghmore. Had the proposed building being sited 5 or 6 kilometres to the south-west, in or beside existing villages and the regional road system and some distance from Mullaghmore itself, there would never have been controversy. The ongoing conflict over a gas terminal and pipeline in Erris, County Mayo can be traced to the purchase by Enterprise Energy Ireland of a 165-hectare site at Ballinaboy. The Corrib Gas Field was discovered in 1996 and several hundred kilometres of coastline, stretching from Clare to Donegal, were investigated for a landfall for the gas pipe and a site for a terminal.⁴ The availability of a large inland site owned by a willing vendor, the state company Coillte, was the decisive locational factor that has set in train the conflict. Having acquired the site, Enterprise

Fig. 6.1. Ballinaboy Bridge, County Mayo, in 2011. The gas terminal is hidden from view in the forestry in the middleground.

Energy Ireland applied for planning permission for a terminal complex in 2000. Kevin Moore, the planning inspector who assessed the application, concluded that 'from a strategic planning perspective, this is the wrong site; from the perspective of . . . balanced regional development this is the wrong site; from the perspective of minimising environmental impact this is the wrong site; and consequently, from the perspective of sustainable development, this is the wrong site'.[5] He recommended refusal of permission but a revised proposal, on the same site, did get permission in 2005. The terminal has now been built but the pipeline connecting the gas field to the terminal has yet to be completed.

Both the Mullaghmore and Ballinaboy projects were subject to very broad locational imperatives. The visitor centre needed to be in or near the Burren National Park which it was 'interpreting' and the Ballinaboy terminal had to be on or near the coastline facing the gas field. There was nothing inherently wrong with either project other than the choice of site, which, in both cases, was made on pragmatic grounds of land availability without much weight being given to other critical considerations. In 2011, An Bord Pleanála, to widespread surprise and consternation, by unanimous decision granted planning permission for a 'Las Vegas-style' casino, sports complex and entertainment resort on a 330-hectare site in the Aherlow Valley near Twomileborris in County Tipperary.[6] The key economic driver in the project is a casino hotel with 500 bedrooms and a 6,000m² casino on the ground floor. The site is near the M8 Cork–Dublin motorway but about as far as it is possible to be from a city or transport hub on the east side of the country. The project location seems only explicable in so far as it is the brainchild of a local businessman who owns a large site that can physically accommodate the quantum of development proposed. The developer and the planning authorities that have granted permission appear to assume that, with its heliport and motorway access, the project is immune to the imperatives of physical accessibility that would otherwise dictate an urban location.

The other side of the coin of the private ownership of land is that it can enable development to take place that is to the broader benefit of society. Expensive capital-intensive projects need security of title to proceed, whether that is achieved by purchase from a willing vendor, through an effective compulsory purchase mechanism or some other secure and generally accepted means. The casino project in Tipperary is supported by horse-racing interests because it includes a Grade 1 horse-racing track to replace existing, lower-standard tracks in Munster. This seems to have significantly influenced An Bord Pleanála to make a positive decision.[7] Large-scale development projects of this kind are impractical in parts of the world where traditional land tenure patterns survive; that is, where land is communally held by a clan or a tribe, unless the traditional system is disregarded or subverted. These traditional systems nevertheless reflect a natural sense of the landscape that we inhabit as a shared and communal resource.

Private property consists of natural and man-made capital. Natural capital is 'God given' and includes everything from genetic codes to minerals, ecosystems and topography. Man-made capital is created by individuals and groups and includes businesses and shares and buildings and roads. In traditional systems, what today we regard as property is the sum of the parts of the territory inhabited by the tribe, held in trust for the tribe by the chief and elders. If that tribal perspective has been consigned to history, mankind, through its religions and philosophical traditions continues to recognise a universal entitlement to the enjoyment of nature and a communal responsibility to protect the heritage handed on by previous generations. However, those instincts and teachings are often poorly served by modern systems of government in which the rights of private property and the operation of the market economy are paramount. In Ireland, Feasta, the Foundation for the Economics of Sustainability, has argued for a community tax on land to capture and redistribute the communal value in property.[8]

What are regarded as traditional values and attitudes about property in Ireland only go back to the eighteenth and nineteenth centuries. A more intimate and more inclusive relationship between Irish society and the land was erased during the preceding centuries of colonisation.[9] In 1804, Ireland was owned by a privileged, predominantly Protestant minority of between 8,000 and 10,000 landlords, about a third of whom were absentees.[10] The system rapidly unravelled in the final decades of the century after the Great Famine, as a result of agrarian unrest and legislative reform. Effectively, a revolution took place with an owner-occupying, Catholic Irish landed class being created within the space of thirty years.[11] But this new order was far from 'The Land for the People' ideal of the Irish National League. There was no place in it for large sections of society – slum-living urban dwellers, the northern unionists or displaced agricultural labourers living in Manhattan, Manchester and elsewhere.[12] At the same time the land question had become inseparable from the struggle for nationhood. By 1920, Ireland was an agrarian society dominated by conservative Catholic owner-occupiers, the majority of whom owned farms that were barely viable. It was a society that could only survive by emigration. 'The west, where the Land War began, [had] proved to be the cradle of the modern Irish nation' while the small farmer had become synonymous with the national identity.[13] This history, first landlordism and then emigration and bare survival as an impoverished, land-owning peasantry, has left an indelible mark on the Irish psyche. It has left behind a preoccupation with the private ownership of land and property that sets us apart from most west European countries and subverts the role of the state as protector of the common good in matters relating to land use and development. We share our fondness for private property with the British where, 'behind all the publicly proclaimed ideals of [the farming and landowning organisations], who describe farmers and landowners as the custodians of the countryside or the stewards of the nation's heritage, are the harsh facts of self-interest and sectional interest'.[14] But that reality in Britain is tempered by countervailing historical factors. Unlike Ireland, there is the legacy of a dense network of legally protected public rights of way to ensure access to the rural landscape. And the environmental and social upheavals of the industrial revolution have left a lasting legacy of powerful conservation bodies and a broad base of support for nature and landscape conservation.

Private property rights are set out in Articles 40 and 43 of the Irish Constitution. Article 40 requires the state to make laws to protect the property rights of its citizens. Article 43 affirms the right of every citizen to own property and directs the state to pass no law that prohibits that right. However, Article 43 balances that right with the principle of social justice, empowering the state to curtail the right of private ownership in the interest of the common good. It is this concept of 'common good' that is intended to capture and safeguard the communal dimension of property. The introduction of a land use planning system in 1963 marked a significant curtailment of private land rights, in the interest of the common good. However, over the succeeding decades the legislative framework has been like the proverbial dyke, having to be repeatedly plugged to curb landowner rights and secure the balance enshrined in Article 43. During the 1980s, public authorities were emasculated in their efforts to curtail suburban sprawl by a fear of incurring crippling compensation claims triggered by refusals of planning permission for the development of sites near towns and cities. At that time, while an authority could zone land for non-profitable purposes such as open space or amenity, it could only ensure those land use outcomes if it was able to compensate affected landowners for loss of a theoretical development potential. If a site could be sewered, the site had development potential regardless of its suitability in other respects. This anomaly was not corrected until 1990 when legislation was amended to make the carrying out of development that was not in accordance with the zoning in a development plan a non-compensatable reason for refusing permission. The 1963 Act largely exempted from the planning code farming, forestry and other rural activities, despite the landscape and environmental impacts of these operations when carried out on an industrial scale. Golf course projects did not require planning permission until 1994 and forestry and peat-cutting operations were not brought fully within the regulatory system until 2000.

While running repairs to the legislation have been ongoing, development has continued apace, sometimes inflicting long-term damage to the landscape and general environment. The recent history of the Old Head of Kinsale in Cork is a salutary tale (see Fig. 6.2). It illustrates both how development trends have frequently outpaced legislative reform and the very limited extent of public access to countryside in Ireland compared to other European countries.[15] When I lived in Cork city in the late 1970s, a visit to Kinsale, combined with a walk across the Old Head, was a popular weekend trip. The headland offered a bracing stroll in a spectacular setting. We used to park above the narrow neck of the peninsula and then walk the track to the lighthouse at the southern end of the Head. There is a wealth of local heritage there, including the ruins of a fifteenth-century castle and a large seabird colony. At that time the Old Head was classified as an Area of National Scientific Importance, was listed as an Area of Visual and Scientific Importance in the county development plan and was included in the national inventory of outstanding landscapes. Here then was a public amenity recognised as part of the national heritage and enjoyed by thousands of citizens every week. However, within the space of a few years public access to the area was closed off and the headland became an exclusive golf course. How could this have happened?

There is a relatively simple answer and also a more complex one. The simple answer is that Michael Roche, a local farmer and the owner of the headland,

Fig. 6.2. The Old Head of Kinsale in 2010. The Supreme Court confirmed in 2003 that there was no right of public access to the headland, even though, for decades, thousands had enjoyed unencumbered access.

decided to sell his land. He sold it to Ashbourne Holdings in 1989, a company owned by brothers John and Patrick O'Connor. They wanted to build a private golf course and at that time the project did not require planning permission. Ashbourne Holdings laid out a course, initially allowing public access to continue, but eventually closed the road to the public. (It transpired that there had never been a dedicated public right of way.) Today the golf course is a commercial success, largely catering to the luxury American market. The club brochure describes it as 'one of the most recognised and sought after golf experiences anywhere on earth. It is a sanctuary for those seeking the finest in personalised service.' Before selling to Ashbourne Holdings, Michael Roche had offered the land to the OPW and to Cork County Council. According to Roche, the OPW were not interested and the council's offer was derisory.

Viewing the recent history of the Old Head in the context of Article 43, the property rights of Michael Roche and the O'Connors have been protected. Just as clearly, 'the common good' has not. The destiny of the Old Head was decided by the contract to purchase the land in 1989. The fact that the Head was an outstanding landscape and a local amenity enjoyed by thousands of people (200,000 annually, according to writer Alannah Hopkin) turned out to have had no bearing on what transpired.

The privatisation of the headland at the behest of the Irish courts came as a shock to the planning authorities. Although, at the time, building the golf course did not require planning permission, building a club house did. Both Cork County Council and An Bord Pleanála granted permissions for a club house on condition that public access to the headland was maintained. However, in 1993, first the High Court and then the Supreme Court found that the planning authorities had exceeded their powers in imposing such a condition. Delivering the judgement in the supreme court, Justice Hardiman quoted from Professor Yvonne Scannell's book *Environmental and Planning Law in Ireland*:

> It should not be assumed, as it sometimes is, that the wide discretion given to planning authorities to attach conditions . . . gives them carte blanche to exact benefits in cash or in kind from the developer in order to reflect the profit which the planning permission confers on him or to further some socially desirable objective promoted by the planning authority.[16]

Ashbourne Holdings had offered public access as part of their proposal, conscious of the strong local sentiment and the line that the council would take in deciding its application. However, the Supreme Court ruled that it was beyond the powers of the planning authority to insist on public access even when such was offered by the applicant and landowner. The judges commented that it was wrong as a general principle for developers to be pressurised into offering a public benefit. Cork County Council could have bought the Old Head of Kinsale when it had the opportunity. Alternatively, it could have made a special amenity area order, a statutory amenity designation, and, by agreement or compulsory purchase, created a public right of way across the headland. The making of a special amenity area order would have bestowed a strong measure of legal protection to the landscape in 1989. It would, for instance, have meant that planning permission would need to have been obtained to construct a golf course. However, since the power to make special amenity area orders was given to local authorities in 1963, none have ever been made outside the Dublin area and, as far as I know, no planning authority has ever used its power to create a public footpath.

Alannah Hopkin recalls a public meeting about the golf course project that took place in Actons Hotel in Kinsale in September 1992.[17] There were about 300 people at the meeting and she observes that 'the polarisation was sharp and uncomfortable', with local professionals living in and near Kinsale declaring against the project and the local farming community supporting it. She remembers the farmers at the back of the hall banging their sticks on the floor, stamping their feet and chanting 'Michael Roche must get his money.'

I recall a similar atmosphere in meetings I organised in west Clare, a few years later. Doonbeg is a coastal parish. The west side of the parish marks the beginning of the attractive coastal scenery of Loop Head while the east side is part of a low-lying coastal belt that stretches north to the Cliffs of Moher and is distinguished by broad sandy bays backed by towering sand dunes. The most impressive dunes are the Carrowmore dunes near Doonbeg where, in 1999, Landmark International, a US leisure company, obtained planning permission to build a golf resort. The company had been lured to Ireland by Shannon Development, which had identified the golf development potential of the site. There was quiet jubilation in the local parish at the prospect of new growth in an area that had suffered decades of economic and demographic decline. With the exception of an increase of just two people between 1981 and 1986, the population of the local electoral district had fallen in every inter-censal period between 1936 and 2002, from a population of over 1,000 in 1936 to 596 by 2002. However, Doonbeg stands out in County Clare as an enterprising and resilient community. It has one of the most successful GAA clubs in the county and the parish also hosts annual drama and jazz festivals. It was no surprise therefore that, as soon as the golf resort project got approval, the local development association began lobbying the council for a local development plan to guide the growth that would ensue. I worked in the council at the time and suggested that,

defect of the market system, almost entirely, if not entirely, cancelling out the benefits, in terms of the common good, of the statutory planning system. The defect was clearly apparent in the 1960s property boom. As a result a government committee was set up to find a method of 'ensuring that all, or a substantial part of the increase in the value of land attributable to the decisions and operations of public authorities . . . shall be secured for the benefit of the community'. 'The Kenny Report', published in 1973, has been part of the planning landscape ever since. The report, which has never been implemented, recommended that local authorities be empowered to acquire land in designated areas at agricultural value plus a premium of 25 per cent. Landowners would get a reasonable profit from selling their land but they would no longer become millionaires simply because they owned land beside a town or city. In 2000, Taoiseach Bertie Ahern, asked an all-party committee to review Kenny and the committee came to almost the same conclusion. According to Fintan O'Toole, every party in government has agreed in principle with Kenny. They have all managed 'to believe that this conviction was like agreeing with Pythagoras' theorem – it was clearly right but you didn't have to do anything about it'.[19]

Until the passing of the National Asset Management Agency (NAMA) Act in 2009, which introduced an 80 per cent windfall tax on rezoned land, the suburban periphery provided the most profitable location to make money out of owning land. A handsome profit could be turned by land speculators and

Fig. 6.4. Terryland suburb, Galway, in 2010, lying outside the city ring road and viewed from the ring road.

those in the business of converting farmland into housing estates. The suburban periphery was the most promising location to extract the commodity value of landscape although, in truth, the landscape aspect was hardly ever recognised, the land typically being treated as a development site, without individual character.

This building process in the outer suburbs has usually paid scant regard to the existing rural landscape. The preferred approach to site preparation until the 1990s was creating a tabula rasa, obliterating surface natural features such as trees, hedgerows, walls, ponds, streams and existing buildings before commencing development. Only belatedly, prodded by planning authorities and a dawning recognition that 'heritage' and 'a sense of place' were marketable assets, has a more sophisticated approach to site development become the norm. 'Prairie planning' and 'concrete jungle' are epithets widely applied to new estates and suburbs when they are first built, the epithets defying forensic scrutiny but nevertheless conveying the notion that these are not attractive places in which to live. However, Irish suburbs, generally built at very low densities by international standards, provide great scope for 'greening up'. In the moist Irish climate which favours the rapid growth of trees, hedgerows and shrubberies, dystopian worlds can be transformed into attractive leafy suburbs within the space of a generation.

A practised eye may discern the utopian ideals underlying adopted standards and regulations, but overwhelmingly the character of Irish suburbia has been shaped by market forces. This is in contrast to other European countries where a more interventionist role by the state in determining the character and quality of housing environments has ensured more design-driven and more ideologically-driven development that has led to more diverse suburban places, with mixed blessings for their inhabitants. Nicholas Taylor, for instance, has described how in Britain 'a perpetual sociological-architectural by-election athmosphere' has reined, leading to 'disastrously contradictory candidates of built form'.[20] In Ireland, by contrast, we have had half-a-century of conservative, architectural stability. The wide belts of low-density suburbs that have sprouted around every city and town and, latterly, many villages, are among the most distinctive Irish landscape creations of recent times.

During the 1960s and '70s, local authorities were leading developers but in recent decades nearly all development has been by the private sector. The new suburbs are strikingly uniform places – row upon row of houses built in identical styles at gross densities of around seventeen dwellings per hectare (seven per acre). The semi-detached, two-storey house with a small front garden and 10-metre deep back garden is the most common dwelling type. The character of the housing reflects the conservative preferences of the Irish consumer. The very low density of the housing is partly a consequence of those preferences but also of the road and open-space standards imposed by planning

Figs 6.5 and 6.6. 1960s housing estate in Skerries, County Dublin. By the time the first photograph was taken in 1995 the roadside trees and garden vegetation had become important elements of the townscape. By 2011, when the bottom photograph was taken, the trees dominate the townscape, creating an attractive degree of enclosure of the public road space.

Fig. 6.7. New estate on the outskirts of the small village of Dualla, near Cashel, County Tipperary in 2007, one of the thousands of estates 'tacked on' to existing small settlements during the first decade of the new century.

authorities. Builders have sought to maximise the number of units on a site while complying with those minimum standards, the resulting layouts having little regard to site topography or orientation. The standards have their origin in building codes mainly developed in Britain after the Second World War. The housing and open-space standards were a reaction to the characteristics of what had become slum housing, built in the nineteenth century, and road and parking standards evolved to meet the challenges of a rapid rise in car ownership from the 1960s onwards. During the last decade, a much greater variety of housing has been built around Dublin, but for most of the last forty years and in most of the country, the semi-detached house is the standard suburban unit. Typically, 25 per cent or more of the ground area of a housing estate is occupied by roadways and junctions. There is also a generous allocation of open space for recreation in the form of tracts of mowed grassland. As a result of the obligatory front gardens and off-street parking spaces and wide road widths, the buildings either side of suburban streets are at least 25 metres apart. This creates streetscapes that lack a sense of enclosure until roadside trees (if they have been planted) mature. Unenclosed spaces, the repetitious character of the buildings, the absence of landmarks and the absence of any sign of human presence for much of the day combine to create bleak places. Until the end of the century, the only evidence of a conscious engagement with urban design, other than road design, was to be found in a small number of public housing projects, such as Ballymun in the 1960s and Darndale in the '70s on the north side of Dublin; Mahon on the east side of Cork in the 1980s and the small-scale housing schemes in the midlands for Bord na Móna, designed by Arthur Gibney.

Figs 6.8 and 6.9.
Above, conventional terraced public housing in Coolock, photographed in 1983, and below, a Ballymun tower block, photographed in 1985. For two decades, from the late 1960s, the north suburbs of Dublin were one of the few places in the country where a variety of new residential environments were created.

Fig. 6.10. Detached 1970s private housing in Blanchardstown, Dublin, photographed in 1984. The large, detached house on a relatively small plot is a popular estate format of this era.

A successful commodification of landscape is a much more difficult task away from towns and cities. The Old Head of Kinsale golf course in Cork and the Doonbeg golf resort described earlier in this chapter are examples of relatively successful commodification. In both cases, the original landowners directly benefited from selling stretches of striking coastal scenery, and development has also brought longer-term benefits for the wider community. At Doonbeg, the population increased by over 100 between 2002 and 2006, the first substantial rise in the area for more than a century and an increase that was undoubtedly due to the new golf resort. In Cork, the Old Head Golf Club employs 250 people during the season from March to October. However, the Old Head and Doonbeg are exceptions to a general rule that it is difficult to translate landscape quality into a material benefit for either the individuals who own land or for the wider local community. At a national level, landscape is a valuable tourism asset, second only to the friendliness of the people as a visitor attractor. However, the revenue stream from tourism to the communities living in scenic areas is probably declining, not increasing. 'The Ring of Kerry', that is, the Iveragh Peninsula, is a premier tourism destination and scenery is its main attraction, according to a 2004 survey. However, very little of the money spent by tourists on Iveragh finds its way to the farmers and other landowners of the peninsula. The 2004 survey found that 49 per cent of tourists stayed in hotels and only 1 per cent opted for farmhouse accommodation.[21] There has been a sharp decline in the bed-and-breakfast business in recent years. Government grants for hotel expansion have led to an over-capacity in the hotel sector. Agri-tourism, a concept promoted by government and by the EU in the last two decades as a solution to the economic problems of peripheral rural areas, has not had much of an impact on Iveragh. In a 2009 study of farmers on the peninsula, only 17 per cent had diversified into tourism-related businesses and, in relation to that 17 per cent, the income generated from tourism was less than a quarter of household income.[22] Landowners, principally farmers (increasingly part time), are the custodians of our exceptional landscapes. If they cannot derive a significant economic benefit from tourism within such a popular tourism area as Iveragh, it is difficult to envisage tourism as the foundation of a viable landscape conservation model in this country. Irish tourism is becoming increasingly urban. The 'Ring of Kerry', a comfortable day's excursion from a hotel in Killarney or Kenmare, is a product of the motor car age. Journalist John O'Dwyer wonders if this 'drive-by tourism' is providing the best recreational experience. He comments that 'even to the casual observer it is clear that Kerry tourism is increasingly an urban phenomenon. Dragging these holidaymakers from their comfortable bar stools and four-star hotels to sample the breezy but hugely rewarding attractions of the countryside will be a formidable challenge'.[23]

More than any other outlook, a property outlook enables an understanding of the mechanism of landscape change in Ireland today. At a 2011 conference entitled

Fig. 6.11. Visitor signage beside the M18 at Drumoland in County Clare in 2009.

'The Burren: What Is To Be Done?' the chairman of Burren Irish Farmers' Association, suggested that the key question should always be 'Will it put food on the table?' However, for a great many people, this materialist perspective is much too narrow and other considerations should be to the fore. These other aspects of our experience of landscape are examined in the next two chapters.

Chapter 7

HISTORY, MEMORY AND DREAMS

———————

There were days during the last decade when the property supplements were bigger than the newspapers themselves and scores of people were buying houses 'off the plans', guided by architects' drawings, artistic impressions and an irrepressible urge to acquire property. These were the boom times for estate agents, advertising executives, lifestyle television producers and other dream purveyors. The collapse of the property bubble in 2008 has left a legacy of unfinished projects across the country, which stand as a powerful demonstration of the potency of the irrational in human affairs.

The photographs below show Ballysadare in County Sligo, a village 8 kilometres to the south of Sligo town. The village has been devastated by the property crash. There are five large unfinished housing schemes there containing over 400 dwelling units, the equivalent of the total housing stock in the village and surrounding countryside in 2006.[1] By the winter of 2010, only fifty-five units in the new schemes were occupied. There are whole streets of empty houses and apartments and there is a poignant contrast between the idealised future represented on the still-standing display boards and the drab reality of the village. The presiding spirit in Ballysadare and other similar places is the fictional Iowa farmer in the 1989 film 'Field of Dreams', played by Kevin Costner, who turned his corn field into a baseball ground, sustained by a philosophy of 'build it and they will come'.

Away from home and the places we know well, our engagement with landscape inevitably possesses a superficial quality. Seamus Heaney has remarked that 'When we go as tourists to Donegal or Connemara or Kerry we go with at best an aesthetic eye, comforting ourselves with the picturesqueness of it all or rejoicing in the fact that it is unspoiled. We will have little felt knowledge of the place, little enough of a sense of wonder or a sense of tradition'.[2] However, that

Fig. 7.1. Display boards advertising new development in the centre of Ballysadare village, County Sligo, photographed in 2010. The board is sited in front of the small park in the artist's impression. No park has been developed and most of the dwelling units are either vacant or unfinished. The fitness centre has been built but it is accessed via a cavernous and nearly empty underground car park.

Fig. 7.2. A built but largely empty precinct in Ballysadare in 2010.

tourist experience and other everyday encounters with landscape also have the capacity to enrich our lives. Paradoxically, connectedness with the surface reality of a place can touch us deeply. Destinations such as the west of Ireland retain an enduring appeal. During the last century the west became one of the famous landscapes of the world. At the beginning of the century, it was an inspiration for Irish poets and painters such as W.B. Yeats and Paul Henry. However, since the middle of the century, the visual celebration has been dominated by outsiders, the most influential being Hollywood directors and cinematographers. Two films in particular, *The Quiet Man* in 1952 and *Ryan's Daughter* in 1970, beguiled two generations of filmgoers. The West is redolent of a better world, part 'rural idyll', part 'romantic landscape'. These utopia belong to a cast of imagined places that conjure up ways of living that both attract and repel and that deeply affect how we see and how we respond to the world around us.

Since classical times, paradise has been imagined as some form of rural idyll. We have an inclination to cast a benevolent eye over farming landscapes, either forgetting or ignoring the drudgery that was an inevitable part of life in a well-managed rural landscape before the mechanisation of farming in the mid-twentieth century. Despite the poverty culminating in the Great Famine, there was ample scope for the portrayal of attractive and productive rural landscapes in Ireland in earlier centuries. The landscape historian Kevin Whelan has written of the real 'hidden-Ireland' of the eighteenth century as 'the

Fig. 7.3. 'The Quiet Man' bridge outside Oughterard in Connemara, just off the N59 national secondary road, photographed in 2004. The empty countryside with its one-off houses is in contrast to the teeming Arcadia portrayed in the film.

comfortable, Catholic strong farm class of south Leinster and east Munster'.[3] Yet in the eighteenth century and the greater part of the nineteenth century, artists did not romanticise Irish rural life to the extent their counterparts did in England and France. That situation changed completely towards the end of the nineteenth century when Irish artists started to champion a nationalist ideal that envisaged a rural Celtic world untainted by English culture. The artistic vision was a thriving and populous countryside, located somewhere in the west, and this came to approximate to the idealised identity of the new Irish state. It was an idyllic world that was believed to have either survived in remote corners of the country or a way of life that had only recently disappeared and was retrievable under the new Irish state. In 1922, Michael Collins described life on Achill in the following terms: '. . . impoverished as people are, hard as their lives are, difficult as the struggle for existence is, the outward aspect is a pageant. One may see processions of young women riding down on the island ponies to collect sand from the seashore, or gathering in the turf, in the shawls and in their brilliantly-coloured skirts. They remain simple and picturesque. It is only in such places that one gets a glimpse of what Ireland may become again.'[4] A famous speech by

Prime Minister de Valera in 1939 expressed a desire for 'a land whose countryside would be bright with cosy homesteads'.[5] In this rural world, people have an innate understanding of, and respect for, the land. They have a natural and unconscious connection with the sacred and mythological dimensions of their landscape.

The work of the American photographer Dorothea Lange, a visitor to Ireland in the 1950s, can be viewed as a visual record of this way of life. Her photographs of rural Ireland show a strong, heroic people with few material comforts, living their lives in landscapes virtually devoid of twentieth-century technology. Lange felt a strong physical relationship between the people and the land. Her son, who accompanied her, recalls that from the start she saw the Irish people as part of their landscape. He remembers her remarking, as she photographed a man walking towards them on a lonely road, 'That's pure Ireland. He was just made out of that wet limey soil. Made out of it!'[6]

A prosperous countryside is a version of the rural utopia. The development of the Irish countryside since the early twentieth century has included an unashamed exploitation of its romanticised, rural idyll character. The Aran Islands were at the epicentre of the literary revival that put the west on the map. The editors of the *Book of Aran*, published in the 1990s, looked at the Inis Oírr waterfront and saw a 'shabby conglomeration that confronts the visitor [that] must – and does – affront the eyes of Arran people as well'. But Father Pádraig Standún, a curate on Inis Meáin and one of the contributors to the book, observed that while 'some people look at Inis Oirr waterfront and see a mini Manhattan, a sprawl of unplanned looking oversized buildings', he saw 'vibrant young families where children were scarce in the seventies'.[7] New construction in the landscape, whether a house, a hotel or a visitor centre, can be seen as heralding prosperity and community wellbeing.

The vitality of the rural idyll is undiminished. The lobby group, the Irish Rural Dwellers Association (IRDA), which was set up in 2002, has assumed custodianship. The IRDA portrays modern 'one-off' housing as a continuation of a Gaelic rural tradition stretching back into the mists of time. The connection is a tenuous one. In the main the dispersed rural settlement of the western seaboard is not a surviving remnant of an older tradition but is a product of population pressure in the eighteenth and early nineteenth centuries when the population of the island soared from a million at the start of the seventeenth century to 8.5 million in 1845.[8] In those times clachans, clusters of farm dwellings, were established by groups of people leasing areas of marginal land. The houses, which were single rooms housing both the families and their livestock, lay at the centre of the settlement. The surrounding area was then farmed communally according to a system known as rundale. Although rundale dates back to the eleventh century, it is possible that it evolved separately in the congested districts of Donegal, Mayo and Connemara in the 18th century as an optimum response to farming densely populated areas.[9]

The architect Dominic Stevens has conceived a utopian, low-density rural settlement on the banks of the Shannon that encapsulates much of the IRDA philosophy in its references to community and its perception of heritage.[10] For the Venice Biennale in 2006, Stevens imagined a linear community of up to 160,000 people stretching along the banks of the Shannon. Families build their homes there on concrete platforms moored by the riverside. They live and work on these platforms, connected to their local communities by rowing boat and motor boat and to the wider world by modern telecommunications. Stevens' vision requires a willing suspension of disbelief to enjoy an elaborate flight of fancy.

The IRDA vision of rural life can only be comprehended in the context of the recent history of Ireland, which is unparalleled in a European context. This is a history of famine followed by rural depopulation and emigration that has lasted until very recent times. In the first half of the eighteenth century, Ireland had one of the densest rural populations in Europe but the rural population

Fig 7.4. Settlement on Achill Island, County Mayo in 2003. Achill was an inspiration for both Micheal Collins and Paul Henry in the early years of the last century. The dispersed settlement of Achill exemplifies the settlement form that has been championed by the Irish Rural Dwellers Association in recent years.

of the country has been in sharp decline for most of the last 150 years. While the population of the island of Ireland increased by over a million during the course of the last century, many rural areas continued to haemorrhage people. It is no coincidence that prominent advocates for new housing in the countryside come from parts of the country where the severest depopulation has occurred and continues. Jim Connolly, a sculptor and community activist from west Clare, and Seamus Caulfield, an archaeologist from north Mayo, are leading spokesmen of the IRDA. In the Kilrush Rural District of west Clare where Jim Connolly lives, the present day population of under 11,000 is less than half the 1911 population, and Ballina Rural District of north Mayo, Seamus Caulfield's home, has seen a 45 per cent decline over the century.[11] There is a yawning gulf between the traditional rural life and values that are espoused by the IRDA and the reality of the urbanised, car-dependent communities they are championing. Nevertheless, such is the shadow cast by rural depopulation that the IRDA message has tremendous potency.

The IRDA vision of a good rural life shares with earlier Irish versions of the rural idyll a hazy sense of place and physical context. By contrast, the competing utopian vision of a romantic landscape is rooted in its physical setting. While much of the landscape art of the eighteenth and nineteenth centuries involved making accurate or complimentary drawings of benefactors' houses and estates, there were also artists and travellers with other interests. They were in the thrall of Romanticism, a broad intellectual movement that emerged in Europe during the second half of the eighteenth century. Romanticism was a reaction to the prevailing ideal of the Enlightenment, that improvements in the human conditions would be secured by advances in knowledge as a result of objective observation and experiment. The focus of Romanticism is the subjective rather than the objective, emotion and instinct rather than the conscious mind. Romantics turn to the natural world, in which the grandeur of nature outstrips the achievements of civilisation, and find there the purest physical expressions of truth and beauty.[12] Ireland was considered to be especially rich in Romantic landscapes 'with its lines of mountains . . . rocks of innumerable shapes . . . passes rugged . . . rivers rapid . . . broadest lakes . . . Nature abundant'.[13] The world-weariness in Doctor Johnson's famous reply to Boswell's question, 'Is not the Giant's Causeway worth seeing?' 'Worth seeing? Yes but, not worth going to see,' has never been the prevailing response.

To a very considerable degree, the geography of what we generally consider to be our most beautiful landscapes was mapped in this early period of cultural tourism. Many of our beauty spots were first drawn and described in this period, for example the Giant's Causeway, the Sugar Loaf and Powerscourt Waterfall in Wicklow and the mountains and lakes of Killarney. Convenience and custom led to some parts of the country becoming better known than others. Leinster, Munster and east Ulster were well visited while much of Connaught and Ulster remained unknown.

The idea of wilderness, a place where nature reigns supreme, is a central theme of romanticism. As recently as 2003, the poet and philosopher, the late John O'Donoghue, was able to ponder about Irish landscapes that 'Perhaps because they are so much themselves, wild landscapes remind us of the unscathed territories of the minds'.[14] That observation belies the ubiquity of human influence, not just in settled landscapes but in every nook and cranny of the planet. More than most countries, Ireland, a small island that has been settled by farming communities for more than 6,000 years, has a dubious claim to wilderness. It is a little hard to credit that it is only three centuries since wolves roamed the Irish countryside (with an estimated wolf population of up to 1,000 in the seventeenth century).[15] But, in the contemporary world, there are still a few places – the uplands, the bogs and much of the coastline – where nature at least appears to hold sway.

The Romantic view of the physical world continues to exert enormous influence, and the extent to which living landscapes in Ireland continue to be regarded as manifestations of a utopian vision is striking. We cling to the vision despite the gap that exists between the vision and reality. We still buy travel guides and calendars with pictures of turf cutters, hay makers, sheep herders and

Fig. 7.5. View of Knocknaree in County Sligo from the far side of Ballysadare Bay (2009).

thatched cottages, not of silage clamps and wind farms. Roy Foster comments on how 'unplanned suburban sprawl and one-off concrete haciendas invade the countryside still resolutely presented as Arcadia by Bord Fáilte and the IDA'.[16] It is only in very recent years that the photographs of Englishman John Hinde, reproduced on countless postcards and calendars from the 1960s onwards, have come to seem anachronistic. Yet tourists continue to visit Ireland, lured by the images and myths of rural beauty and tranquillity. What is more, these visitors leave Ireland satisfied by what they have seen. Observers seeking evidence of a decline in landscape quality will look in vain in the Bord Fáilte visitor survey data.

By and large, therefore, the changes wrought to the Irish landscape over the last two centuries have not destroyed its romantic allure. Places such as Connemara, west Mayo, the interior of the Wicklow massif and the islands off the west coast have been protected by relative inaccessibility. But even where manifestations of urbanisation are very evident, the physical majesty of a romantic landscape continues to assert itself. Knocknaree, crowned by the massive Queen Maeve's Cairn, is near Sligo town but it still commands the coastal plain just as it did when the cairn and tomb were constructed more than 4,000 years ago. It is only when you draw close to the mountain that the modern development lapping against its base becomes apparent and the romantic vision is comprehensively subverted. Unlike in other Western countries, in Ireland the rural idyll has not had

Fig. 7.6. A housing estate in Strandhill at the foot of Knocknaree in 2009. It is only close up that the majesty of the hill is diminished by twentieth-century housing development.

to compete with an attractive alternative. At the end of the nineteenth century, Dublin had the reputation of being the worst-housed and unhealthiest city in the British Isles. Many writers have commented on the anti-urban sentiment of the new Irish state in the last century.[17] Before and after independence in 1922, the needs of Irish cities were badly neglected.[18] Cities cast their spell but the cities in question were London and Birmingham, New York, Boston and Sydney rather than the towns and cities of Ireland. It was only towards the end of the century that the larger Irish cities, Dublin in particular, recovered their allure as places to live but many provincial towns have been abandoned by the middle classes. They have become hollowed-out places ringed by housing estates and, beyond the estates, a penumbra of one-off housing. The rural homestead has remained centre stage in conservative settlement mythology in contrast to Britain and America where the small town is equally popular. Former Prime Minister John Major's wordscape of a future Great Britain as 'a country of long shadows on cricket grounds, warm beer, invincible green suburbs and pools fillers and, as George Orwell said, "Old maids bicycling to holy communion through the morning mist" comes to mind as an example of a strand of conservative urban imagery that is almost entirely absent in this country.[19]

Fig. 7.7. Ennis town centre in 2007. The medieval street pattern remains but the function and character of the historic core have changed completely in the last half century. There are now virtually no families living there and the public spaces are largely given over to road space and car parks.

An idyllic dream of suburban living has never flourished in Ireland. The suburb as a place to live was discredited in the 1960s and '70s by the experience of the Dublin 'new towns' and of other outer suburbs built at that time. Local government demonstrated that it could demolish inner-city slums with considerable efficiency but that it was incapable of planning and creating attractive suburbs in their place. Whether it was state-led low-rise, low-density housing in Tallaght in Dublin or Knocknaheeny in Cork or high-rise in Ballymun or private estates in Blanchardstown or Swords, the new suburbs generally did not live up to expectations. They were laid out according to housing, road and open-space standards that had their genesis in utopian models developed in Britain and in the United States, but Ireland has generally lacked the organisation and resources to build attractive, liveable places.

In other parts of the Western world, particularly the United States, where the suburban dream of a good life has had considerable power, an influential counter-mythology emerged in the second half of the last century. In this suburban nightmare, the newly settled suburban dweller comes to acquire the negative superficial traits of the suburban environment. In the 1950s version of the myth, American women were transformed by their move to the suburbs into

Fig 7.8. Turn-of-the-century, upper income housing in Ballybeg, Ennis. This is an uncharacteristically attractive new estate but Ballybeg suburb has few local services and is more than 2 kilometres from the centre of a town which has no public transport.

colourless clones, preoccupied with their children and a facile social life of coffee mornings and drinks parties. Despite research which has found no substance to the notion of a suburban sub-culture, the myth keeps resurfacing and fuelling the fears of American intellectuals that their society is under threat.

An Irish version of this myth has not developed, probably for two reasons. Firstly, Ireland is a small country of small cities. Even in Dublin the suburbs remain intimately connected to the city and have not developed lives of their own. Visits into the city are part of the normal life of most households. In large American cities, a significant proportion of suburban dwellers never visit the city at all. Secondly, the suburban myth feeds on the fear that a culture, enriched by its diversity, is under threat from a process creating uniformity.[20] A 1960s sociological study of urbanisation in Ireland fifty years ago, identified the same profound organisational changes in family life that were common to the urbanisation process across the world.[21] But the study also found that in Ireland, in contrast to other countries, values were hardly changed by the move from the countryside. Irish people, whether living in the country, in city centres or suburbs, shared the same basic outlook on life. It remains to be seen whether the dramatic and very visible transformation of the settlement pattern in Ireland over the last decade will come to be associated with a new type of Irish person and sub-culture.

The absence of an attractive suburban alternative has enhanced the appeal of rural living in Ireland. In part, the enormous growth of one-off rural housing over the last forty years is testimony to the potency of a rural idyll. It is only recently that more ambitious ideas about suburban living, matched with a more accomplished execution, notably Adamstown in south Dublin and a re-invented Ballymun in North Dublin, are beginning to appear as attractive alternatives. However, these are unlikely to be more than footnotes in the history of Irish settlement given the scale of dispersed rural housing development that is taking place.

If it is accepted that seeking out and creating earthly paradises are mainsprings of human endeavour, the question has to be posed why there is so little evidence of such endeavour in contemporary Ireland. It would seem that history has fractured and distorted the relationship that exists between Irish society and the landscape that it inhabits to such an extent that a constructive engagement with landscape is severely compromised. So-called 'landscapes of shame', a label applied to the Burren by geographer Eileen O'Rourke, are an extreme manifestation of the condition.[22] These are landscapes, that may be highly valued by visitors but that have been so tainted by impoverishment and colonial oppression that they cannot be enjoyed by their inhabitants. F.H.A. Aalen has wondered if throughout Ireland 'there has been a collective subconscious breaking with the past, a feeling that the rural landscape is not a genuinely Irish thing but something irredeemably tainted by impoverishment, with colonial dispossession and landlord oppression: "a data bank of humiliation".[23]

I would have difficulty acknowledging these insights were it not for a project I carried out in County Kilkenny. I was commissioned by the county council to prepare a local area plan for Woodstock, an historic demesne beside the picturesque village of Inistioge in the Nore Valley. Woodstock House was burned down in 1922 by the local IRA and the ruins of the house lie at the centre of the plan area. Today there is a scattering of houses but most of the area is either farmland or forestry plantation. Captain William Sweete, an astute property speculator, acquired the 6,717-acre estate of Woodstock in 1703. The biggest project in the early years of the estate was the planting of an oak plantation that covered the southern half of what is now the plan area. The estate was inherited by William Tighe in 1793. The Tighes were a wealthy English family that settled in Ireland in 1640 and prospered during Cromwell's rule. Richard, the first Tighe

Fig. 7.9. Fahee North in the upland Burren, both a 'landscape of shame' and also a landscape of world renown. The signboard has been erected by Burren Connect, a current multi-agency tourism development project led by Clare County Council.

in Ireland, had a contract to supply wheat for Cromwell's army and became High Sheriff and Lord Mayor of Dublin. As recently as 1900 the Tighes owned 22,000 acres of land, spread over six counties. However, the family's present-day legal interest in Woodstock is restricted to the hunting and shooting rights over the land, which the state, now Coillte, acquired on a 150-year lease in 1926.

Woodstock estate was designed and managed as both a commercial operation and a place to be enjoyed by its occupants and admired by its visitors. There was ambition and ingenuity in its creation and embellishment during the eighteenth and nineteenth centuries. Woodstock had all the accoutrements of an eighteenth-century country estate: a walled demesne, a fine house, a deer park, a home farm, walled garden and picturesque follies, walks and rides. These various elements were planned with close attention to the natural setting of the Nore Valley and of nearby Brandon Hill and the medieval landscape of the valley. In the nineteenth century, Lady Louisa Tighe and her gardeners Pierce Butler and Charles McDonald further enhanced the estate by creating extensive gardens and an arboretum. This phase included the construction of an ingenious spring-fed surface water system to supply the needs of the farm and the gardens. During the last century, after the house burnt down and the Department of Lands took over what was left of the estate, the landscape fell into rapid decline. A basic forestry operation replaced the integrated management system of the estate. The tide began to turn only at the very end of the century when the county council, with the support of the Tighe family, started the restoration of the gardens. However, despite decades of neglect and destruction, the modern landscape retains the imprint of the designed landscape that was created over the previous centuries. This is the most fascinating aspect of the Woodstock landscape today.

It is unusual for a statutory local area plan to be prepared for a tract of countryside, particularly countryside in a rural backwater. I suspect that the impetus for a plan primarily came from Coillte, which was interested in extracting maximum commercial value from its lease and required the backing of the local planning authority to execute its plans. The company wanted to market part of its plantation as a site for a hotel-spa development, a fairly commonplace rural commercial venture in recent years. Over a six-month period, through fieldwork and public meetings, meetings with landowners, and reviewing available literature, our planning team built up an understanding of the area. Although we identified two sites that we thought would be suitable for new commercial development on a substantial scale, including the Coillte hotel site, the thrust of our plan was the conservation of the designed landscape of Woodstock and protection of the tranquil character of this part of the Nore Valley. In our view these were the most attractive and distinctive aspects of the area, which could underpin sustainable development over the long term.

Fig. 7.10. Inistioge Bridge on the River Nore viewed from Woodstock estate in 2005. Robert Lloyd Praeger wrote that 'no river scenery that Ireland can offer excels [the lower reaches of the Nore and the Barrow]'. The bridge, which was built at the end of the eighteenty-century, has an important practical transport function but it is also the centrepiece of a view from the large Gothic window of Mount Sandford Castle, a folly within the Woodstock estate. The scenic role of the bridge is indicated by the ornamented character of this side of the bridge in contrast to the plain treatment of the other side.

Fig. 7.11. Woodstock viewed from the eastern side of the Nore Valley in 2005. The former home farm of the estate occupies the centre and right side of the view. Woodstock House and Gardens lie under the tree cover on the far side of the fields. The left side of the view shows Coillte forestry which is on the site of the oak wood that was planted by William Sweete in 1703. There is more Coillte forest on the higher ground of Mount Alto on the skyline.

I expected some adverse response to our draft plan and people who support a plan rarely write letters of congratulation. However, I was taken aback by the vehemence of the negative reaction. Here are extracts from three of the submissions that we received:

> *This plan is only about one thing, the re-establishment of an era best forgotten and the tyrants that it contained. A lot of people are seeing the Woodstock estate through rose tinted glasses, mine must have been lost in the post, this estate should be seen for what it is, a crumbling monument to British imperial colonial power and the people that were crushed under its heel . . . I object [to] this plan and for the most part find it wholly offensive.*

> *My earliest impression of Woodstock was that it is was a dreadful place as my father was imprisoned there in February 1921 and later transferred to Spike Island until December 1921 . . . For too many years landlords were in control in this country and I do not want that situation to arise again.*

With these stones the walls of Woodstock Estate were built, to keep in the deer – and to keep out the Irish peasant.

When Rome was burning Nero played the fiddle. When the Thatch was burning the Tighs played in their garden . . . I reject this plan because it fails to address sustainability for all. A new plan and a more inclusive approach is needed.

Our draft document had touched raw nerves in a way that I can hardly comprehend. As we were preparing the plan, Thomas Whyte, a local historian, was completing a history of the estate and its family. When his account reaches the War of Independence and the destruction of Woodstock House, he explains that the names of those involved and specific details of the operation have been omitted 'because the memories are still relatively fresh even after eighty-five years'.[24]

Kilkenny County Council has since adopted a Woodstock Local Area Plan. The adopted plan has a conservation focus but it represents a less comprehensive and less coherent approach than the one we had proposed.[25] Although the council owns the ruin of Woodstock House, it has not committed to finding a new role for the house, which was a key aspect of our recommendations. Woodstock will not regain its place as a landscape of national importance while there is a crumbling ruin at its centre.

Fig 7.12. The entrance to Woodstock, Inistioge, County Kilkenny, displaying the wolf's head of the Tighe crest.

The demesne landscape has provoked a complex response from contemporary Irish society. On the one hand, the colonial heritage holds an abiding fascination for society's movers and shakers. In the 1980s, Taoiseach C.J. Haughey ran the country while residing at 'Abbeville' in north County Dublin, a mansion he had bought in 1969 when he was Minister for Finance. 'Abbeville', set in 230 acres of parkland and farmland, was designed by James Gandon, the foremost architect in Ireland in the late eighteenth century. Roy Foster refers to the 'sanctimonious self-delusion' of Patrick Gallagher, justifying the bankrolling of the former Taiosoeach by Gallagher's father, developer Matt Gallagher. Patrick Gallagher claimed that 'Haughey was financed in order to create the environment which the Anglo-Irish enjoyed and that we as a people could never aspire to'.[26]

Frank McDonald and James Nix have recounted the travails of dancer Michael Flatley and financier Dermot Desmond while trying to modernise their Georgian homes (respectively Castle Hyde in County Cork and No. 71 Merrion Square in Dublin) in the face of restrictive conservation codes.[27] There is nothing remarkable about a close association of heritage, power and wealth in a society. But what is noteworthy is how a new elite has simultaneously appropriated and pillaged the country's built heritage, acquiring big houses as trophy homes while exploiting houses and demesnes as sites for lucrative development projects. Paddy Kelly, one of the country's largest property developers in the Celtic Tiger era, proclaimed that 'It was time the Irish went through the front gate', referring to the housing estate he had built in the grounds of Castletown in County Kildare, perhaps the finest Early Georgian mansion in the country. It seemed, according to Fintan O'Toole, that in Kelly's eyes,

> *Property development was the new armed struggle, the war of independence by other means. Where Paddy Kelly's great-grandfather and his generation had taken on the landowning aristocracy with boycotts and rent strikes, and the next generation had burned down their big houses, now the people's struggle against the aristocracy was best conducted by building lucrative office blocks and densely profitable housing estates on the sites of their former townhouses and mansions.*[28]

On Achill in County Mayo, local developer and builder, Joe McNamara, has drawn inspiration from a much earlier era. In 2010, Mr McNamara, who is reported to owe the Irish Bank Resolution Corporation (formerly Anglo-Irish Bank) several million euro, won notoriety by a series of high profile protests, including blocking the main entrance to Leinster House with a cement mixer emblazoned with the words 'toxic bank' and 'anglo', and abandoning a poster-strewn, cherry picker hoist outside the Anglo-Irish Bank's headquarters in Dublin. But on

Figs 13 and 14. The 'Achill Henge' outside Pollagh, Achill, and the derelict hotel site in Keel, Achill, photographed in 2012.

Fig 7.15. Allihies in West Cork, photographed on a summer's evening in 1985, with a 300mm lens. The compact village and simple house forms, nestling under the rock face of Slieve Misk-ish (the physical characteristics accentuated by the telephoto lens) is a strong visual represen-tation of a West of Ireland rural idyll. Allihies, more properly the village of Cluin in Allihies, has since had a colourful makeover and more than doubled in size, but it retains a physical allure that is accentuated by its continuing physical remoteness.

Achill that defiance has taken the form of a massive landscape installation in the style of Stonehenge. With a diameter of 30 metres and a circumference of nearly 100, 'Achill-henge' is a striking feature on the lower slopes of Slievemore. Mr McNamara has never satisfactorily explained the purpose of the henge, which was built without planning permission or any other kind of sanction.[29] But if the henge stands as an enigmatic memorial to developer hubris, another of his projects, a 'boutique' hotel in nearby Keel, represents a more prosaic memorial. The hotel was to replace a pub and guesthouse in the village. The planning permission expired in 2010, with construction not advanced beyond demolishing the old premises and excavating an underground car park. The site now stands as an ugly and dangerous eyesore in the centre of the village.

This chapter, exploring our emotional response to landscape, has been dominated by negative emotions and consequences. However, reactions to Irish landscape remain overwhelmingly positive. The recognition of beauty, the highest expression of that response, is the subject of the next chapter.

Chapter 8

BEAUTY

I do not find my local landscape, the inland Burren, as beautiful or seductive as other places that I know. This is disconcerting because the Burren is an exceptional place and I am often in the company of people who are enthralled by it. Paul Clements from Belfast finds leaving the Burren a trial: 'each time I prepare to leave – my mind unsatiated – I point the car in the direction of home and the humdrum world of work that imprisons the spirit, I am loath to depart. A wistful and soft tristesse comes over me.'[1] There are other places that have affected me strongly. The western tip of the Beara peninsula is one such place.

I remember a family holiday there in 1985 when we rented a bungalow that a farmer and his family had vacated for the summer. The first problem we encountered when we arrived late one evening from Dublin was that the views from every window were so stunning that we could not decide where to park the car, that is which view to sacrifice. Then it rained most of the rest of our holiday. Over the fortnight we seemed to receive the sympathy of the whole local community but in fact the rain did not matter. We enjoyed every day, revelling in the beauty and otherness of the place. As a young adult living in Dublin, the west of Ireland was a wondrous realm at the end of a long car journey, but now that I live here I rarely register the moments of unalloyed pleasure that I had come to associate with the western seaboard. I have feared that this signals a weakening life force as I grow older. However, a visit to Dingle last summer has reassured me. I had to do some work in Dingle town, a place where I have never stopped before. In the past it was a night-time blur through a car window, a marker on the final leg of a journey to somewhere further west. When I finished my work that day I had time to take a leisurely drive to Slea Head and further along the coast to Ballydavid, places that I had not seen for more than twenty years. It was a warm, sunlit evening and three hours quickly passed as I reacquainted myself with the extremities of the peninsula, finding myself as enchanted as I had ever been. Of course I should have realised that the west of Ireland has many faces and that my favourite places are the ends of the rocky peninsulas and the outlying islands, places where mountains, sea and sky vie to dominate expansive vistas. These are wide open places that face the broad Atlantic, tenuously connected to the rest of the country by winding mountain roads. My ideal western landscape as a place to visit therefore does not begin to materialise until I have passed beyond Schull, Castletownbere, Sneem and Dingle and the other outposts of my ordinary world. That enjoyable sense of separation is further enhanced by going a step further, to one of the offshore islands, perhaps to the Aran Islands, referred to by Tim Robinson as 'Ireland raised to the power of two' or to Skellig Michael, one of the great destinations of the world where the actual experience of the place exceeds the expectation.[2] The western seascapes therefore inspire me, more so than the quieter beauty of the inland Burren, and I suspect that this predilection reflects a relatively conventional taste.

It was Immanuel Kant in *Critique of Judgement*, published in 1790, who elucidated that beauty is created by the pleasure of the onlooker and not by an intrinsic quality of the object on view. This explains how concepts of beauty change in time and space and that an ability to appreciate beauty is, to some extent, a matter of discernment.[3] Kant further explained that while beauty gives pleasure, not all pleasure is the result of beauty. We may therefore take pleasure from a view or place for many reasons other than for its beauty. It could be

Figs 8.1 and 8.2. Different versions of beauty. Above, the quiet beauty of the inland Burren at Carran, on a winter's day, the turlough filled with water. Below, the dramatic beauty of Slea Head on the Dingle Peninsula on a summer's evening.

because it is our home or because we own it or because we like the people who live there. We can take displeasure for the same variety of reasons, none of which have anything to do with beauty or the lack of beauty but which nevertheless may deeply affect the way we feel about a place.

Beauty has engaged philosophers for centuries. Plotinus, the last great pagan philosopher, teaching in Rome in the second century AD, had an appealing explanation of beauty. He believed that the soul is a fragment of the divine being that has fallen into matter and taken human form. Stunned by the fall and burdened by its physical state, the soul almost loses touch with its divine self and its natural inclination to return to the divine is upset. However, 'when the soul sees anything of its kin [the divine] or trace of that kinship, it thrills with an immediate delight, takes its own to itself, and thus stirs anew to the sense of its nature and all its affinity' (*The Enneads*, 1.6.2). The less damaged the soul, according to Plotinus, the more quickly it is able to recognise this kinship and the more quickly it is healed and able to become fully itself once more. It is this thrill of recognition that is our experience of beauty.

The idea of beauty as an intrinsic quality has endured through the ages, and for more than two centuries that quality has strongly adhered to Irish landscapes. Ireland began to acquire an international reputation for its landscapes at the end of the eighteenth century. A visitor in 1839 'was particularly struck with the rich and vivid colouring of the scenery of Ireland. When the sun shines after one of the frequent showers, the whole landscape resembles a highly finished and freshly varnished picture, not by any well-known master, for the composition, to speak technically, is totally different, though I think quite as fine as any ideal image of Claude, Hobbings or Poussin'.[4] We can enjoy landscapes as works of art, the artist in this instance a divine creator. We sometimes think so highly of a view that we do not believe that it can be improved upon, that it is perfect as it is. This is a demonstration of 'aesthetic necessity', a concept formulated by German poet and dramatist Friedrich Schiller in the eighteenth century. It is the idea that a work of art is perfect and that it cannot be any different than the way it is. John Anderson suggests that it is the gulf between the edited perfection of a great art and the messy, unedited quality of our lives that produces such strong emotions when we look at a beautiful object. We are made happy and sad, happy because of the perfection rendered and sad because that perfection highlights how unsatisfactory ordinary life is.[5] However, Armstrong suggests that 'aesthetic necessity' is a conceit that can only be sustained by critics who are relatively ignorant of the creative process. That process is usually full of u-turns and blind alleys with a far from certain ending. Aesthetic necessity would therefore seem to be an especially inappropriate concept in the context of landscape because landscape, even if it may appear to have a timeless quality, is in a state of perpetual flux. The fact that we are able to experience landscapes in this way illuminates the paradoxical nature of the landscape experience. On the one hand, it is a visual experience which is prone to being superficial and false in so far as it leads to unfounded conclusions about the nature of what is being viewed. On the other hand, the experience has the potential to convey beauty, the pleasure as profound as any created by a great work of art.

In the eighteenth century, landscape became a favourite subject of artists and their patrons and the custom grew of viewing the landscape itself as a work of art. Contemporary society's appreciation of landscape beauty is connected to the history of landscape painting. A Flemish painter, William Van der Hagen, who probably arrived in Ireland in the 1720s, began the Irish tradition of landscape

Figs 8.3 and 8.4. Beauty and pleasure at Ladies View, Killarney, in 2010. Ladies View is named after Queen Victoria's ladies-in-waiting who went there during the royal visit of 1861. The top photograph is composed in the Romantic tradition, a carefully constructed 'timeless' vista of dramatic natural scenery. The bottom photograph, taken in the car park a few metres from the other photograph, records a prosaic tourist activity, the capture of a moment in time for future enjoyment.

painting. The artists painted idealised rural landscapes, the most accomplished in the eighteenth century being Thomas Roberts from Dublin (1748–77), who had a short but prolific professional life. The paintings of this era show rugged mountains, towering cliffs, wave-battered shores, waterfalls, fast-flowing streams and tranquil lakes, ruins and ancient trees. There is a notable absence of people and, if there are human figures, they are dwarfed by their surroundings, to emphasise the scale and grandeur of nature. Travellers were educated to view landscape as a series of picturesque compositions. Particularly influential were the rules of composition formulated by the Reverend William Gilpin on his travels in Britain in the 1760s and 1770s. Gilpin could take his enthusiasm about landscape as a subject for sketching and painting to extremes. When he saw the thirteenth-and fourteenth-century ruins of the Cistercian abbey at Tintern, on the banks of the River Wye in Gloucestershire, he famously suggested that 'a mallet judiciously used' would improve their picturesque quality. Although Gilpin is easily satirised, his way of seeing landscapes has had a lasting effect. Ireland was a much-visited place by English travellers and artists in the late eighteenth and nineteenth centuries when continental wars curtailed the 'Grand Tour' of the upper classes. Some areas did remain remote, and unvisited. For instance, none of the well-known eighteenth-century travellers considered the Aran Islands worth the detour, where, as Tim Robinson puts it 'a web of cultural nationalism' came to be spun in the middle decades of the nineteenth century.[6]

Given the extent that we are habituated to seeing landscapes as works of art, we can usefully apply principles of art appreciation to landscape appreciation. There is, for instance, a recognised impulse for the eye to make a connection between form and function. If there is an aspect of an action portrayed in a work of art that does not appear quite right, or some element of a piece of furniture or a building that does not seem properly shaped to carry out its intended purpose, the eye will spot the weakness and be distracted by it. We also appreciate this marriage of form and function in landscape. There is an underlying sense of order in an agricultural landscape. The eye makes sense of what it sees. It cannot see that a bank manager now lives in the old farmhouse, that the farmer has moved into one of the new houses on the roadside nor can it see the sites, occupied by the other new houses, which have been sold to underpin the economic viability of the rest of the landscape on view. We are heavily influenced by what we see in front of our eyes and are inclined to draw conclusions about places that are based on appearance alone.

The law of the whole states that, when viewing an art object, we have to consider the whole object. We cannot divide it into component parts and expect to expose its beauty in this way. This insight has a telling relevance to landscape. The quality of a landscape cannot be conserved or sustained by safeguarding only those elements of the landscape that make it special. For instance, we place a high value on views of seas and lakes. These views are protected in statutory development plans but they are also the most sought-after locations for new houses. As a result there are numerous coastal and lakeside roads in Ireland where views of water are intact but where the landward side of the roads is lined

Figs 8.5 and 8.6. Two photographs taken from a laneway outside Doolin in north Clare in 2011. The top photograph shows an uninterrupted view of Galway Bay and the Aran Islands from the seaward side of the lane. The photograph below, taken from the same place, shows the bungalows on the landward side of the lane. The planning policy in the county development plan was 'to prohibit developments located between the road and the sea . . .'

with housing. In these places, although the view of water has been protected, our perception is one of landscape spoliation because we take in the whole vista, not just the view of the sea or the lake. When we photograph these places we consciously opt for an edited reality, omitting the offending housing from view.

Over the last three decades, an idea has gathered pace that our aesthetic appreciation of landscape has an underlying biological basis. Hominins evolved in Africa some seven million years ago. Our species, *Homo sapiens*, evolved around 200,000 years ago and migrated out of the continent in the last 50 to 100,000 years.[7] Thereafter it spread across the globe, not arriving in Ireland until after the last ice age, about 9,000 years ago. Following the development of agriculture in the Near East, the first urban civilisations emerged about 6,000 years ago. Before that time Man and Woman lived on their wits and skills as hunter-gatherers. In other words, for more than 97 per cent of its existence, our species has survived as a hunter-gatherer, and for most of that time has inhabited the African savanna and nowhere else. It is therefore not unreasonable to posit that contemporary behaviour and attitudes are heavily influenced by that hunter-gatherer legacy and that as a species we have hardly begun to adapt, in an evolutionary sense, to the sedentary, urban, technological lifestyle that we now pursue. An obvious example of disjunction is the prevalence and potency of primordial phobias, such as fears of the dark, open spaces, snakes, spiders and wild animals, all of which seem out of place in our urbanised world.

A less obvious example is the enduring attraction of certain types of landscape. This has led to the formulation of the savanna hypothesis. Basic assumptions of the hypothesis are that 'a crucial step in the lives of most organisms, including humans, is selection of a habitat' and 'if a creature gets into the right place, everything else is likely to be easier'.[8] The savanna was such a habitat for early man. Compared to the forest it offered more abundant plant and animal food for a ground-dwelling species and lower risks for ground-dwelling humans because of its visual openness, more escape opportunities and lower probabilities of encountering close hidden predatory threats. The human species is therefore a savanna species and as a result, 'given a completely free choice, people gravitate statistically toward a savanna-like environment'.[9] Knowledge of the best places to survive within the savanna's mosaic of habitats was a crucial survival trait and as such has been inherited through natural selection. The trait no longer bestows a survival advantage but continues to manifest itself in our preference for certain types of landscape and landscape experience. Today, when we enjoy a commanding view over a fertile plain or valley in Ireland we are not just enjoying the view in a superficially pleasurable sense. We are also stimulated by a primordial affection for a safe viewing place and the sight of territory that is replete with refuges, safe passages, water holes and game.

Irish environmentalist John Feehan describes our evolutionary journey in the following terms.

> *A few tens of thousands of years ago we moved out of Africa, to slowly conquer the world. But we also took Africa with us, because wherever possible we have shaped the natural landscapes we made our own to resemble those in which our minds as our bodies are most at home . . . Our mind and spirit as our body are most at home in the traditional agricultural landscape which is the cultural counterpart of the open natural landscapes of our origins . . .*[10]

Figs 8.7 and 8.8. Top, suckler herd on improved pasture in north Clare and, below, a herd of buffalo on the Masai Mara in Kenya. Environmentalist John Feehan has suggested that the innate attraction of traditional agricultural landscapes is related to their visual resemblance to the natural landscape in which the human species evolved.

The savanna hypothesis incorporates the idea that biological differences and the sexual division of labour within hunter-gatherer communities would produce different landscape responses according to sex.[11] Females would be more likely to avoid open spaces where large predators hunted and where there would be a higher risk from attack by human males seeking to gain a reproductive advantage. To protect themselves and their children, females would be inclined to seek out enclosed refuges with good views of the surrounding countryside. In their role as gatherers of fruit, nuts and tubers, they would be attracted to more vegetated areas. Males by contrast were hunters who would seek out the open plains where large herds of game roamed and would value the vantage points of hills and rock outcrops that overlooked the plains. The gender hypothesis has been tested by a content analysis of landscapes painted by French and Irish painters during the heyday of landscape painting in the eighteenth and nineteenth centuries. As predicted, a much higher proportion of the paintings by women contain refuge symbols (houses, other buildings or vegetation cover, especially in the foreground) while a much higher proportion of the paintings by men contain prospect symbolism (hills, mountains, rock outcroppings). All the painters were more likely to show women in refuge locations and men in open spaces. The researchers acknowledge that some of their findings could have a cultural rather than an evolutionary explanation, for example the paintings could reflect the more restricted scope of life for women in eighteenth- and nineteenth-century society than a predisposition determined by evolutionary psychology.[12]

The extent to which Ireland's traditional agricultural landscape is an unconsciously created counterpart of the African savanna has not been investigated by empirical research. But the savanna hypothesis has been tested against another landscape type in Ireland, the parkland landscapes that were created in the eighteenth and nineteenth centuries.[13] For hundreds of years garden creation has been a potent demonstration of power and taste in European society. The early eighteenth century saw a strong reaction against the geometrical formal approach that had previously prevailed. The English landscape park was born and rapidly became popular across Europe and especially in Ireland. Some 320,000 hectares (nearly 4 per cent of the country) were enparked. There are over 7,000 Irish houses associated with parks of 4 hectares or more.[14]

The English landscape park is characterised by its informal, picturesque and 'natural' quality. Irregular groupings of trees are dispersed in open areas of meadow containing streams and bodies of water. Viewers typically discern an attractive, naturalistic quality even though the landscape park resembles no natural habitat found anywhere in Europe. In visual terms the landscape park most resembles the savanna, a habitat of which its original creators would have had no direct experience.

Figs 8.9 and 8.10. Savanna/parkland landscapes. Above, the herd of fallow deer in the Phoenix Park in Dublin and below, herds of zebra and springbok at Nxai Pan in Northern Botswana. Once a royal hunting ground, the Phoenix Park is the largest enclosed city park in Europe while Nxai Pan is a national park which attracts an annual concentration of game at the onset of the rainy season.

Humphry Repton was one of the most famous designers of parks. Rather than designing and then building them like Lancelot 'Capability' Brown, Repton made his living by selling 'before' and 'after' sets of drawings, usually leaving it to the client to interpret and implement the vision. Repton's Red Books provide a valuable resource to examine the savanna hypothesis. Heerwagen and Orians have tested the following propositions against a sample of eighteen Red Books:

1. Landscapes are changed to make them more savanna-like.
2. Closed woods are opened up in ways that increase visual access and penetrability.
3. Distant views, especially to the horizon, are opened up.
4. Refuges are added if none presently exist.
5. Cues signalling ease of movement – paths, bridges, roads – are added.
6. Water and large, grazing mammals are added if they are not already present.[15]

The researchers found that the content analysis confirmed the hypothesis and quote Repton's comment that 'it is only by such deceptions that art can imitate the most pleasing works of nature'.[16]

Is it wholly fanciful to suggest that in contemporary times these recreated hunting grounds hold a special attraction for the country's male-dominated, business elite? A new chapter in the history of the landscape park in Ireland

Fig. 8.11. Carton House and golf course, County Kildare, in 2011.

Fig. 8.12. View of the Hill of Tara from Skryne Hill in 2012, looking across the Gabhra Valley and the newly constructed M3 motorway. This settled countryside, with a remarkable archaeology and history, but an unassuming topography without romantic character, lies at the heart of a proposed Tara–Skryne Landscape Conservation Area (LCA). Meath County Council's decision in 2007 to prepare an LCA was a belated recognition of the national importance of the local landscape. A draft LCA plan, published in 2010, attracted over 300 submissions, nearly two-thirds of which opposed designation, mainly on the grounds that it would inhibit housing and farm development. The objectors included the three sitting TDs in the Meath East constituency.[20] The council has yet to designate the area as an LCA.

unfolded at the end of the twentieth century with the retro-fitting of existing parklands as golf courses and the design of new ones. Sean Fitzpatrick, chief executive and then chairman of Anglo Irish Bank, the bank at the epicentre of Irish business in the last decade, apparently queried the appointment of a new head of lending in 2007 solely on the basis that the candidate did not play golf.[17] Several of the bank's developer clients not only played golf but were financed to buy and/or build their own parkland courses (Paddy Kelly at Tulfarris and Carton House, Joe O'Reilly at Killeen Castle, Gerry Gannon at the K Club and Seán Quinn at the Slieve Russell).[18]

The romantic appeal of our landscapes endures with particular tracts of country standing out as exceptional places. In the Republic, these areas were first collated and described in an *Inventory of Outstanding Landscapes*, published by the government research body, An Foras Forbartha, in 1977. The inventory was intended as a first attempt only. Very detailed but at the same time rather uneven and unreliable in its description of the landscape resource, the inventory (which was never revised) has to be carefully interpreted. A somewhat more reliable guide, in the sense that it makes no attempt to be a detailed statement, is the schematic map of landscapes produced by Bord Fáilte in 1994, which shows twenty-four scenic landscapes. Those and the eleven existing and proposed Areas of Outstanding Natural Beauty (AONBs) in Northern Ireland, broadly summarise Ireland's scenic landscape resource (See Fig. 8.13).

Most of these landscapes have a romantic landscape character that has been appreciated and celebrated over a long period, in the case of places like Killarney,

Fig. 8.13. The scenic landscapes of Ireland.

	SCENIC LANDSCAPES KEY		
1	Cooley Peninsula	19	Lakelands-W. Meath
2	Wicklow Mts	20	Slieve Blooms
3	SE River Valleys	21	Silvermines
4	Comeragh-Knockmealdowns	22	Lough Derg
5	Galtees-Comeragh	23	Lough Ree
6	SW Cork	24	S. Cork-Kinsale
7	Iveragh Peninsula-Killarney	A	Fermanagh Caveland
8	Dingle Peninsula	B	Erne Lakeland
9	Burren	C	Sperrin Mts
10	Connemara	D	North Derry
11	Mayo-West/Newport/Achill	E	Causeway Coast
12	NW Mayo	F	Antrim Coast and Glens
13	L. Key – L. Arrow/L Allen	G	Lagan Valley
14	Sligo-Leitrim	H	Strangford Lough
15	Slieve League	J	Lecale Coast
16	L. Eske	K	Mourne Mts.
17	NW Donegal	L	Ring of Gullion
18	Inishowen		

Figure 8.13 Key to scenic landscapes, based on a 1994 Bord Fáilte compilation and designated and proposed Areas of Outstanding Natural Beauty in Northern Ireland.[21]

the Wicklow Mountains and the Causeway Coast for more than two centuries. There is a strong and on-going attachment to these places that is demonstrated by a resistance to landscape change. Had the countryside around the Hill of Tara possessed the physical attributes of a Killarney Lakeland or a Connemara it seems doubtful that the decision in 2003 to route the M3 motorway through the Tara–Skryne valley would have been so casually taken. Ian Russell notes that George Petrie, who surveyed the area in 1839, had written that Tara was 'undistinguished either for altitude or picturesqueness of form'. Russell has commented that while universal and 'obvious' qualities have been ascribed to the sacred terrain of Tara in recent times, 'there is nothing either obvious or universal about such claims'.[19] By contrast our romantic landscapes retain that 'obvious' appeal and are universally acclaimed.

In Chapter 3 I referred to the rapid suburbanisation of the Howth peninsula in Dublin in the early part of the last century. The headland is a pocket-sized scenic landscape on the north side of Dublin Bay that is included in the national inventory but not the Fáilte Ireland list, presumably because of its small size. In the late 1990s, when I worked for Fingal County Council, I drafted a Special Amenity Area Order (SAAO) for the locality (see Figs. 8.15 and 8.16). This was after Brendan Howlin, then Minister for the Environment, had instructed the council to prepare an order. The minister was reacting to a local campaign for designation that had been spearheaded by Jean Finn, an indefatigable organiser and activist. At that time orders could be made for places that possessed any or all of three qualities: outstanding natural beauty, special recreation value or a need for nature conservation. In the council we decided to show that Howth qualified for designation under all three criteria. Landscape architect Conor Skehan was engaged to help make the aesthetic argument. Conscious that the SAAO would be strongly resisted by some landowners and also conscious of the failure of a previous attempt by Dublin Corporation to make an order for the whole of Dublin

Fig. 8.14. The romantic scenery of Hag's Glen in the Macgillycuddy's Reeks, Lough Gouragh in the foreground and Lough Callee behind. The Killarney National Park is 7 kilometres to the east, on the far side of the Gap of Dunloe.

Fig. 8.15. Doldrum Bay and the Baily, Howth, viewed from Drumleck Point in 2011. This is part of the Howth Peninsula coastline that is covered by the special amenity area order.

Bay, we believed that a strong technical case for designation was essential. This led us to consider in some depth the meaning of 'outstanding natural beauty', the legislation itself shedding no light on the matter. Conor Skehan devised a definition that was based on the possession of the three characteristics of distinctiveness, establishment and consensus. For 'distinctiveness' Howth had to have a 'unique, rare, noteworthy, unmistakeable or easily recognisable landscape character'. This was relatively easy to demonstrate by reference to the geology and geomorphology of the headland in the context of its urban setting. There are only a few areas of rugged coastal scenery on the east coast. Howth and Bray Heads are the only places where you find such scenery in a metropolitan setting. For establishment Howth had to have been noted and valued for its beauty over a long period of time. We cited more than 1,500 years of literary and artistic references, beginning with Saint Colmcille in the sixth century and including the works of two Nobel laureates, Oscar Wilde and George Bernard Shaw in the nineteenth and twentieth centuries. Finally, there had to be consensus; that is, we had to show that Howth's scenery was valued by a broad spectrum of society. We did this by evidence of an involvement in the conservation of Howth of a diverse group of government and non-government organisations. These included the local authorities that had designated large parts of the peninsula as 'special amenity' in their development plans; An Taisce, which had acquired land on the headland to protect it and the unremitting campaigns of local residents' groups for designation. Having assessed the order drafted by the council, An Bord Pleanála recommended to the minister that the SAAO be made and The Howth Special Amenity Area Order came into effect in 2000.

As we had expected, in the council there was opposition to the order, the opposition coming from a handful of landowners, most notably two companies that were part of the Treasury Holdings group which owned 85 hectares of heathland at the eastern end of the peninsula. When the order was confirmed these companies initiated proceedings in the High Court against the minister and the council on the basis that the order was unconstitutional. The two companies sought damages of over €2 million for loss of development potential. However, six years later, by which time Treasury Holdings had more pressing concerns in relation to Nama and the viability of their property empire, the case was dropped. What has turned out to be noteworthy about Howth (and later Bray) is the relative ease with which the landscape designations were eventually made. Once the initial institutional inertia was overcome (there had been talk

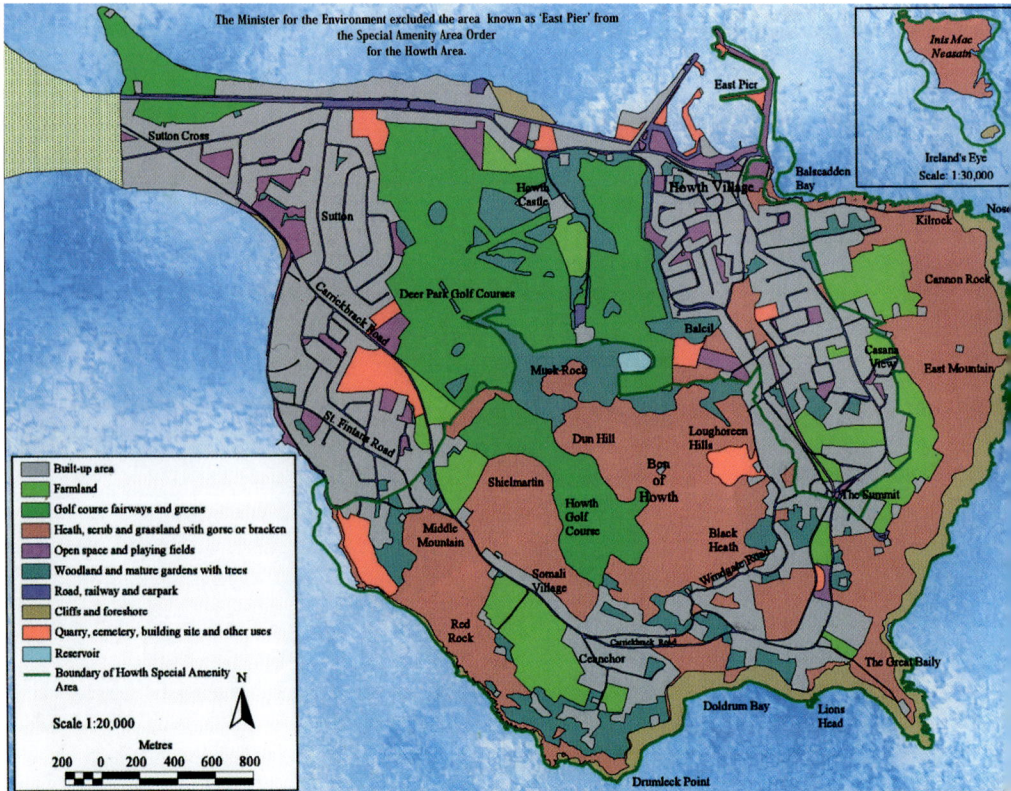

Fig. 8.16. The Howth Peninsula showing the Howth Special Amenity Area Order area.

of SAAOs for Howth and Bray for decades), the designations went through without that much difficulty.

That experience does not portend a generally more proactive official approach to landscape conservation more generally. Howth and Bray are special cases, populous, scenic suburban areas where there was strong support for designation in the local communities. The level of support was such that there was little likelihood that disaffected landowners would be able to enlist the assistance of politicians to block designation. Unusually, in the case of Howth, two landowners with large properties either actively supported the designation or did not seriously contest it. John Bellingham, whose farm at Ceanchor is the last working farm on the peninsula and therefore a vital feature of the diversity of the Howth landscape, actively supported the SAAO. Christopher Gaisford St Lawrence, 'Earl of Howth', and the largest landowner on the peninsula, viewed the order from the perspective of 800 years of family occupation. From that perspective he decided not to oppose the fundamental principles of the order. In Howth there was a substantial group of local people who passionately supported landscape designation while the remainder of the peninsula's population probably had no strong views either way. But this is an unusual scenario and in most places in Ireland (such as those described in Chapters 5 and 6), routinely described as 'close-knit communities' with an abundance of community spirit and social capital, deep-seated divisions about the landscape are liable to emerge as soon as the status quo is threatened.

In the rest of the country, therefore, statutory landscape designations have come to appear as increasingly irrelevant and anachronistic features of the Irish planning systems and are rarely attempted these days. Nevertheless, there is no doubt that the visual character of the Irish landscape matters to many people. To understand that sensitivity and to explore further ideas of landscape beauty and quality it is necessary to examine responses provoked by developer-driven change. The next chapter considers the response to the intrusion of large-scale technology in the landscape and the following chapter the ubiquitous and controversial impact of one-off housing. The final chapter returns to the issue of landscape designation and explores different options for the future.

Chapter 9

NEW TECHNOLOGY AND BEAUTY

———

We have seen that studying the arcane world of landscape designation does not throw much light on contemporary attitudes to landscape beauty. Dramatic landscape change or the prospect of such change is a more promising focus of enquiry because it involves situations that provoke strong reactions. Most landscape change is incremental, the resulting changes hardly rippling the surface of established practice and convention. However, two widespread technologies have arrived on the scene over the last quarter of a century that, by virtue of the sheer size and visibility of the engineering structures involved, have caused the transformation of landscapes and upset aesthetic conventions.

The roll-out of mobile telephony in Ireland is now substantially complete and wind farm development, which began in 1992, has gathered pace since the turn of the century.

Ireland has one of the highest rates of mobile phone usage in the world, enabled by a network of over 4,500 phone masts. Historian Roy Foster is scathing about a decision of Kerry County Council in 2006 when '. . . not content with rezoning unspoilt landscapes for one-off housing, [the council] enthusiastically gave permission for the erection of a 123-metre receiving mast in front of the marvellous 'Ladies View' of Killarney, to help with mobile-phone reception in the Black Valley'.[1] Foster recounts only the beginning of the story. The council decision was subsequently appealed by An Taisce and in 2007 An Bord Pleanála overturned the decision by a majority of six to one, endorsing its inspector's recommendation, who had described the proposed mast setting as 'breathtaking' in her report. Therefore this particular example shows a planning regime in force that is predisposed towards protecting scenic landscapes. At Ladies View, the planning authorities had to give weight to a national economic policy to improve the mobile phone network and also a safety argument for better mobile phone coverage for walkers and climbers in the Reeks. Nevertheless, a concern for the established beauty of the landscape prevailed.

Phone masts have tended to be controversial not because of their visual impact but because of a perceived health threat. Mobile telephony is the latest wave of electronic technology to be assimilated into the landscape, the previous one resulting in the ESB wirescape created in the middle of the last century. Nowadays we hardly notice electricity lines and poles until perhaps we try to frame a photograph without them. Both phone masts and power lines generate electromagnetic fields of low frequency, non-ionising radiation (as opposed to the destructive, high-energy radiation of gamma rays and x-rays). The modern world is saturated by this type of radiation which is produced by electrical appliances, power lines and telecommunication systems. There is no scientific evidence of a health risk from normal exposure to the radiation but this has not prevented a widespread belief that there is a serious risk.[2] That perceived risk is associated with the large physical structures that enable transmission, that is, radio and telephone masts and the pylons and cables of high-tension power lines. Here is an example of the irrepressible urge of the human psyche to draw inference, mistaken or otherwise, from physical appearance. Lattice-type phone masts and electricity pylons are ugly, intimidating structures, out of place and out of scale in most landscape settings. It seems that by being ugly and visually unwelcoming to this degree, they bestow substance and credibility to an otherwise unsubstantiated health risk. In marked contrast, while alarmist headlines about phone masts and pylons proliferate, the message promulgated by the Radiological Protection Institute of Ireland about the serious and widespread health risk posed by the build-up of radon gas in dwellings and workplaces has failed to gain any traction. Radon, a naturally occurring radioactive element, goes unnoticed because it is invisible. Ireland has one of the highest rates of naturally occurring radon in Europe and the risk of death from exposure to radon is of the same order as dying in a road traffic accident.[3]

There is also widespread opposition to wind farm development in this country. Virtually the whole of this island has a viable wind energy resource potential, on the assumption that there is a potential commercial return from any site where there is an average wind speed of 7.5 metres per second or more at 100 metres above ground level. The first Irish wind farm came into operation in 1992 and is situated on low-lying cutaway bog at Bellacorrick in north Mayo. The farm generates 6.45 MW of electricity. The industry progressed slowly in the following decade with only a further 120 MW of installed capacity.[4] More recently change has accelerated. By 2011, there was 1,900 MW of installed capacity at 163 wind farms in 27 counties. This is equivalent to 11 per cent of national electricity production and compares with a mandatory EU target of 16 per cent renewable

Fig. 9.1. A tower in a 400kV transmission line in north Clare, one of two lines constructed in the 1980s from Moneypoint power station to Dublin. The lattice-type towers, typically standing 57 metres high, are more than seven times the height of nearby dwellings. In the immediate vicinity the audible crackle of air breaking down into charged particles along the surface of the conductors contributes to the sensory impact of the line.

where the modern wind energy industry began building wind farms with virtually no regard to landscape setting. In response to that experience, a group of American experts organised an international, multi-disciplinary symposium to clarify the landscape issues and devise solutions. The product of the symposium is *Wind Power in View*, published in 2002. One of the contributors is Gordon Brittan, an American philosopher, who offers a philosophy of landscape and wind energy.[17]

Brittan endorses a landscape aesthetic based on evolutionary biology rather than the eighteenth-century romantic landscape tradition. He refers to natural philosopher Aldo Leopold, who saw the beauty of a swamp in its ecosystem, a web of interrelationships developed over time to create a beautiful dynamic equilibrium. We have insight into such complex systems because of the scientific knowledge gathered over the last two centuries. This then is an aesthetic based on how a place functions rather than how it looks. The concept embraces both spectacular and humdrum visual manifestations of nature. From this perspective, bogs, marshes and mudflats are as inherently attractive as the rugged coasts, forests and lakelands beloved by Romantics. The approach chimes with older traditions of viewing the world in which the physical landscape is an inseparable aspect of an environment divinely created.

Brittan ponders whether, in the way that we are able to appreciate the beauty of a superficially unattractive marshland, we could see beyond the external appearance of a wind turbine to something that is inherently attractive. Somewhat surprisingly, considering the objective of the symposium, he concluded that we cannot. He classes turbines as 'devices' rather than 'things', a distinction that has been explored by Albert Borgman, another American philosopher. Most of our modern technology consists of devices which are defined by their function, for example televisions and mobile phones, whereas 'things' have the potential to engage us, such as cars and dwellings. There used to be windmills, which are 'things', and now there are wind turbines, which are 'devices'. Turbines are anonymous and the only way they engage us is visually. We cannot get inside them, we cannot tinker with them. By contrast windmills were things; we knew how they worked, we could go inside them and we may have known who worked in them.

Brittan acknowledges that he is writing from an American perspective, where the wind energy sector is dominated by large corporations and, typically, installations consist of large arrays of turbines owned and operated by remote corporations. By contrast, in other countries, Denmark being the best example, wind installations are small scale and locally owned and managed. This fosters engagement and, as a result, a positive view. Brittan allows the possibility for wind turbines to become 'things' by new approaches to design and management.

Fig. 9.2. Field trip participants on a visit organised by the Sustainable Energy Authority of Ireland to the Knockawarriga Wind Farm in County Limerick in 2010. An organised visit with the opportunity to meet wind farm workers is an untypical wind farm experience. The turbine in view behind the control room is one of nine in this wind farm. The tower stands 75 metres high and the blades have a diameter of 45 metres.

Fig. 9.3. Glenmore in County Limerick near the Kerry border in 2009.

The Western Development Commission in Ireland has studied the cooperative experience in Denmark and other countries.[18] Denmark is comparable to Ireland in several ways. It is a small country with a similar population to Ireland's. It also has a strong rural economy and a cooperative tradition and it has a good wind resource. Some 80 per cent of wind farms in Denmark are community owned, 22 per cent of Danish energy is supplied by community wind farms and more than 100,000 Danish families are 'wind guild' members. By contrast, a community-based approach has made little progress in this country, where typically wind farm developers are companies that do not have a local connection other than leasing agreements with the landowners on which a wind farm is built. The Danish movement has its roots in an initiative in 1979 by three families living outside Århus. The families already shared a snowplough and they decided to put up a wind turbine together to meet their own energy needs, the turbine to be sited where their properties met. Their plan had been to sell surplus electricity to the local electricity company but the company was completely unsympathetic to that proposal and it was not until there was high-level political intervention that the families were given a grid connection. There then followed two years of negotiation to work out the terms of the connection. It was finally agreed that they would deliver all the power they generated to the grid, for which they would be paid 85 per cent of the household price and that they would buy back all the electricity they needed at the full price. These terms were very attractive and created a lot of interest. With that agreement as a benchmark and funding supports from government to build turbines, wind power guilds began to be set up all over the country. Nowadays anybody living within 10 kilometres of a wind farm can become a guild member and have a financial stake in the operation of the wind farm. In Denmark therefore the guild movement originated as an initiative by landowners but quickly became a vehicle for the involvement of a geographical community, first people living within 3 kilometres of a wind farm site and then within 10 kilometres.[19] Landscape architect Frode Birk Nielson, who has been heavily involved in the development of the industry, believes that 'if, for some reason, we were to remove Denmark's 6,000 turbines, there would be a public outcry'.[20] The Western Development Commission report examined the Danish experience and experience in other countries with a view to promoting a community approach in the west of Ireland. Their report emphasises the difficulties of a community-based initiative in Ireland but does conclude that 'given a policy environment that facilitates community-owned projects, Ireland could have a similar wind farm [a community-supported large-scale wind energy project in Denmark] within a few years'.[21] Being a 'late developer', Ireland has benefitted from lessons learnt in America and elsewhere in respect of wind farm and turbine design. However, it has not been able to address the issue of a fairer distribution of the costs and benefits of the new technology.

Trying to appreciate the beauty of a wind farm development in the same way that Aldo Leopold could enjoy the beauty of a swamp offers one alternative viewpoint. Another is the perspective of global sustainability. This stretches the aesthetic connection to its limits because the relevant visual image is the earth viewed from space, a view of a whole planet rather than its individual ecosystems. As of June 2011, only 523 astronauts from thirty-eight countries have had the privilege of seeing that view for themselves but millions of us have seen the films and photographs.[22] That beautiful view has helped to change the way we think about the world at the turn of the millennium. As James Lovelock wrote in 1979:

> The apologists for space science always seem over-impressed by engineering trivia and make far too much of non-stick frying pans and perfect ball-bearings. To my mind, the outstanding spin-off from space research is not new technology. The real bonus has been that for the first time in human history, we have had a chance to look at the Earth from space, and the information gained from seeing from the outside our azure-green planet

in all its global beauty has given rise to a whole new set of questions and answers.[23]

Can a global perspective affect how we feel about major landscape change in our own back yard? Could a landscape dominated by wind farms come to seem beautiful because we appreciate the sustainable quality of the landscape? Michael Viney tells the story of a visit to his home in Mayo in 2008 by a renewable energy entrepreneur. He spread his maps on the dining table and enthusiastically described the ten-turbine wind farm he intended to build on the hillside by the Vineys' home.

> *We swallowed our misgivings, wished him success with the county planners and began to reorder the landscape in our minds; we'd still have the ocean, after all. And hadn't we been green supporters of wind energy from back in the 1970s when Ethna was editor of* Technology Ireland? *She still finds the turbines beautiful, and sometimes I agree.*[24]

Viney describes the guilty sense of relief he felt when he rang their visitor in 2011 for news of the project and was told that the project was 'dead' because Mayo County Council had 'unzoned' the mountain for wind developments (in the county's new wind strategy referred to above).

One landscape academic has suggested that sustainable landscapes will 'serendipitously come to be seen as beautiful'.[25] But deciding whether a landscape is sustainable, never mind beautiful, is a far from easy judgement, especially in relation to developments like wind farms, which have so many environmental implications. Probably several recently constructed Irish wind farms will prove not to have been sustainable in retrospect. A 2009 survey found that thirty-nine of the seventy-three existing wind farms had been built in upland bog areas.[26] It is only very recently that the important role of bogland as a major carbon sink has come to be recognised. Where wind farms have been built on deep peat, they may have negative carbon budgets. The positive consequence of a reduction in carbon emissions as a result of using the clean energy generated by the wind farm will be cancelled out by the effects of the release of carbon from the bog during construction of the farm and by the permanent loss of the bog's sequestration capacity. The promotion of wind farms on upland bogs has now been described as one of the main obstacles to sustainable peatland management in Ireland.[27]

The complexity of landscape challenges the rigour of a rational decision-making process. Beauty is part of the decision equation and, as Michael Viney has remarked, 'deciding what is beautiful has created all kinds of problems for decision-makers, who feel helpless without the framework of numbers and

Fig. 9.4. View across a large wind farm planning application site near Casla (Costelloe) in east Connemara. The 27-turbine project was refused planning permission in 2011.

boxes'.[28] In 2011, An Bord Pleanála, in a unanimous decision, refused permission for a large wind farm comprising twenty-seven 139-metre-high turbines on low-lying bogland in east Connemara (see Fig. 9.4). The board decided that the proposal would be an 'excessively dominant feature and visually obtrusive form of development' in 'this highly scenic landscape'.[29] But the clarity of that statement masks the serendipitous quality of the decision-making process that preceded it. The wind farm site is on land zoned specifically for wind farm development by Galway County Council and the council, in the person of a senior official, had granted permission for the scheme, against the advice of the council planner. The board's decision was also contrary to its own inspector's recommendation. The inspector, who had visited the site (unlike the board members), had written a detailed assessment, 108 pages in length, that offered the board four decision options: to grant permission for a slightly modified scheme (the inspector's preferred option), to grant permission for a much smaller wind farm in response to environmental and landscape issues; to refuse permission on the ground of prematurity in advance of the adoption of a wind strategy; and to refuse permission because of adverse landscape and environmental impacts.

In Mayo, Ireland's newest national park at Ballycroy occupies a large part of the Nephin Beg mountain range. The county council's energy strategy, adopted in 2011, sandwiches the park between two large areas that have been identified for wind energy development over the next ten years.[30] In the strategy the area bordering the western boundary has been set aside for large wind farms and the area on the eastern boundary has been identified as an area where wind farms are 'open for consideration' (see Figs 9.5 and 9.6).

The Park brochure contains a description of the district by Robert Lloyd Praeger:

> *Indeed the Nephinbeg range of mountains is I think the very loneliest place in this country, for the hills themselves are encircled by this vast area of trackless bog . . . I confess I find such a place not lonely or depressing but inspiriting. You are thrown at the same time back upon yourself and forward against the mystery and majesty of nature.*[31]

Fig. 9.5. View towards Ballycroy National Park from the N59 south of Bangor in 2007.

Fig. 9.6. View north-east towards Ballycroy National Park in 2011, across degraded boglands which have been selected for large wind farm development in the Mayo Energy Strategy.

The brochure advises visitors to 'not venture into the hills alone'. This is not idle advice; Praeger's description of seventy-five years ago still resonates. Comprising more than 11,000 hectares of bog and mountain, Ballycroy is the only protected landscape on this island where it is possible to enjoy an extensive wilderness experience. It is hard to put a value on that experience, one that will undoubtedly be devalued, if not destroyed, by the presence of vistas dominated by wind turbines.

Wind energy policy making and project assessment are becoming increasingly sophisticated technical tasks yet it is not clear that the quality of the decision-making about wind energy is improving. The Connemara example described illustrates the high level of unpredictability there is in the decision-making process. One can deduce from this both an increasing divergence of viewpoint about the aesthetic merits of wind farm developments and a consequence of a decision making process balancing so many disparate criteria. Many of those

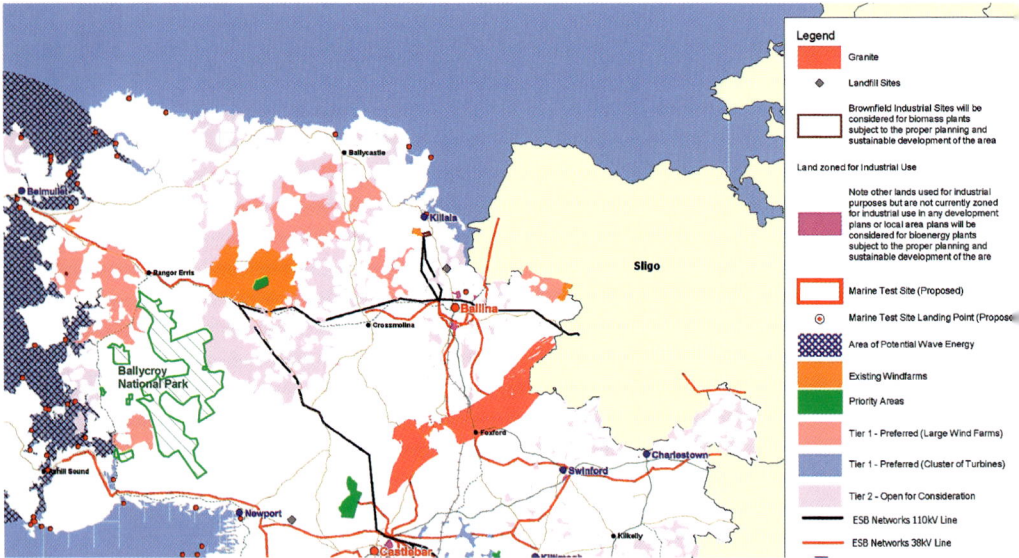

Fig. 9.7. Extract from the 2011–2020 County Mayo Energy Strategy Map showing the location of Ballycroy National Park in relation to areas selected for wind farm development.

criteria are readily susceptible to measurement and mapping, for example wind speeds and the distribution of Natura 2000 sites, but others such as community cohesion, amenity, 'the common good' and beauty are stubbornly resistant to assimilation into a rational decision-making process. The apparently casual manner in which the state, in the guise of the Department of the Environment, has put forward the bogs of north-west Mayo as a candidate World Heritage Site and promotes Ballycroy as a last wilderness, yet at the same time, in the form of Mayo County Council, identifies the locality for major wind farm development points to a weakness of governance.

Physical beauty enriches our lives. The beauty of another person, the beauty of a work of art and the beauty of the natural world have the power to stop us in our tracks. The romantic landscape tradition remains significant and important and explains the continuing allure of our iconic landscapes. The other perspectives described in this chapter feed in to a much more complicated notion of landscape but one with ancient roots. The Greeks did not have a word for physical beauty, their word 'kalos' being better translated as 'delightful' or 'fine' or 'excellent'. In Plotinus' world, 'beauty' did not equate to physical beauty but to the beauty of the spirit, and before the eighteenth century in Ireland, there was probably no distinction made between physical beauty and the presence of the divine. In their deliberations about wind turbines, aesthetics and landscape Gordan Brittan and the other contributors to the wind farm symposium could not agree about very much. The only unqualified agreement was that their meeting was being held in a beautiful place. That was the Rockefeller Foundation center that overlooks Lake Como in Northern Italy. Nearly two centuries earlier the Romantic poet Percy Bysshe Shelley had written about Como that 'This lake exceeds anything I ever beheld in beauty with the exception of the arbutus islands of Killarney.'[32]

This chapter has introduced different notions of landscape beauty, notions that are relevant not only to the lakeland of Killarney but also the lakelands of Cavan. The next chapter examines different perspectives in relation to rural housing, the most divisive planning issue in Ireland in recent years.

Chapter 10

LANDSCAPE AND RURAL HOUSING

We moved west, out of Dublin, in 1999. The house we bought had been built as a holiday home for letting. When we arrived here there were eighteen other dwellings within a kilometre of our house, now there are twenty-eight. Most of the new dwellings are dormer bungalows sitting on half-acre and one-acre sites. This had been an area with an aging population but now there is a good mix of families, many with young children. There are also several houses that are vacant or empty most of the time. Some 20 kilometres to the west, along the Atlantic coast, the pace of change was more dramatic.

Since the 1960s, there have not been that many places in Ireland where, if the will is there, there has not been a way to build a house with all 'mod cons'. Access, sanitation, power and water became virtually ubiquitous during the course of the last century. Ireland had a dense road network at the start of the twentieth century though many of the roads were of poor quality. However, during the first half of the century most roads were tarred, 'a striking example of the dominance of rural values in post-independent Ireland' according to transport geographer James Killen.⁹ The Frenchman Louis Mouras is credited with the invention of the septic tank around 1870. The septic tank provides a safe means to treat sewage on a well-drained site (although a large number, perhaps the majority of rural houses, do not have properly constructed sewage systems). Several other treatment systems appeared on the market in the 1980s and '90s that increased the options available and allowed sites to be developed that were not suitable for septic tank systems. Meanwhile, in 1978, the ESB completed its rural electrification programme when it brought power to the Black Valley in Kerry. While less than a fifth of rural households had a piped water supply in 1960, most rural areas had piped water by the end of the century. The rugged topography of parts of the country has ceased to be an obstacle to site development. As a result of the great expansion of the construction industry and the easy credit that once

Fig. 10.3. A ribbon of new housing off the N17, 15 kilometres north of Galway city, in 2010.

Fig. 10.4. Dispersed housing in 2004 on the hillside above Lough Nafooey on the Mayo-Galway border.

was available, there is nearly always a man with a digger on hand to tame and level the most unpromising of sites. For several decades now there has been no engineering barrier to building new houses in most places.

It may be possible to attribute wayward property projects, including golf and spa resorts, shopping centres and suburban housing estates, to 'the new gentry', the errant sub-culture of the Celtic Tiger years that is described by Fintan O'Toole in *Ship of Fools*.[10] But there is no escaping the fact that building dispersed rural housing is a shared endeavour, involving everyone from merchant prince to small farmer, from government minister to county councillor and from bank manager to 'the man with a digger'. The British Channel 4 programme *Grand Designs*, which charts the trials and tribulations of home builders in Britain, has been compelling reality TV in Ireland for ten years. *Grand Designs* takes its audience into a world of private enterprise and achievement in which the dream of creating a beautiful home is invariably successful. Many of the projects are rural houses. The dream of self-build may be universal but it is entirely beyond the grasp of most Europeans. *Grand Designs* therefore has a unique appeal in Ireland, where a relatively large number of the viewers of the programme both aspire to the dream and have the opportunity to turn their dream into reality.

For all the heat that the bungalow bliss/bungalow blitz debate generates among Irish commentators, it makes little dent on outsider perceptions. As we have seen in earlier chapters, guidebooks and annual Fáilte Ireland surveys of visitors continue to reflect a timeless landscape and a green and pleasant land. The visitor sees the country's famous landscapes, and that experience is almost entirely a visual one, hardly affected by the nature of modern settlement. In contrast, many residents are powerfully exercised by one-offs and explain their opposition or support in visual terms, even though, according to Conor Skehan, the visual impact of one-offs, assessed in strictly objective terms, is not that significant.[11] The visual dominates the debate and it is no coincidence that the labels attached to the different sides of the argument – 'bungalow bliss' and 'bungalow blitz' – have a strong visual flavour. Numerous rural house-design guides have been published by local councils in recent years to try to improve design standards. The most authoritative is that written by Cork architect Mike Shanahan and Colin Buchanan and Partners, British planning consultants.[12] But at best the guides have been greeted with lukewarm enthusiasm by local politicians. When Clare County Council published its guide in 2002, its officials got no thanks from councillor P.J. Kelly, who compared them to 'the deposed Taliban' for their intended 'suppression of house designs' in the county.[13]

In 2001, the architect and planner Fergal MacCabe, a founder member of the Irish Planning Institute, retraced a bicycle trip in County Offaly that he had made as a 15-year-old, forty-five years before, to find the house in which Myles na gCopaleen had grown up. He remembered as a teenager cycling thirteen miles out of Tullamore on a lonely road through woods and bogs. But in 2001

> All had changed – changed utterly. From Tullamore to Croghan, the road was lined with bungalows and the sites in between festooned with notices seeking to build more. None of the bungalows had any architectural merit and, thanks to affluence and garden radio and television programmes, their vulgarity extended to the gardens, which abounded with swans, swings and illuminated fountains. While the houses were uniformly awful, the gardens were individually awful. The few farmhouses I remembered were now abandoned and decayed . . .[14]

Others making the same bicycle journey would have an entirely different reaction. Jack Fitzsimons from County Meath, the author of *Bungalow Bliss*, a bungalow-design book which went through eleven editions after it first appeared in 1971, believes that the new housing has given 'an opportunity to many who would be condemned to the housing list and the housing scheme to transpose themselves on the magic carpet of their dreams to a situation where they could be monarchs of all they surveyed'.[15] The Irish Rural Dwellers Association celebrates 'dream

Fig. 10.5. The settled landscape of An Cheathrú Rua (Carraroe) in 2011. Visiting the area a quarter of a century ago led journalist Frank McDonald to coin the phrase 'bungalow blitz' in 1987.

houses' in which 'home owners are proud to express their new-found economic freedom, creativity and modernity'. The IRDA rejoices in a new order in which 'colonial and outmoded authoritarian structures and alien ideologies have been overturned'.[16] Economist Ethel Crowley cites historical geographer E. Estyn Evans and travel writer Pete McCarthy to make the case that the ostentation of the new housing is a pent-up response to centuries of rural poverty.[17] She quotes Pete McCarthy, arguing that the self-confident synthetic consumerism of the new houses is a response to the history of deprivation. 'Look,' the new bungalows are saying, 'we're not peasants anymore. We buy things now rather than digging them up. We've been sitting on bare wooden benches for centuries, but we've got Dralon sofas now, just like you.'[18]

In the last book of his Connemara trilogy, Tim Robinson describes meeting environmental journalist Frank McDonald shortly after he had coined the phrase, 'bungalow blitz'.[19] McDonald had written an article on rural housing following a visit to An Cheathrú Rua (Carraroe). This was an area which Robinson himself had only recently surveyed, cycling every road and boreen and talking to everyone he met. Robinson had been appalled by the 'ugliness' of the new bungalows there but had ventured to suggest to McDonald that there might also be something good to write about the area. McDonald riposted that Robinson had 'gone native'. Robinson acutely observes that McDonald's viewpoint had come about from 'driving through' the area, while he had begun

The Republic has a hierarchical plan-making structure which has now been further elaborated and clarified by the Planning and Development Act of 2010. At the top of the hierarchy lies a national spatial strategy which sets population targets for the different regions of the country and for the cities and towns that have been earmarked for major growth. The next tier consists of eight regional authorities which periodically issue guidelines to ensure that development takes place in accordance with the national strategy. Every county and city planning authority is required to make plans that are in accordance with these guidelines. A primary purpose of this planning framework is to decide where new housing should be built. The regional authorities have recently issued their guidelines for the period to 2022. The guidelines include population and housing targets that are based on detailed statistical forecasts. But this target-setting entirely ignores the fact that, outside the Dublin region, a large proportion of the housing stock is being, and will continue to be, built in the countryside. For example, the Mid-West Guidelines for Clare, Limerick and north Tipperary assume that 'a *small* amount of development will continue in the countryside'.[29] This is a convenient deceit that helps to manage the massive over-zoning of lands that has taken place. The 'headroom' created in the guidelines, that part of projected growth which, in reality, will take the form of one-off houses but which is counted as future urban development, provides a justification for the retention of a much higher proportion of zoned urban lands than would otherwise be the case. The guidelines therefore ignore the ingrained pattern of development over the past half century. They note that during the previous census period, 2002–2006, a high proportion of towns lost population, which was a repeat of the pattern in the census period before that, 1996–2002. The guidelines express surprise at the declining growth rates of the designated regional growth centres of Limerick and Ennis since 2002 and the fact that, between 2002 and 2006, more than 10,000 people settled in the villages and countryside around those urban centres.[30] The guidelines therefore perpetuate the notion of one-off housing as a marginal phenomenon when it is, in fact, one of the dominant growth features of the region (and of the whole country).

Statutory development plans do not promote ribbon development and the suburbanisation of the countryside near towns and villages. Nevertheless, ribbons of housing and a dense scatter of houses around towns and villages are characteristic products of the Irish planning regime. Development plans typically have a policy to protect the countryside. However, that policy is invariably negated by other policies in the same plan to facilitate rural housing. The end result is the gradual development of a low-density pattern of one-off housing. In County Clare it has been policy in four statutory plans, adopted over a thirty-year period, that development is to be 'gathered where possible into settlements and other existing groups'.[31] The plans have all included policy along the lines that 'a high priority will be given to the protection, conservation, enhancement, appearance and character of the open countryside'. However, near towns and villages these policies have been countered by another plan policy 'to meet the needs of local communities for rurally generated housing'.[32] The outcome is low-density settlement such as the area in Figure 10.6, 3 kilometres outside Ennis, the nearest town.

Plans for rural areas around towns and villages in County Donegal illustrate a more straightforward approach, but an approach that surrenders any claim to scientific rationality. For more than thirty years in Donegal there has been a policy to 'normally grant permission for appropriate development on zoned lands within town development control points'.[33] There are control points around all the towns and villages of the county. While one might have expected that the control points would be near the edges of built-up areas, they are generally in open countryside, often coinciding with speed limit signs on the approach roads to settlements. In Donegal, therefore, the countryside around towns and villages is zoned for development as though it was an urban area. In the example

Fig. 10.6. Rural housing near Ennis in 2010 in an area where successive development plans have sought to both protect the character of the open countryside and to provide for 'rurally generated housing'.

illustrated, which is outside Buncrana, there is a control point about 2 kilometres up the Crana valley, so that a chaotic suburbanisation of the lower part of the valley (shown in Fig. 10.7) has been inevitable. Housing estates are marooned on the valley sides, lacking basic services and facilities, separated from each other by individual house plots and reedy fields and not a footpath in sight. It is impossible, short of demolition and restoration, to envisage a credible planning policy for such areas. It is no wonder therefore that the current plan policy resorts to fairly meaningless technical 'gobbledegook'. The policy is

> to provide for a spatial development pattern that is reflective of a dispersed rural settlement pattern and that is related in form and scale to the level of existing physical and social infrastructure in the area and that can be integrated and absorbed into the landscape.[34]

A rationale for dispersed rural housing is heavily based on the premise that it is

Fig. 10.7. The Crana valley outside Buncrana, County Donegal in 2008, a hotchpotch of rural laneways, reedy fields, housing estates and individual house plots.

associated with very high levels of residential satisfaction. As Martin Mansergh has put it, 'it is what people want'. Surveys carried out in the eighties and again in the last decade have found high satisfaction levels. [35, 36] Based on a comparative survey of people who had either bought new houses on estates or had built houses in the countryside during the early 1980s, housing economists Robert Jennings and Stephaney Bissett concluded that:

> *Rural housebuilding (bungalow bliss) provides access for lower-income households to good-quality housing at low cost. The costs of curtailing such development, in terms of welfare loss to the household and resource cost to the state, would be high. Negative environmental impacts (if or where they exist) should be dealt with by a policy of advice/guidance/ assistance regarding siting, screening and external environs rather than by curtailing development.*
>
> *Self-build or self-initiated housebuilding has considerable potential for providing good-quality housing at low cost . . .*[37]

Twenty years later the authors of a report for the EPA found the same high levels of satisfaction. This more recent report does not deliver the same ringing endorsement of rural housing growth as its predecessor but it is nevertheless a surprisingly muted critique given the much greater awareness there is these days of the external costs associated with a dispersed pattern of development. It takes a relatively close reading of the report to find a conclusion that 'there are very considerable social or external costs to scattered rural residential development' and it is 'clearly inequitable that private benefits should be allowed to dominate the wider public good'.[38]

The current dependence on one-off housing as a source of new housing stock and the implications of that dependence, in terms of a heavy reliance on fossil fuel consumption for everyday living, are alarming. At the present time the environmental benefits of eco-house construction are completely offset by the environmental costs associated with even a very short car commute.[39] Car travel accounts for by far the greatest energy expenditure of Irish families. There is no prospect of replacing the private car as the dominant mode of transport in rural Ireland and very little likelihood that car travel will become an inherently sustainable everyday transport mode. The externalities associated with car dependence are just part of a wide range of costs, costs that may not be shared by the individuals and families building houses in the countryside but which are ultimately borne by Irish society.[40]

Table 10.1. The annual energy consumption (kWh) of an average Irish household.	
Energy use	kWh p.a.
Heating	20,000
Light and power	20,000
Car travel	30,000
Total	70,000

Source: Pat Stephens, 'Settlement Patterns and Energy Consumption', paper presented at Irish Planning Institute national conference, 2009.

Rather than Irish society in the latter decades of the twentieth century and the early twenty-first century choosing to renew its settlement pattern by reinforcing the urban hierarchy, it has built dispersed rural houses as a high proportion of new housing stock. It does not require a crystal ball to see outcomes in the near future in the shape of greater numbers of impoverished rural dwellers and of an Irish countryside increasingly characterised, not so much by the picturesque ruins of the nineteenth century, but by a scattering of empty and abandoned concrete-block houses that were erected in the late twentieth and early twenty-first centuries (Fig. 10.8). More than a quarter of the housing stock of counties Kerry, Donegal and Leitrim was vacant in 2011.[41]

A by-product of the building free-for-all is the creation of a substantial rural population without legal or economic ties to rural land other than the ownership of a small house plot. This will increase the frequency of damaging and divisive landscape conflicts in the future that are precipitated by the prospect of major rural development projects. While landowner interests are protected by the established legal framework, rural residents have limited options open to them. The development programme that immediately comes to mind in this regard is Grid 25, the planned strengthening of the national grid by Eirgrid. Grid 25 involves building 1,000 kilometres of new overhead high-tension power lines by 2025. Some of those lines will have to traverse the wide commuter belts that have grown up around Dublin and Cork.

The Irish rural landscape, envisioned as a place of farms and farmsteads, exemplifies a 'paper landscape', a place that only exists in a John Hinde postcard or between the covers of some official planning documents. The blind eye turned to one-off housing illustrates a strand of 'wishful thinking' that has been evident in spatial planning in Ireland for decades. Another example of this kind of thinking is the 'paper park', found throughout the world and so named by Adrian Phillips of the International Union for the Conservation of Nature and Natural Resources (IUCN). This is a designated protected landscape which is

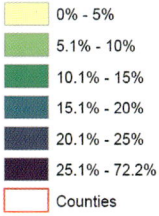

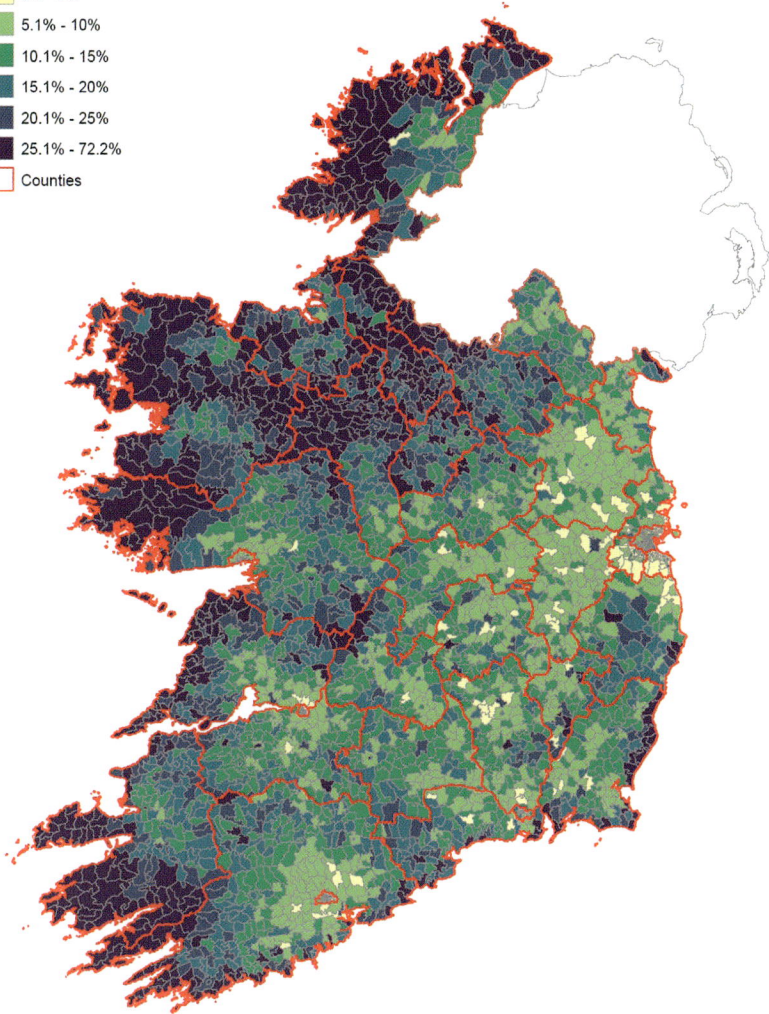

Figure 10.8. Vacancy dwelling rates in the Republic of Ireland in 2011.
(© *Ordnance Survey Ireland/Government of Ireland*)

protected in name only, its substance little more than the coloured-in area on a map.[42] Real parks and paper parks are among the landscape choices that are examined in the final chapter.

Fig. 10.9. Bungalows overlooking Killary Harbour, County Mayo, in 2011. Two of the five bungalows have not been completed and are unoccupied.

Fig. 10.10 and 10.11 (above and opposite page). Different types of abandoned structure in the north Clare countryside in 2011: nineteenth-century stone-built cottages and a twenty-first-century concrete-block-built house.

Chapter 11

MAKING THE MOST OF LANDSCAPE

––––––––

This year our village re-entered the Tidy Towns competition after a gap of several years. The local committee has been active since the late spring. As well as tidying up the village itself, work parties have also gone outside the village. They have made flower beds beside the main approach road from Ennis and spruced up the picnic tables at Lake Inchiquin. Our contribution was designing a map board with heritage information for residents and visitors that was erected in the main street. While the geographical range of the work parties is a short stroll from the village, the map covers a wider area, about 100 square kilometres.

It includes part of the Burren National Park which is to the north of the village, Dromore Wood to the west, and the ancient settlement of Dysert O'Dea to the south. The top of the map corresponds to the edge of the Burren uplands and the left side to the start of the boggy hill country of west Clare. However, to the south and east, where the land merges seamlessly into the low-lying heartland of the county, the map edges are arbitrary lines across the land. Somewhere between the area covered by our map and the territory overseen by the work parties of the Tidy Towns committee there is an imprecise entity that, for most purposes, passes muster as the Corrofin area. This is the area of the parish, the catchment area of Corrofin national school and the area from where the Corrofin GAA, camogie and soccer clubs and the drama society draw most of their members. This is the place, larger than the farm and the townland and smaller than the county, within which social and cultural relationships and landscape intertwine. Beyond this local scale, fervent attachments to county sports' teams notwithstanding, the strength of affiliation and knowledge of place wane.

At the local scale, landscape is less an abstract concept and more an amalgam of ingredients of everyday life that share place as a common denominator. It is an idea of landscape that finds expression in the maps and writings of Tim Robinson that have been frequently referred to in this book. This is landscape at its simplest and most profound, an interaction of people with the places they inhabit. Few of us possess the literary and cartographic skills of a Tim Robinson, but while unravelling a landscape narrative requires patience and persistence, it is not a complicated skill and one that is well adapted to communal enterprise. Terry O'Regan, a Cork landscape architect, has devised a simple landscape survey method for community groups to follow, called 'The Landscape Circle'.[1] Depending on the resources that are available to the community, the circle can be between 1 and 5 kilometres in radius, 'small enough to be studied having account of the time and resources available, but large enough to encompass a range of landscape diversity'.[2]

Beyond the scale of O'Regan's circle, landscape becomes more abstract but retains its pedagogical power. Landscape offers an age-old means of making sense of the world. From the perspective of an archaeologist, Conor Newman explains that 'in so far as the landscape is constructed in, and according to our likeness, it is capable therefore of being a classroom, a storehouse of personal, tribal and communal knowledge'.[3] Of most pressing concern in our times, landscape provides an accessible route to an understanding of the interdependence of culture and environment, offering a powerful alternative to the prevailing paradigm of academic specialisation. The notion of a geographical area serving as a basic educational tool has always been appreciated. Over forty years ago, Lewis Mumford proposed it as a means to educate people so that they 'will know in detail where they live and how they live . . . united by a common feeling for their landscape, their literature and language, their local ways'.[4]

At a local scale, therefore, landscape is within our grasp as something that can be enhanced and enjoyed in modest and satisfying ways. All landscape has this local dimension but there are several parts of Ireland where landscape possesses such a striking character that it also has national and international significance. This is landscape as national heritage, something to be treasured and safeguarded as a source of pride for future generations, and also something that can be exploited as a tourism asset for short-term economic benefit. At this scale landscape cannot be managed by piecemeal local interventions but requires a national engagement. This has not happened in Ireland, which is in marked contrast to other European countries.

The Burren is one of those Irish landscapes that stand out. In 2005 Liam Lysaght, a former ranger in north Clare and now director of the National Biodiversity Data Centre in Waterford, proposed a 'landscape scale' national park for the Burren, 'a landscape like no other in north-west Europe'.[5] Lysaght observed that landscape scale initiatives work elsewhere in Europe so why not in Ireland. He cited the National Park of Abruzzo, Latium and Molise in the Apennine Mountains, east of Rome, as a comparable example. That park, now about 500 square kilometres in extent, began life as a small 500-hectare protected site in the 1920s, that is, about the same size as the Burren National Park is today.

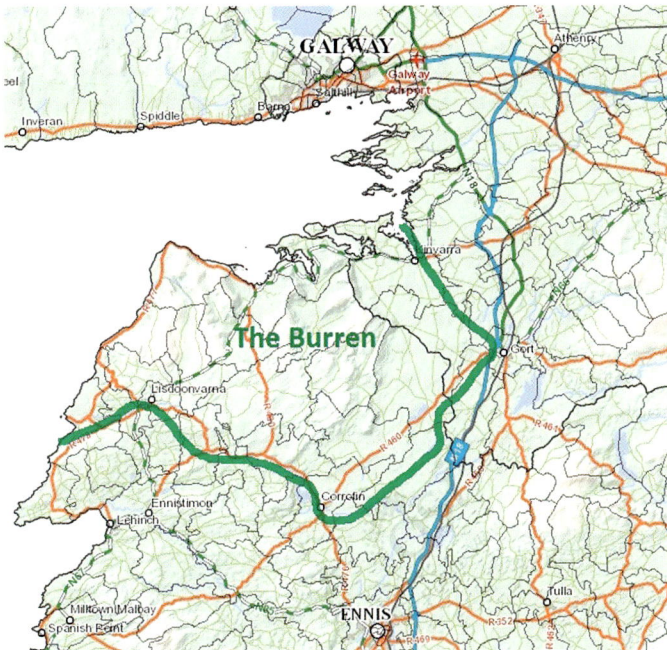

Fig. 11.1.
The extent of the Burren National Park proposed by Liam Lysaght in 2005.
(© Ordnance Survey Ireland/ Government of Ireland)

Lysaght lists failed initiatives of recent times – Tourism in the Burren: A Strategic Plan, The Burren Monuments Strategy and the Burren Consultative Committee. They failed, according to Lysaght, because there is no management structure for the area, an organisation that can 'reconcile national policies with local needs' that 'would straddle the area between ensuring that the needs and expectations of local communities are realised while also protecting this special place'.[6] If such a body were to be created it would be staffed not just by people with expertise in nature conservation management but also 'teachers, tourism specialists and even business advisors to assist the proper development of the area'.[7]

Nothing has come of Lysaght's suggestion but much has been happening in the Burren over the last half dozen years. Working out of an office in Carran in the centre of the Burren, scientist Brendan Dunford is leading a three-person team implementing the Burren Farming for Conservation Programme, a four-year project funded by the Departments of Agriculture and Heritage. The programme, which builds on the successful Burren LIFE project,[8] currently covers 40 per cent of the designated SAC land in the Burren. The aim of the programme is to help farming practices which benefit the environment, with a special emphasis on the conservation of species-rich grasslands. In its second year of operation, the programme has disbursed nearly €1 million in grants to farmers for environmental improvements. The 143 farmers involved have received average payments of €7,000 in 2012.[9] Carol Gleeson, meanwhile, is running Burren Connect from the area offices of Clare County Council in Ennistymon. Burren Connect is a multi-agency project that was begun in 2007 to develop local tourism. The project has set up the Burren Ecotourism Network, a network of accredited local businesses committed to sustainable tourism practice. The network was launched in 2011 in Gregan's Hotel at the foot of Corkscrew Hill, the hotel being one of the network members. That proved an auspicious choice of venue, with the hotel going on to win restaurant and hotel of the year awards in 2011 from the Restaurant Association of Ireland and Automobile Association. Burren Connect has also helped to secure Geopark status for the area. On the Galway side of the Burren, Kinvara is the base of Burrenbeo. Burrenbeo was founded in 2002 by Brendan Dunford and Ann O'Connor and re-launched as a charitable trust in 2008. The trust is dedicated to the conservation of the Burren landscape. With just one full-time staff member, the trust sustains an impressive information, conservation and educational programme. Burrenbeo, Burren Connect, Burren Farming for Conservation and the Burren IFA are all currently involved in drawing up a community charter, an initiative that is supported by the Heritage Council. Michael Starrett, its chief executive, hopes that the charter will mark 'a new dawn' and show that 'within the existing frameworks . . . landscape management and conservation measures can play a central role in sustaining us all'.[10] There can be no doubt, as Paul Clements has commented, that 'the Burren has a large number of people fighting its corner'.[11] But in the absence of a Burren Park or a similar area-based organisational structure to enable policy integration, implementation and continuity, can that progress be sustained?

The Burren has a 'sister' limestone landscape, about the same size, on the island of Öland in the Swedish Baltic and here too much has changed in the past decade. This is another stony place that has been moulded into a distinctive landscape by generations of farmers. The Stora Alvaret on the island is the outfield part of an infield-outfield agricultural system that had largely died out on mainland Europe in the nineteenth century. Through a quirk of geography, the system survived on Öland well into the twentieth century but by the end of the century it was about to disappear. This prompted Kalmar County, the Swedish administrative area where Öland is situated, to embark on a four-year conservation project to restore the grasslands of the Stora Alvaret. The project involved clearing bush vegetation and re-establishing grazing. The project was grant aided by LIFE, the EU conservation body. The Swedish authorities were also interested in achieving the designation of the whole agricultural landscape of Öland – infields, outfields and the linear villages – as a UNESCO World Heritage Site.[12] World Heritage Sites are places with an 'outstanding universal value' and applications for designation must be accompanied by comprehensive management plans. Kalmar County set up a multi-disciplinary team (biologist,

Fig. 11.2. Mullaghmore in the Burren in winter, 2010.

cultural geographer and agronomist) to prepare an application to UNESCO. Two years of consultations and negotiations followed that involved local authorities, landowners and farmers. This culminated in a plebiscite of local members of the farmers' federation and a vote for designation. In 2000, while communities in the Burren and the Irish government were coming to terms with the Mullaghmore debacle (see Chapter 5), the Agricultural Landscape of Southern Öland, an 'outstanding example of human settlement', was inscribed as Sweden's eleventh World Heritage Site. The largest part of the site is the Stora Alvaret, but the site also contains eighty-seven villages and intensively farmed arable and pasture lands in private ownership. The plebiscite was not a foregone conclusion. Support from a local farm leader and an undertaking by the Swedish government to continue financial support for the local farm economy, irrespective of EU agricultural reform, were probably crucial factors in securing a 'yes' vote.[13] Southern Öland has now celebrated its twelfth birthday as a World Heritage Site. An adjoining area on the island, which voted against designation in 2000, has since requested inclusion in the site, an indication of the local popularity of the designation. The successful outcome of the designation process on Öland can be attributed to a number of factors. The cultural landscape of Öland met the UNESCO criteria and was carefully presented by the Swedish authorities to reflect UNESCO philosophy. The application received local support because it was seen as a solution to social and economic problems of job loss and emigration from the island. Most important, local farmers, who had initially regarded the proposal with suspicion, came to the conclusion that designation was in their interests because it would guarantee the continuation of agriculture.[14]

Southern Öland is just one of many examples of contemporary landscape-scale management initiatives in Europe. Scotland provides two more. After the Second World War there was an expectation in Westminster that parks would be created in Scotland along the same lines as the ones in England and Wales. But there was a notable lack of enthusiasm for national parks among politicians north of the border. In the 1970s, 'special parks' were proposed, national parks on the British model in all but name, as the top tier of a recreational park system. But this idea too was discarded and instead forty 'national scenic areas' were identified and then designated to protect their visual beauty. Anne and Malcolm McEwen, writing at the time, in an authoritative review of national parks in the United Kingdom, believed that Scotland had 'taken the wrong turning. There is a gaping hole in its protective and recreational systems where national parks . . . could have been.'[15] Yet within a relatively short time, in the wake of the re-establishment of the Scottish parliament in 1999, an appetite for an ambitious national landscape management programme emerged. The passing of the National

Fig. 11.3. Pasture near the village of Stenåsa, on the east coast of Öland in the Southern Öland World Heritage Site.

Fig. 11.4. Farmland on the west side of Öland, near the village of Mysinge, in the Southern Öland World Heritage Site.

Parks Scotland Act was one of the first acts of the new administration. Two years later, the Loch Lomond and The Trossachs National Park was created, followed by the Cairngorms National Park in 2003.

The Loch Lomond and The Trossachs and the Connemara national parks make an interesting comparison. They both lie in settled, upland areas of comparable iconic status. Connemara, when defined as the old barony of Ballynahinch, that is, most of the land in County Galway west of Maam Cross, has an area of over 1,000 square kilometres. About 9,000 people live there.[16] Of the total area, 20 square kilometres (2 per cent), is occupied by the state-owned park outside Letterfrack. The Loch Lomond and Trossachs National Park in Scotland, by contrast, has a population of 15,600 and covers an area of 1,865 square kilometres.

Connemara National Park is owned by the state and was set up in 1980 with the primary objective of conserving and promoting biodiversity. The park, like all the Irish parks, is managed by a career civil servant, a principal officer in the Department of Arts, Heritage and the Gaeltacht, who is based in Dublin. There is a small visitor centre, which is open between April and October. There is also a National Park and Wildlife Service (NPWS) office and another in nearby Clifden. A district conservation officer (DCO), based in the park, is responsible for the park's day-to-day management. There are ten permanent staff, including three rangers, operating from the two offices. The rangers, together with the DCO, provide a wildlife service not just for the small park but for the whole of west Galway and south Mayo.

The Scottish park administration is much larger. The park is run by a board whose seventeen members are either directly elected by postal ballot, appointed by Scottish ministers or are nominees of the local authorities within the park area. The headquarters of the authority are inside the park and there are also three visitor centres. The authority has an annual budget of over £7 million and a permanent staff of 130, including a 40-strong ranger service.[17] Its remit covers not just heritage conservation, the sustainable use of natural resources and environmental education – the same work as the ranger service in Galway – but also the promotion of the economic and social development of the Loch Lomond and The Trossachs area.

Governments have been protecting landscapes for more than a century. The idea has its roots in the national park movement in the United States during the nineteenth century. There the objective was to preserve spectacular wilderness landscapes. But the desire to protect landscapes has been as strong, if not stronger, in Europe, where, although landscape has a more equivocal natural character, landscapes are nevertheless prized and celebrated. In the early 1990s, international recognition of such landscapes was placed on a more formal footing by the World Heritage Committee of UNESCO deciding to make 'cultural landscape' a new category of World Heritage Site and the International Union for the Conservation of Nature and Natural Resources (IUCN) recognising a new form of protected landscape. A Category V landscape is:

> *an area where the interaction of people and nature over time has produced an area with a distinct character with significant aesthetic, ecological and/or cultural value, and often with high biological diversity. Safeguarding the integrity of this traditional interaction is vital to the protection, maintenance and evolution of such an area.*[18]

The national park east of Rome described by Lysaght, Southern Öland in Sweden and Loch Lomond and The Trossachs are examples of Category V protected landscapes. About two thirds of European protected landscapes fall into this category. They occupy more than 10 per cent of the land area of the Czech Republic, France, Italy, Latvia, Luxemburg, Slovakia, Switzerland and the United Kingdom and they account for more than 20 per cent of Germany and Austria.[19] By contrast, less than 1 per cent of the land area of the Republic is covered by landscape designations. There are four small national parks, two larger ones (Wicklow and Ballycroy) and a handful of areas around Dublin that are covered by Special Amenity Area Orders including the Howth SAAO described in Chapter 8. There are just three World Heritage Sites on the island: The Giants Causeway (inscribed in 1986), The Bend in the Boyne (inscribed in 1993) and Skellig Michael (inscribed in 1996). The three sites are all relatively small, by far the largest of them being the Bend of the Boyne (770 hectares). The 2000 Planning Act provides for the making of Landscape Conservation Areas (LCAs). This is a statutory development tool in the old conservation tradition (draw a line around somewhere and stop further development), but to date only a single draft LCA has been made (for Tara-Skryne, briefly described in Chapter 8). With understandable exasperation, given the wealth of the landscape heritage, a report for Fáilte Ireland in 2007 stated that 'It is high time the Irish landscape is afforded the level of attention and concern that it so deserves. Future generations will not thank us if we needlessly erode the special character and quality of Ireland's landscape'.[20]

Landscape designation, however, is not a conservation panacea and the motivation for designation is frequently ambiguous. It has been suggested, for instance, that the impetus behind creating national parks in the United States had more to do with a search for a national identity and a glorification of the natural wonders of the West than a desire to protect natural beauty.[21] Historically, designation in Britain was tainted by class prejudice. William Wordsworth, who inspired the national park movement in England, opposed construction of the Kendal to Windermere railway because it would improve access to the Lake District for the 'lower classes'. He believed that the Lake District would be ruined if 'artisans, labourers and the humbler class of shopkeepers' whose 'common minds precluded pleasure from the sight of natural beauty' were tempted by the railway to 'ramble at a distance'.[22] If not class prejudice, a high culture aura adheres to protected sites and areas in Ireland. Here the concept of a national park is further coloured by negative historical associations. In the South the 'national park' label is a handicap to any conservation initiative because it implies a slavish imitation of English culture. In the North, national park designation is 'tied up with complex politics' and was 'originally an attempt to strengthen unionist ties by mirroring legislation in Britain in the wake of the Second World War'.[23]

Protecting landscape as heritage is an ambitious endeavour of the modern state. The fact that so much has been achieved in this policy arena in Europe during the twentieth century is an unsung achievement of modern European civilisation. Fifty years ago, the scale of the endeavour was not properly understood. Governments believed that they could protect landscape simply by drawing lines on maps and passing laws to stop things happening within the lines. The first Irish SAAO for the Strawberry Beds stretch of the Liffey Valley in Dublin and the AONBs in the North are legacies of that era. Even a review in 1982 of the much-admired national park system in Britain concluded that it was then a largely cosmetic enterprise.[24] But it is necessary to draw a distinction between landscape conservation initiatives in the past and what has been happening over the last two decades. A new paradigm has taken shape which reflects a more realistic understanding of the demands of landscape conservation and provides a more solid basis for effective intervention. That paradigm is summarised in the table below, taken from an IUCN guidance document.

The Howth Head SAAO that was made in 2000 and is described in Chapter 8 is one example of the new paradigm in practice in this country, albeit on a very small spatial scale. Unlike earlier SAAOs, the Howth designation was preceded by extensive consultation with the local community and affected landowners and the order itself established a long-term cooperative management process for the area. The order requires the area to be managed to 'realise the exceptional potential [of Howth] as a place for informal recreation, tourism and environmental education, to ensure that all sections of the local community have an equal opportunity to enjoy the natural attractions of the area and to ensure effective local participation in the management process'.[25] The order required the local authority 'to establish a partnership structure to manage the area'. In 2002, Fingal County Council set up a management committee comprising five landowner and local community representatives and seven elected members

Table 11.1. A new paradigm for protected areas	
As it was: protected areas were . . .	As it is becoming: protected areas are . . .
Planned and managed against people	Run with, for, and in some cases by, local people
Set aside for conservation	Run also with social and economic objectives
Managed without regard to local community	Managed to help meet the needs of local people
Developed separately	Planned as part of national, regional and international systems
Managed as 'islands'	Developed as 'networks' (strictly protected areas, buffered and linked by green corridors)
Established mainly for scenic protection	Often set up for scientific, economic and cultural reasons
Managed mainly for visitors and tourists	Managed with local people more in mind
Managed reactively within short timescale	Managed adaptively with long-term perspective
About protection	Also about restoration and rehabilitation
Viewed primarily as a national asset	Viewed also as a community asset
Viewed exclusively as a national concern	Viewed also as an international concern
(Source Phillips (2000), p.14)	

of the council. The committee meets quarterly. Recent and ongoing projects overseen by the committee include the maintenance and expansion of the extensive public footpath system on the peninsula, a project to conserve the headland's red squirrel population, the eradication of alien flora and the drafting of management plans for the peninsula's heathlands.

The Howth SAAO stands in stark contrast to the prevailing inertia about landscape conservation. The SAAO for nearby Bray Head, made eight years later, has all the hallmarks of the old mindset of drawing a line on a map and leaving it at that. The draft order that was brought forward by Bray Town Council for confirmation by An Bord Pleanála incorporated no mechanisms for effective community participation or ongoing management. However, at confirmation the board amended the order to require the preparation of a management plan.[26]

Measured by statutory designation initiatives, the Irish government commitment to landscape protection rarely extends beyond the aspirational. The Burren is on a tentative list of World Heritage Sites that was submitted by the government to the World Heritage Commission in 2010. Most of the sites on the list have the restricted dimensions of a site in the generally accepted sense of that word. Only the Burren, the north-west Mayo boglands and Clonmacnoise are of 'landscape' scale. In 2007 the government decided to proceed with the designation of 'Clonmacnoise and its Landscape Setting' as a World Heritage Site. To that end a draft management plan was drawn up for consideration by the UNESCO technical committee and for public consultation over the summer of 2009.[27] The Clonmacnoise site has an area of nearly 30 square kilometres, and comprises not only the monastic settlement itself but also the surrounding callows, farmland and bogland. There are an estimated 200 people living in the area and a further 500 in a buffer zone around it. Most of the land is in private ownership. When the draft plan was presented to a public meeting in Athlone in 2009, there was 'an IFA-inspired walkout and the intimidation of a Department official in a highly charged atmosphere'.[28] Then toaiseach and local politician Brian Cowen subsequently met the Clonmacnoise Action Group and assured it that no proposal would go to UNESCO without local support. In 2010, Minister John Gormley launched a new website, World Heritage Ireland. With detailed information about the Bend in the Boyne and Skellig Michael World Heritage Sites, but no mention at all of Connemara or Iveragh, the website is a very narrowly bounded version of the landscape heritage of the Republic of Ireland.

World Heritage Sites Tentative List submitted in 2010 by the Irish Government
1. The Burren
2. Ceide Fields and NW Mayo Boglands
3. The Monastic City of Clonmacnoise and its Cultural Landscape Setting
4. Dublin – The Historic City of Dublin
5. Early Medieval Monastic Sites (Clonmacnoise, Durrow, Glendalough, Inis Cealtra, Kells and Monasterboice)
6. The Royal Sites of Ireland (Cashel, Dún Ailinnne, Hill of Uisneach, Rathcroghan Complex and Tara Complex)
7. Western Stone Forts (Aran Island forts, County Galway group of forts, Caherconree in Clare, Charerconree and Benagh on Dingle, Staigue in Iveragh)

The only national park initiative in Ireland in recent times was an ill-fated 'solo run' in 2002 by Northern Environment Minister Dermot Nesbitt. Nesbitt resurrected an idea that had been around since the 1940s of a national park for the Mournes. The Mournes cover an area of 570 square kilometres, about half of which is farmed. There are about 1,500 landowners but much of the higher land is in large holdings held by public agencies, the National Trust and the Mourne Trustees.[29] The government appointed consultants to carry out various studies and also set up a Mournes National Park Working Party to prepare for designation. But the working party was disbanded in 2007 at the end of a divisive and unsuccessful public consultation process, and after that the official enthusiasm for designation faded away.

The contrasting experience of other European countries invites two questions. Why does Ireland not put more resources into conserving its landscapes? And in terms of landscape conservation, does this matter? Designation, which seems to be a natural impulse of government elsewhere, does not happen here. There are a number of possible explanations and much of this book can be read as a discourse on this issue. It can be argued that designation has not been as necessary here because development pressures have been lower compared with more populous and more urbanised parts of Europe. Alternatively, we do not care enough about our landscapes to want to protect them or we care but lack the institutional structures for effective intervention. The reasons are not that clear but what is clear is that the nature of our response does not reflect a lack of landscape heritage but is symptomatic of a distinctive cultural legacy which inhibits a constructive engagement with that heritage.

Jim Connolly from the IRDA once told the *Irish Letter*, an Irish-American subscription newsletter, that 'if people want to see the green fields they should go to places like Scotland', that off-the-cuff remark revealing a degree of alienation that cannot be discounted.[30] In 2004, Fintan O'Toole suggested that 'Irish society has skipped the evolutionary stage when a society rediscovers the sacred'. O'Toole believed Ireland had 'become a post-modern society in which landscape is viewed only as a commodity'.[31] He is also of the view that 'one of the legacies of our history of dispossession is that we've never, collectively, taken ownership of the place we inhabit. We don't belong to it and it doesn't belong to us.'[32] But if alienation is an issue, governance is too. The Heritage Council, originally set up by C.J. Haughey in 1988, and established as a statutory body in 1995 charged with advising the government on heritage matters, has consistently promoted a landscape conservation agenda. The council ensured that Ireland signed up to the European Landscape Convention and continues to lobby the government for action on landscape.[33] Yet very little has happened in this policy area in the last two decades. This may reflect a pervasive alienation but it also reflects a weakness in the institutions of state, which characteristically demonstrate an 'intervening' as opposed to a 'managing' capability.[34] Given the centralised nature of power in Ireland, it seems essential that effective landscape initiatives are driven from the centre, but at the same time these initiatives have also to find a way of bolstering local democracy.

I have already referred to old and new paradigms of protected areas described in the IUCN guidance. In the old paradigm, landscapes are set aside for conservation and are planned and managed without much regard for the interests of local people. In the new paradigm, which has come to the fore in Europe in the past two decades, protected areas are run with, for, and in some cases by local people and they are run with social and economic objectives in mind alongside the more traditional conservation ones. Loch Lomond and The Trossachs and Southern Öland are examples of the new paradigm in practice. In Ireland, however, the debate about protected areas continues within the old framework of thought. If anything, the prospect of a paradigm shift in Ireland has receded. In recent years the state has been obliged to comply with EU environmental directives and this has led to the extensive designation of areas for nature conservation. The Natura 2000 network, which is now substantially in place, is a product of two EU directives, the 1979 Birds Directive to protect endangered birds and the 1992 Habitats Directive to protect endangered habitats, fauna and flora. While less than 1 per cent of the land area of the Republic is covered by landscape designations, 14 per cent is now affected by nature designations, the bulk of which are located in the western seaboard counties.[35] Most of the Burren, for instance, is covered by either SAC or Special Protection Area (SPA) designations. We have arrived at a situation where landscape conservation is a by-product of an EU-driven nature conservation strategy. Unfortunately, that strategy has had all the hallmarks of the outmoded protected areas paradigm. The SACs and SPAs are viewed as creations of 'Brussels' and 'Dublin', and little to do with local people other than the restrictions that they place on the use of their land. This is how Conor Skehan describes the situation.

> The [Irish] landscape is becoming a place to receive and reflect the value systems of an increasingly urbanised European population. These value systems are scientific – ecological designations – and aesthetic – scenic areas and drives, national parks. Control of the countryside is changing hands. Not the ownership, just the control. The landscape is beginning to become a patchwork quilt of designations which determine where and how the land uses of the future will be arranged. It will be a very new landscape, one that is emerging very haphazardly as a result of the well

intentioned but uncoordinated imposition of such designations. These problems are rapidly becoming apparent and there are already signs of the emergence of a 'planned landscape' in Ireland.[36]

Skehan's critical viewpoint is completely in tune with popular rural sentiment. The Uplands Forum is a voluntary group pursuing a partnership approach to the management of upland areas (more than 300m above sea level). In 2009 the Forum commissioned a questionnaire survey of communities and individuals living in three upland areas: the North Sligo/North Leitrim Uplands, the Comeragh Mountains in Waterford and the Twelve Bens and Benchoonas in north-west Connemara.[37] In all the areas the survey revealed a strong antipathy towards landscape and environmental designations.

We seem to have arrived at an impasse. State intervention of any kind in landscape is regarded with suspicion at best and at worst as an unwarranted intrusion into the lives of individuals and of local communities. State institutions appear to be relatively impotent as guardians of the common good, except, that is, when that duty is underpinned by European directives. From a landscape perspective, the recent record of the wholly state-owned company Coillte is not good. The Office of Public Works has a fine record of managing heritage sites but a poor record of landscape-scale interventions – witness the interpretative centre fiascos in the 1990s and the failure to make progress on World Heritage Sites in recent times. The area-based tax incentive schemes of the 1990s and the 2000s, such as the 1995 scheme for renewal and improvement of certain resort areas (the 'seaside resort scheme') and the 1998 Rural Renewal Scheme for the Upper Shannon, dreamed up by ministers and officials in the Department of Finance, have had serious adverse landscape consequences. Meanwhile, local authorities are immersed in land matters, their official roles undermined by a decision-making culture that is preoccupied with the interests of landowners and developers. Even where local authorities are directly involved in successful initiatives such as Clare County Council's lead role in Burren Connect and Fingal County Council's management of the Howth SAAO, there is the impression of a 'semi-detached' mentality, of officers and members playing a part and turning up for meetings but without much conviction, believing that their priorities and obligations lie elsewhere.

Recent successes in the Burren might suggest that in Ireland we can do without area-wide approaches and integrated planning. Brendan Dunford believes that the foundations have already been laid in the Burren for a sustainable future and that those foundations are more solid than they would have been as a result of a statutory designation process.[38] Michael Viney, a patron of the Burrenbeo Trust, has written that a major achievement of Burren LIFE has been 'the sense of meaningful identity it has helped to foster in the region's communities – a sense reinforced by a whole network of new activities, contacts and events'.[39] There can be no doubt that the increasing support for a conservation agenda in the local farming community is an enormous step forward. However, as an interested citizen of the Burren, I am not as sanguine as Brendan Dunford and Michael Viney about how things are shaping up. I have only once met a local councillor at any of the conservation events and meetings that I have attended and I don't recall seeing a single politician in the throng of people that celebrated the launch of Burrenbeo in Ballyvaughan in 2008. The 3½-year period from 2007 to 2011, when there was an environment minister (John Gormley) who espoused environmental principles and when Tony Killeen, the local TD, was also a minister and for a time a minister of state in the Department of the Environment, seemed to present an exceptional political opportunity for the Burren, but nothing of significance transpired.

There is conflicting evidence of progress in my own village of Corrofin. This summer in 2012, in the depth of the recession, the NPWS has opened an attractive information point, staffed by young graduates, in the village and has begun a free summer bus service, albeit on a trial basis, from the information point into the national park. But, at the same time, a handsome building that is owned by the Office of Public Works stands boarded up and empty. It was supposed to have been the refurbished headquarters of the ranger service for north Clare but the planning permission has long since expired and the rangers have been relocated to offices in Ennis.

There is little evidence of a concerted approach to managing the Burren, which is hardly surprising in the absence of a management framework. My own impression is of not so much the laying of foundations for a sustainable future, but of a positive momentum that is being sustained through the work of a few, exceptionally able and committed individuals, despite the absence of a supportive framework. At times the Burren seems like a place where 'projectism' is running riot, where things happen because they are project deliverables but where there is no lasting effect. Only the passage of time will enable a reliable judgement to emerge about what is currently happening. However, I think it is unlikely that a sustainable pathway can be fashioned without an institutional structure to support it. It seems to me that, contrary to Michael Starrett's hope, lasting progress is not achievable within the 'existing frameworks'.[40] Eileen O'Rourke's research in the Burren documents the failure of a top-down sectoral approach to landscape management but also what she has described as the 'naivety of consensual community participation' in the context of a community that is anything but homogenous. Neither top-down nor bottom-up models of development will work in most places in Ireland. As O'Rourke has concluded, an approach has to be developed that enables 'grassroots dialogue within enabling institutional structures'.[41]

I began this book with reference to the Dutch landscape architect Han Lorzing. Lorzing celebrates the imaginative power of the human mind in landscape but his enthusiasm for that idea leads to an extreme conclusion.[42] He believes that 'fake heritage can be just as genuine as real heritage if we want it to be that way'.[43] His book is full of examples of successful fake environments such as the new 'historic' town of Seaside in Florida, founded in 1981, downtown Leavenworth in Washington State which recreated itself as a Bavarian village in the 1960s, the Nagasaki 'Holland Village' in Japan and Poundbury in Dorset, England, built by the Duchy of Cornwall and labelled by Lorzing as 'nostalgia by royal appointment'. Lorzing imagines a future 'archipelago of well-designed, well-kept islands in a sea of dreariness, crime and decay. There will be a huge demand for places that look like real environments but in fact are skilful remakes. Bogus experience will not only replace the real world; it will be the real world for us.'[44]

Ersatz heritage can be relevant and pleasurable. In north Clare 'The Ledge' at the Cliffs of Moher visitor centre, which opened in 2007, is a CGI simulation of a gannet's eye view of the cliffs. It is a minute or so of diverting imagery for visitors, an accessible substitute for real experience of a place that is not infrequently enveloped in mists and Atlantic gales. A few kilometres inland the Burren Perfumery is a more subtle ersatz encounter. At first glance, set within the floral abundance of the high Burren, the perfumery seems a perfect congruence of nature and artisanal enterprise. But it only takes a moment's thought to realise that most of the high Burren is SAC, its flora, common and uncommon, protected, and that therefore all the ingredients of the perfumery's creams, fragrances and soaps are imported from far and wide. As a manufacturing business, the perfumery would be better located on an industrial estate in Ennis but there, of course, nobody would visit it.

Such small fabrications are inconsequential. However, for myself and, I suspect, for most people, Lorzing's 'archipelago of well-designed and well-kept islands' is an intolerable prospect of society in the future. We can glimpse this vista in the guise of new additions to our built environments in recent years – the gated communities with their high walls and tidy lawns and the shopping malls with their climate control and CCTV. These may be fine places to visit, even places in which to live, but unimaginable as the sum physical expression of our culture. It is beyond the resources of any culture to create landscape-scale pastiche on the scale of a Burren, a Connemara or Mourne Mountains. And such a venture would, of course, be preposterous given that we still have the real thing.

The effective management of outstanding landscape areas requires a hitherto unseen level of engagement with this issue by Irish society. It requires political and financial commitment by national government and the creation of local management structures that can command a sufficiently broad base of community support. It requires radical initiatives that would probably have been inconceivable in the recent past. The IUCN paradigm for the participatory management of landscape areas to achieve social, economic and heritage objectives offers an attractive template provided that it incorporates a realistic approach to local participation. With annual visitor surveys conducted by Fáilte Ireland consistently confirming that 'landscape', in its broader sense of people and scenery, is why people choose to visit Ireland, there is an obvious economic rationale for the pursuit of a landscape-based development strategy. What has been happening in the Burren in recent years, where a range of different initiatives – the work of a handful of committed individuals – is beginning to bear fruit, shows what can be achieved without sustained institutional support. Embracing landscape conservation as a core philosophy would signal a change in perspective from the short term to the long term, from an opportunistic outlook to a sustainable one, from a narrow materialistic perspective to a broader vision for the future. This perspective would bring other landscape projects to the fore of a national agenda in addition to the conservation of outstanding landscapes. Here are just a few examples. The EPA BOGLAND report proposes a National Peatland Park in the Midlands and the re-use of degraded bogs there for wind farms as an alternative to building more wind farms on vulnerable and more environmentally valuable boglands further west.[45] Michael Viney believes that

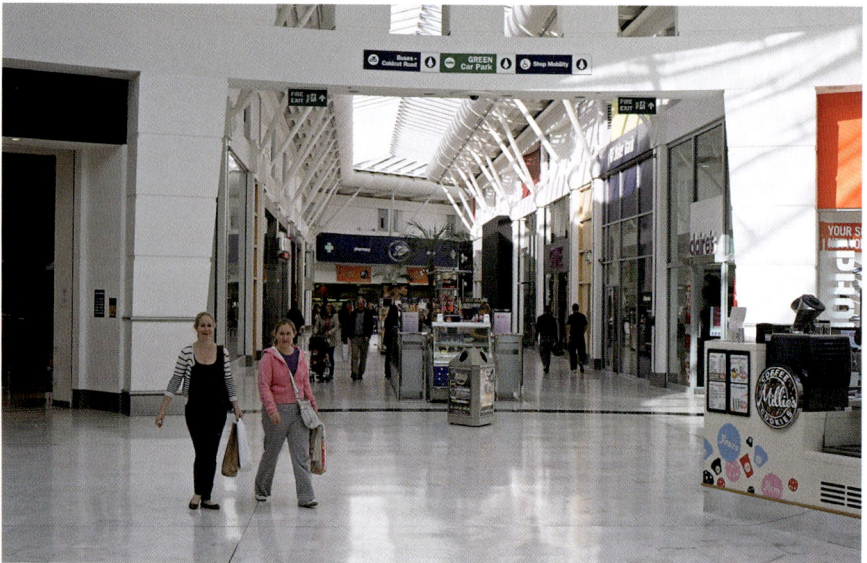

Fig. 11.5. A mall in the Liffey Valley shopping centre in 2011.

'We must also find room in Ireland for at least one sizeable broadleaf forest – big enough to get lost in – which is not planted for any kind of timber and in which nature alone holds sway'.[46] In the last decade it was fashionable to envisage Dublin-Belfast as an economic growth corridor but a potentially more enduring vision is to place those cities in a region with a 5000-year history of settlement and a rural landscape that is unsurpassed in the urbanised regions of Western Europe in terms of physical variety and cultural wealth. This region stretches 130 kilometres from the Antrim coastline to Glendalough and Avonmore in the Wicklow massif. Its landscape heritage includes not only the more obvious delights of the Mournes and Wicklow Mountains and some magnificent coastal scenery but also places of more subtle charm such as the Ring of Gullion, Lecale and the Boyne valley. Few cities in Europe can compete with either Dublin or Belfast in terms of the quality of their immediate physical settings or the calibre of the landscapes of their hinterlands yet this competitive advantage has not yet been fully appreciated. In Britain, the official biography of the national park movement acknowledged that setting up the parks was considered by a post-war government as a cheap and easy option after the cataclysm of war to meet expectations of a better, brighter future for everyone in society.[47] We know better today that landscape conservation is neither a cheap nor an easy objective to realise but it is almost certainly one that is both desirable and achievable.

Chapter 6
Fig. 6.2 Photograph taken by John Finn

Chapter 7
Fig. 7.11 and 7.12 Photographs taken by Dr John Olley

Chapter 8
Fig. 8.13 Map derived from 1994 Bord Fáilte Development Plan and Department of the Environment (NI), Northern Ireland Landscape Character Assessment, 2000
Fig. 8.14 Photograph taken by John Finn
Fig. 8.16 Fingal County Council, Howth Special Amenity Area Order (1999)

Chapter 9
Fig. 9.7 Map derived from Mayo County Council, *County Mayo Wind Energy Strategy, 2011*

Chapter 10
Fig. 10.8 Central Statistics Office and All-Island Research Observatory (AIRO)

Chapter 11
Fig. 11.1 Derived from *Heritage Outlook*, the journal of the Heritage Council (2005)
Fig. 11.3 Photograph taken by Susanne Forslund
Fig. 11.4 Photograph taken by Markus Forslund

BIBLIOGRAPHY

Aalen, F.H.A., Kevin Whelan and Matthew Stout, *Atlas of the Irish Rural Landscape*, 1st edn (Cork: Cork University Press, 1997)

An Taisce, *State of the Nation: A Review of Ireland's Planning System 2000–2011* (Dublin: An Taisce, 2012)

Armstrong, John, *The Secret Power of Beauty: Why happiness is in the Eye of the Beholder* (London: Allen Lane, 2004)

Baker, F.D., *An Angler's Paradise: Recollections of Twenty Years with Rod and Line in Ireland* (Ashburton, Devon: Flyfisher's Classic Library, 2000)

Bannon, Michael, *Planning: The Irish Experience, 1920–1988* (Dublin: Wolfhound Press, 1989)

Barker, Richard, *Coming Down from the Mountains: Landscape Challenges Arising from Recent Trends in Wind Farm Development* (Dublin: Sustainable Energy Authority of Ireland, 2011)

Bartlett, Thomas, *Ireland: A History* (Cambridge: Cambridge University Press, 2010)

Bond, Valerie, *An Taisce: The First Fifty Years* (Dublin: The Hannon Press, 2005)

Bourke, Simon, 'Media and Heritage in Ireland: Representations of Heritage in Irish Newspapers and the Praxis of Determination', PhD thesis, Dublin City University, 2009

Brinkerhoff, Derick W. and Arthur A. Goldsmith, 'Clientelism, Patrimonialism and Democratic Governance: An Overview and Framework for Assessment and Programming', DocID/Order No: PN-ACR-426, December 2002 (http://www.dec.org/pdf_docs/PNACR426.pdf (Washington, DC: US Agency for International Development, Office of Democracy and Governance, 2002))

Brody, Hugh, *The Other Side of Eden* (London: Faber & Faber, 2001)

Brown, David Blayney, *Romanticism* (London: Phaidon Press, 2001)

Buckley, Inge, 'Wind Energy in Ireland: The Present Situation', in Richard Douthwaite (ed.), *Before the Well Runs Dry: Ireland's Transition to Renewable Energy* (Dublin: Feasta, 2003)

Carswell, Simon, *Anglo Republic: Inside the Bank that Broke Ireland* (Dublin: Penguin Ireland, 2011)

Clare County Council, *Clare County Development Plan, 1988* (Ennis: Clare County Council, 1988)

Clare County Council, *Ennis and Environs Development Plan, 2008* (Ennis: Clare County Council, 2008)

Clements, Paul, *Burren Country* (Cork: The Collins Press, 2011)

Collins, Timothy (ed.), *Decoding the Landscape: Contributions towards a Synthesis of Thought in Irish Studies on the Landscape* (University College Galway, 1994)

Cork County Council, *Cork Rural Design Guide: Building a New House in the Countryside. A Design Guide by Colin Buchanan and Partners and Mike Shanahan and Associates* (Cork County Council, 2003)

Countryside Agency, *Landscape Character Assessment for England and Scotland* (Cheltenham: Countryside Agency, 2002)

Crowley, Ethel, *Land Matters: Power Struggles in Rural Ireland* (Dublin: The Lilliput Press, 2006)

Crowley, John and John Sheehan, *The Iveragh Peninsula* (Cork: Cork University Press, 2009)

Department of the Environment, Heritage and Local Government (DEHLG), *The Monastic City of Clonmacnoise and its Cultural Landscape: Management Plan, 2009– 2014* (Dublin: DEHLG, 2009)

Department of the Environment, *Wind Energy Guidelines for Planning Authorities* (Dublin: Government Publications, 1996)

Department of the Environment, Northern Ireland (DOE (NI)), *Northern Ireland Landscape Character Assessment* (Belfast: DOE (NI), 2000)

Dixon, Daniel, *Dorothea Lange's Ireland* (London: Aurum Press, 1996)

Donegal County Council, *Buncrana and Environs Development Plan, 2007* (Lifford: Donegal County Council, 2007)

Donegal County Council, Donegal County Development Plan, 2000 (Lifford: Donegal County Council, 2007)

Duffy, Patrick J., *Exploring the History and Heritage of Irish Landscapes*, Maynooth Research Guides for Irish Local History, No. 12 (Dublin: Four Courts Press, 2007)

Ekeh, Peter P., 'Colonialism and the Publics in Africa', *Comparative Studies in Society and History*, vol. 171 (1975), pp. 91–112

Environmental Protection Agency (EPA), *Bogland: Sustainable Management of Peatlands in Ireland*. STRIVE Report 75 (Wexford: EPA, 2011)

Environmental Protection Agency, *Sustainable Rural Development: Managing Housing in the Countryside*. STRIVE Report 44, Mark Scott ed. (Wexford: EPA, 2010)

European Environment Agency (EEA), *Urban Sprawl in Europe: The Ignored Challenge*, EEA Report No. 10/2006, 2006

European Foundation for the Improvement of Living and Working Conditions (EFILWC), *The Journey from Home to the Workplace: The Impact on the Safety and Health of Commuters/Workers* (Dublin: EFILWC, 1983)

Fáilte Ireland, *Feasibility Study to Identify Scenic Lands in Ireland*. Report by MosArt (Dublin: Fáilte Ireland, 2007)

Feehan, John and Grace O'Donovan, *The Bogs of Ireland: An Introduction to the Natural, Cultural and Industrial Heritage of Irish Peatlands* (Dublin: University College Dublin (UCD), Environmental Institute, 1996)

Feehan, John, 'Beyond 2000: The Price and Place of Landscape Heritage in Ireland', John Jackson Memorial Lecture, Occasional Papers in Irish Science and Technology (Dublin: Royal Dublin Society, 1995)

Feehan, John, *Farming in Ireland* (Dublin: UCD Faculty of Agriculture, 2003)

Feehan, John, 'Urban Nature and Human Nature', Natura 2000 and Biodiversity in the City (Dublin: Urban Institute Ireland, 2002)

Fine-Davis, M. and E.E. Davis, 'Predictors of Satisfaction with Housing and Neighbourhood: A Nationwide Survey in the Republic of Ireland', *Social Indicators Research*, vol. 9 (1981), pp. 477–94

Fingal County Council, 'Howth Special Amenity Area Order' (Swords: Fingal County Council, 1999)

Fitzsimons, Jack, *Bungalow Bashing* (Meath: Kells Publishing, 1990)

Foster, R.F., *Luck and the Irish: A Brief History of Change since 1970* (Oxford: Oxford University Press, 2008)

Foster, R.F., *Modern Ireland* (London: Allen Lane, 1988)

Garavan, Mark (ed.), *Our Story: The Rossport Five* (Knocknaquirk, Wicklow: Small World Media, 2006)

Government of Ireland, *Sustainable Development: A Strategy for Ireland* (Dublin: Government Publications, 1997)

Harding, Jesmond, *Discovering Irish Butterflies and their Habitats* (Privately published, 2008)

Heaney, Seamus, *Preoccupations: Selected Prose, 1968–1978* (London: Faber, 1980)

Heritage Council, *Proposals for Ireland's Landscapes* (Kilkenny: Heritage Council, 2010)

Heritage Council, *Valuing Heritage in Ireland: Report by Keith Simpson and Associates* (Kilkenny: Heritage Council, 2007)

Hickey, Kieran R., 'A Geographical Perspective on the Decline and Extermination of the Irish Wolf *Canis Lupis*: An Initial Assessment', *Irish Geography*, vol. 33, no. 2 (2000), pp. 185–98

Hickie, David, *Native Trees and Forests of Ireland* (Dublin: Gill & Macmillan, 2002)

Holland, Charles Hepworth, *The Irish Landscape: A Scenery to Celebrate* (Edinburgh: Dunedin Academic Press, 2003)

Hopkin, Allanah, *Eating Scenery: West Cork, The People and the Place* (Cork: The Collins Press, 2008)

Horner A.A., J.A. Walsh and V.P. Harrington, *Population in Ireland: A Census Atlas* (UCD Department of Geography, 1987)

Hourihan, K., 'Urban Change in the Republic of Ireland', *Cities*, vol. 6, (1989), pp. 209–25

Humphreys, A.T., *New Dubliners: Urbanisation and the Irish Family* (London: Routledge & Kegan Paul, 1966)

Huntley, Brian, Rhys Green, Yvonne Collingham and Stephen G. Wills, *A Climatic Atlas of European Breeding Birds* (Barcelona: Lynx Edicions, 2007)

Irish Planning Institute (IPI), *A Census of the Planning Profession in Ireland* (Dublin: IPI, 2007)

Irish Rural Dwellers Association (IRDA), *Positive Planning for Rural Houses* (IRDA, 2004)

Irish Timber Growers Association (ITGA), *Forestry and Timber Year Book* (Dublin: ITGA, 2009)

Irish Uplands Council (IUC), *Challenges, Changes and Opportunities in Irish Uplands*, Research project report by Zena Hoctor (Dublin: IUC, 2009)

Jennings, Robert and Stephaney Bissett, *A Study of New House Purchasers* (Dublin: Environmental Research Unit, 1989)

Jones, Carleton, *The Burren and the Aran Islands: Exploring the Archaeology* (Cork: The Collins Press, 2004)

Kellert, Stephen R. and Edward O. Wilson, *The Biophilia Hypothesis* (Washington: Ireland Press, 1992)

Kohn, Marek, *Turned Out Nice: How the British Isles will Change as the World Heats Up* (London: Faber & Faber, 2010)

Lorzing, Han, *The Nature of Landscape: A Personal Quest* (Rotterdam: 010 Publishers, 2001)

Lysaght, Liam, 'The Burren: The Case for a Different Kind of National Park', *Heritage Outlook* (Summer/Autumn, 2005), pp. 8–12

MacEwen, Ann and Malcolm, *National Parks: Conservation or Cosmetics?* (London: George Allen & Unwin, 1982)

MacMahon, Michael, 'The Cult of Inghin Bhaoith and the Church of Killinaboy', *The Other Clare* (2000), pp. 12–17

Macnamara, Dr George U., 'Inchiquin, Co. Clare. With a Pedigree of the O'Quins of Thomond', *Journal of the Royal Society of Antiquaries of Ireland* (1901), pp. 204–7

Maddock, Fidelma, 'The Cot Fishermen of the River Nore', in William Nolan and Kevin Whelan (eds), *Kilkenny History and Society: Interdisciplinary Essays on the History of Irish Society* (Dublin: Geography Publications, 1990), pp. 541–66

Mayo County Council, *Renewable Energy Strategy for County Mayo, 2011* (Castlebar: Mayo County Council, 2011)

McAreavy, Ruth, 'Towards a Mourne National Park: Emergent Prospects and Pitfalls from Articulating Needs in a Local Context', ISEP Working Paper 2 (Belfast: Queen's University, 2002)

McCabe, Bernard and Alain Le Garsmeur, *W.B. Yeats: Images of Ireland* (London: Little Brown, 1991)

McCabe, Fergal, 'How We Wrecked Rural Ireland in the Latter Part of the Twentieth Century', *Pleanáil*, no. 15 (2001), pp. 64–6

McDonald, Frank and James Nix, *Chaos at the Crossroads* (Kinsale: Gandon Books, 2005)

McGahern, John, *Memoir* (London: Faber & Faber, 2009)

McGrath, Brendan, 'Suburban Development in Ireland, 1960–1980', *Planning Perspectives*, vol. 77 (1992), pp. 27–46

McGrath, Brendan, 'The Sustainability of a Car-Dependent Settlement Pattern', unpublished MSc thesis, Trinity College Dublin, 1996

McKibben, Bill, *The End of Nature* (New York: Random House, 1989)

Mid-West Regional Authority (MWRA), *Mid-West Regional Guidelines 2010–2020* (Nenagh: MWRA, 2010)

Mitchell, Frank and Michael Ryan, *Reading the Irish Landscape* (Dublin: Town House, 1997)

Mumford, Lewis, *The Culture of Cities* (New York: Harcourt Brace Jovanovich, 1970)

National Parks and Wildlife Service (NPWS), *The Status of EU Protected Habitats and Species in Ireland* (Dublin: NPWS, 2008)

Newman, Conor, 'Landscapes 'Я' Us', Proceedings of the Irish National Landscape Conference 2009 (Kilkenny: Heritage Council), pp. 8–14

O'Brien, L.M. and T.J. Baker, *The Irish Housing System: A Critical Overview*. Broadsheet 17 (Dublin: Economic and Social Research Institute, 1979)

O'Connell J.W. and Anne Korff, *The Book of the Burren*, 2nd edn (Kinvara: Tir Eolas, 2001)

O'Donohue, John, *Divine Beauty* (London: Bantam, 2003)

O'Regan, Terry, *A Guide to Undertaking a Landscape Circle Study in Seven Easy Steps* (Dublin: Landscape Alliance, 2008)

O'Rourke, Eileen, 'Landscape Planning and Community Participation: Local Lessons from Mullaghmore, the Burren National Park, Ireland', *Landscape Research*, vol. 30, no.4 (2005), pp. 483–500

O'Rourke, Eileen, 'Socio-economic Interaction and Landscape Dynamics in the Burren, Ireland', *Landscape and Urban Planning* (2005), pp. 69–83

Orr, David, 'Love It or Lose It: The Coming Biophilia Revolution', in Stephen R. Kellert and Edward O. Wilson (eds), *The Biophilia Hypothesis* (Washington: Island Press, 1992) pp. 415–40

O'Sullivan, Philip and Katherine Shepherd, *Irish Planning Law and Practice* (Haywards Heath: Bloomsbury Professional, 2012)

O'Toole, Fintan, *Black Hole, Green Card: The Disappearance of Ireland* (Dublin: New Ireland Books, 1994)

O'Toole, Fintan, *Ship of Fools: How stupidity and Corruption Sank the Celtic Tiger* (London: Faber & Faber, 2010)

Pakenham, Valerie, *The Big House in Ireland* (London: Cassell, 2000)

Parr, Sharon, 'Striking a Balance: Orchid-Rich Grasslands and Atlantic Hazel Woodland in the Burren', *Burren Insight* (2011), pp. 12–13

Parsons, Aengus, Jackie Hunt and Brendan McGrath, *Review of the Implications for Heritage of the Expansion of the Wind Energy Industry in Ireland* (Kilkenny: Heritage Council, 2002)

Pasqualetti, Martin J., Paul Gipe and Robert W. Righter (eds), *Wind Power in View: Energy Landscapes in a Crowded World* (San Diego: Academic Press, 2002)

Peace, Adrian, 'A Sense of Place, A Place of Senses: Land and Landscape in the West of Ireland', *Journal of Anthropological Research*, vol. 61 (2005), pp. 495–512

Peillon, Michel, 'State and Society in the Republic of Ireland: A Comparative Study', *Administration* (1987), pp. 190–212

Petrash, Jack, *Understanding Waldorf Education* (Gateshead: Floris Books, 2003)

Phillips, Adrian, *Management Guidelines for IUCN Category V Protected Areas* (Gland: International Union for Conservation of Nature (IUCN), 2002)

Praeger, Robert Lloyd, *The Way That I Went*, with an introduction by Michael Viney (Cork: The Collins Press, 1997)

Rackham, Oliver, *The History of the Countryside* (London: Phoenix Press, 1986)

Radiological Protection Institute of Ireland (RPII) and Health Service Executive (HSE), *Radon Gas in Ireland* (Dublin: RPII/HSE, 2010)

Robinson, Tim, *Connemara: A Little Gaelic Kingdom* (Dublin: Penguin Ireland, 2011)

Robinson, Tim, *Connemara: Listening to the Wind* (Dublin: Penguin Ireland, 2006)

Robinson, Tim, *Connemara: The Last Pool of Darkness* (Dublin: Penguin Ireland, 2008)

Robinson, Tim, *Stones of Aran* (Dublin: The Lilliput Press, 1995)

Runte, Alfred, *National Parks: The American Experiment* (Lincoln, NE: University of Nebraska Press, 1979)

Schön, Donald A., *The Reflective Practitioner: How Professionals Think in Action* (Aldershot: Ashgate Publishing, 1983)

Selman, Paul, 'What Do We Mean by Sustainable Landscape?', *Sustainability: Practice and Policy*, vol. 4, no. 2 (Fall/Winter 2008), pp. 23–8

Siggins, Lorna, *Once Upon a Time in the West: The Corrib Gas Controversy* (London: Transworld Ireland, 2010)

Skehan, Conor, 'New Planning Perspectives on the Assessment and Protection of Landscape', *Pleanáil*, no.16 (2002), pp. 42–58

Starrett, Michael, 'The Burren: A New Dawn?' *Burren Insight*, no. 3 (2011), p. 4

Stevens, Dominic, *Rural* (Leitrim: Mermaid Turbulence, 2007)

Synge, J.M., *The Aran Islands*, with an introduction by Tim Robinson (London: Penguin, 1992)

Turtinen, Jan, 'Världsarvets Villkor: Intressen, Forhandlingar och Bruk i Internationell Politik', doctoral thesis in Faculty of Humanities, Stockholm University, 2006

Viney, Michael, *A Living Island: Ireland's Responsibility to Nature* (Dublin: COMHAR, 2003)

Viney, Michael, *Ireland: A Smithsonian Natural History* (Belfast: Blackstaff Press, 2003)

Waddell, John, J.W. O'Connell and Anne Korf, *The Book of Aran* (Kinvara: Tir Eolas, 1994)

Western Development Commission (WDC), *To Catch the Wind: The Potential for Community Ownership of Wind Farms in Ireland* (Ballaghaderreen, Roscommon: WDC, 2004)

Whyte, Thomas J., *The Story of Woodstock in Inistioge* (Dublin: Cappagh Press, 2007)

Wickham, James, *Gridlock: Dublin's Transport Crisis and the Future of the City* (Dublin: TASC/New Island, 2006)

NOTES

Chapter 1

1   Fintan O'Toole, *Black Hole Green Card: The Disappearance of Ireland* (Dublin: New Ireland Books, 1994).

2   J.W. O'Connell, 'Introduction' in J.W. O'Connell and A. Korff (eds), *The Book of the Burren* (Kinvara: Tír Eolas, 2001).

3   Preamble to European Landscape Convention, Florence, 20 October 2000.

4   Quotation cited in Han Lorzing, *The Nature of Landscape: A Personal Quest* (Rotterdam: 010 Publishers, 2001), p. 24.

5   Breandán Ó Madagáin, 'The Picturesque in the Gaelic Tradition', in Timothy Collins (ed.), *Decoding the Landscape* (Galway: Social Sciences Research Centre, UCG, 1994), Chapter 5.

6   Lorzing, *The Nature of Landscape*.

7   Conor Newman, 'Landscapes 'Я' Us' in *Proceedings of National Landscape Conference, 2009* (Kilkenny: Heritage Council, 2009), pp. 8–14.

8   Lorzing, *The Nature of Landscape*, Chapter 3.

9   Ibid.

10   Burren Spring Conference (2009), Burren College of Art, Ballvaghan.

11   Newman, 'Landscapes 'Я' Us'.

12   Seamus Heaney, 'The Sense of Place', in *Preoccupations: Selected Prose 1968–1978* (London: Faber, 1980).

13   Laurence Short, 'Wind Power and English Landscape Identity', in Martin J. Pasqualetti, Paul Gipe and Robert W. Righter, *Wind Power in View: Energy Landscapes in a Crowded World* (San Diego: Academic Press, 2002), pp. 43–58.

14   Keith Simpson and Associates, et al., *Valuing Heritage in Ireland: A Report for the Heritage Council* (Kilkenny: Heritage Council, 2007), Figure 4.

Chapter 2

1   Seamus Heaney, 'The Sense of Place' in *Preoccupations: Selected Prose 1968–1978* (London: Faber, 1980).

2   Roy Foster, *Modern Ireland* (London: Allen Lane, 1988), p. 340.

3   S. Ó Duilearga, 'The Gaelic Story-Teller', The Sir John Rees Memorial Lecture, 12, 1945.

4   Dr. George U. Macnamara, in *Journal of the Royal Society of Antiquaries of Ireland* (1901), pp. 204–27.

5   Foster, *Modern Ireland*, p. 10.

6   Hugh Brody, *The Other Side of Eden* (London: Faber & Faber, 2001), p. 320.

7   Paddy Bushe, in John Crowley and John Sheehan (eds.) *The Iveragh Peninsula* (Cork: Cork University Press, 2009), pp. 69–79.

8   Ethel Crowley, *Land Matters: Power Struggles in Rural Ireland* (Dublin: The Lilliput Press, 2006.)

9   Tim Robinson, *Stones of Aran* (Dublin: The Lilliput Press, 1995), p. 117.

10   Éamon Lankford, Kerry Placenames Survey, Local Studies Unit, Kerry County Library, 2010.

11   Fidelma Maddock, 'The Cot Fishermen of the River Nore' in William Nolan and Kevin Whelan (eds) *Kilkenny History and Society: Interdisciplinary Essays on the History of an Irish Society* (Dublin: Geography Publications, 1990), pp. 541–66.

12   Breandán Ó Ciobháin, 'The Toponomy of the Peninsula of Uíbh Ráthach' in John Crowley and John Sheehan (eds) *The Iveragh Peninsula* (Cork: Cork Univeristy Press, 2009), pp. 81–92.

13   Ibid.

14   Michael MacMahon, 'The Cult of Inghin Bhaoith and the Church of Killinaboy', in *The Other Clare*, vol. 24 (2000), pp. 12–17.

15   Tim Robinson, *Connemara: The Last Pool of Darkness* (Dublin: Penguin Ireland, 2008), pp. 124–135.

16   David Hickie, *Native Trees and Forests of Ireland* (Dublin: Gill & Macmillan, 2002).

17   Oliver Rackham, *The History of the Countryside* (London: Phoenix Press, 1986).

18   Patrick J. Duffy, *Exploring the History and Heritage of Irish Landscapes*, Maynooth Research Guides for Irish Local History, Number 12 (Dublin: Four Courts Press, 2007), p. 42.

19   Irish Timber Growers Association, *Forestry and Timber Yearbook 2009.*

20   Ibid

21   Sharon Parr, 'Striking a balance: Orchid-rich Grasslands and Atlantic Hazel Woodland in the Burren' in *Burren Insight*, vol. 3, pp. 12–13.

22   Hickie, *Native Trees and Forests of Ireland.*

Chapter 3

1   Jack Petrash, *Understanding Waldorf Education* (Gateshead: Floris Books, 2003).

2   Edward O. Wilson, 'Arousing Biophilia: A Conversaton with E. O. Wilson', cited 26 January 2004, http://arts.envirolink.org/interviews_and_conversations/EOWilson.html. [accessed 25 July 2012].

3   David Orr, 'Love it or lose it: The coming Biophilia Revolution' in Stephen R. Kellert and Edward O. Wilson (eds), *The Biophilia Hypothesis* (Washington: Island Press, 1992) pp. 432–433.

4   Heritage Council, *Valuing Heritage in Ireland* (Kilkenny: Heritage Council, 2007).

5   Stephen R. Kellert, 'The Biological Basis for the Human Values of Nature' in Stephen R. Kellert and Edward O. Wilson (eds), *The Biophilia Hypothesis* (Washington: Island Press, 1992) p. 65.

6   F.H.A. Aalen, Kevin Whelan and Matthew Stout (eds), *Atlas of the Irish Rural Landscape* (Cork: Cork University Press, 1997), p. 34.

7   Alain Le Garsmeur and Bernard McCabe, *W.B. Yeats: Images of Ireland* (London: Little Brown & Company, 1991).

8   Tim Robinson, 'Connemara' in F.H.A. Aalen, Kevin Whelan and Matthew Stout (eds), *Atlas of the Irish Rural Landscape* (Cork: Cork University Press, 1997).

9   Michael Viney, *Ireland A Smithsonian Natural History* (Belfast: Blackstaff Press, 2003), p. 27.

10   Frank Mitchell and Michael Ryan, *Reading the Irish Landscape* (Dublin: Town House, 1997); Viney, *Ireland: A Smithsonian Natural History*.

11   Mitchell and Ryan, Reading the Irish Landscape, pp. 26–31.

12   Tim Robinson, 'A Suspect Terrane', in *Connemara: The Last Pool of Darkness* (Dublin: Penguin Ireland, 2008).

13   Ibid., p. 13.

14   John Feehan, 'Beyond 2000: The Price and Place of Landscape Heritage in Ireland', Occasional Papers in Irish Science and Technology, 1 (John Jackson Memorial Lecture, Royal Dublin Society, 1995).

15   Environmental Protection Agency, (EPA), *Millenium Report* (Wexford: EPA, 2000).

16   Michael Viney, *A Living Ireland. Ireland's Responsibility to Nature* (Dublin: Comhar, 2003).

17   National Parks and Wildlife Service (NPWS), *The Status of EU Protected Habitats and Species in Ireland* (Dublin: NPWS, 2008).

18   Michael Viney, 'Why ecologists always fall for this wild wedge of coast', *The Irish Times*, 6 November 2010.

19   Ibid.

20   Ibid.

21   Environmental Protection Agency, *Bogland: Sustainable Management of Peatlands in Ireland*, a STRIVE report by UCD (Wexford: EPA, 2011), p. 19.

22   John Feehan, *Farming in Ireland* (Dublin: Faculty of Agriculture, UCD, 2003), Chapter 2.

23   Ibid.

24   Environmental Protection Agency, *Bogland*, p. 31.

25   Ibid.

26   Ibid.

27   John Feehan and Grace O'Donovan, *The Bogs of Ireland: An Introduction to the Natural, Cultural and Industrial Heritage of Irish Peatlands* (Dublin: UCD Press, 1996), p. 477.

28   Environmental Protection Agency, *Bogland.*

29   Ibid

30   Ibid.

31   National Parks and Wildlife Service (NPWS), *The States of EU Protected Habitats and Species in Ireland.*

32   The Countryside Agency, *Landscape Character Assessment Guidance for England and Scotland* (Sheffield: The Countryside Agency, 2002).

33   Northern Ireland Department of the Environment, *Northern Ireland Landscape Character Assessment* (Belfast: Department of the Environment, 2000).

34   Department of the Environment, Heritage and Local Government, *Draft Landscape Character Guidelines, 2000* (Dublin: Department of the Environment, Heritage and Local Government, 2000).

35   For a critique of the guidelines refer to Conor Skehan, 'New Planning Perspectives on the Assessment and Protection of Landscapes', a paper presented to the Irish Planning Institute national conference in 2007.

Chapter 4

1   F.D. Baker, *An Angler's Paradise: Recollections of Twenty Years with Rod and Line in Ireland* (London: Faber & Gwyer, 1929. Republished in 2000 in Flyfisher's Classic Library).

2   John Feehan, John Jackson Inaugural Lecture: Occasional Papers in Irish Science and Technology (Royal Dublin Society, 1995).

3   Michael Viney, 'Introduction', in Robert Lloyd Praeger (1937), *The Way That I Went* (Cork: The Collins Press, 1997), p. iv.

4   Ibid.

5   Ibid., p. 260.

6   www.earlscliffe.com [accessed 25 July 2012].

7   Valerie Pakenham, *The Big House in Ireland* (London: Cassell, 2000).

8   Oliver Rackham, *The History of the Countryside* (London: Phoenix Press, 1986).

9   Shaun Quinn, *Landscape and Tourism, Irish National Landscape Conference Papers* (Kilkenny: Heritage Council, 2006).

10   Tom Kelly, Peter Somerville Large and Seamus Heaney, 'Introduction', in *Ireland: The Living Landscape* (Schull: Roberts Rinehart Publishers, 1992).

11   Roy Foster, *Luck and the Irish. A Brief History of Change from 1970* (Oxford: Oxford University Press, 2008).

12   Michael Starrett, 'Looking After the Landscapes Where We Live Work and Play', in *Landscape Highlights* (Kilkenny: Heritage Council, 2009) pp. 87–89.

13   Paul Clements, *Burren Country* (Cork: The Collins Press, 2011) p. 145.

14   Ibid., p. 110.

15   *The Irish Times*, 13 March 2004.

16   Paul Gray and Geoff Wallis, *The Rough Guide to Ireland* (London: Rough Guides, 2006).

17   Alison Healy, *The Irish Times*, 28 December 2011.

18   John Feehan and Grace O'Donovan, *The Bogs of Ireland: An Introduction to the Natural, Cultural and Industrial Heritage of Irish Peatlands* (Dublin: UCD Press, 1996) p. 479.

19   F.H.A. Aalen, Kevin Whelan and Matthew Stout (eds), *Atlas of the Irish Rural Landscape* (Cork: Cork University Press, 1997), pp. 106–116.

20   John Feehan, *Farming in Ireland* (Dublin: UCD Press, 2003), p. 489.

21   Ibid., p. 238.

22   Justin Gleeson, Rob Kitchen, Brendan Bartley, John Driscoll, Ronan Foley, Stewart Fotheringham and Chris Lloyd, *The Atlas of the Island of Ireland: Mapping Social and Economic Change* (All-Island Research Observatory and International Centre of Local and Regional Development, AIRO Maynooth and ICLRD Armagh, 2008).

23   Ethel Crowley, *Land Matters: Power Struggles in Rural Ireland* (Dublin: The Lilliput Press, 2006), p. 32.

24   Eileen O' Rourke, 'Socio-Economic Interaction and Landscape Dynamics in the Burren, Ireland', *Landscape and Urban Planning*, vol. 70 (2005), pp. 69–83.

25   Conor Skehan, Paper presented to the Burren Law School, Ballyvaughan, May 2004.

26   A.A. Horner, J.A. Walsh and V.P. Harrington, *Population in Ireland: A Census Atlas* (Dublin: UCD Press, 1987).

27   European Environment Agency, *Urban Sprawl in Europe: The Ignored Challenge*, EEA Report No. 10/2006.

28   Fintan O'Toole, *The Irish Times*, 19 June 2007.

29   Department of the Environment, *Irish Bulletin of Vehicle and Driver Statistics, 1995* (Dublin: Department of the Environment, 1996).

30   Department of Transport and the Marine, *Irish Bulletin of Vehicle and Driver Statistics, 2010* (Dublin: Department of Transport and the Marine, 2011).

31   James Wickham, *Gridlock: Dublins Transport Crisis and the Future of the City* (Dublin: TASC/New Island, 2006), p. 66.

32   Ibid., p. 55.

33   Brendan McGrath, 'The Sustainability of a Car-Dependent Settlement Pattern', unpublished Masters thesis, Trinity College Dublin, 1996.

34   European Foundation for the Improvement of Living and Working Conditions (EFIKWC), *The Journey from Home to the Workplace: The Impact on the Safety and Health of Commuters/Workers* (Dublin: EFILWC, 1983).

35   John McGahern, *Memoir* (London: Faber & Faber, 2009).

36   Brendan O'Sullivan, 'Contemporary Change and Planning in the Iveragh Peninsula' in John Crowley and John Sheehan (eds), *The Iveragh Peninsula* (Cork: Cork University Press, 2009), p. 426.

37   Frank McDonald, *The Irish Times*, 12 September 2011.

38   Minutes of Kerry County Council, special meeting, March 2011.

39   Bill McKibben, *The End of Nature* (New York: Random House, 1989).

40   Marek Kohn, *Turned Out Nice: How the British Isles will Change as the World Heats Up* (London: Faber & Faber, 2010).

41   Ibid., p. 268.

42   Ibid., p. 208.

43   Ibid., pp. 283–4.

44   Brian Huntley, Rhys Green, Yvonne Collingham and Stephen G. Wills, *A Climatic Atlas of European Breeding Birds* (Barcelona: Lynx Edicions, 2007).

45   Kohn, *Turned Out Nice*, p. 164.

46   Ibid., p. 11.

47   Ibid. p. 286.

48   Brian Motherway, 'National debate on renewable energy policy urgently needed' *The Irish Times*, 28 August 2011.

Chapter 5

1   Eileen O'Rourke, 'Landscape Planning and Community Participation: Local Lessons from Mullaghmore, the Burren National Park, Ireland, *Landscape Research*, vol. 30, no. 4 (2005), p. 495.

2   Adrian Peace. 'A Sense of Place, A Place of Senses: Land and Landscape in the West of Ireland', *Journal of Anthropological Research*, vol. 61 (2005), pp. 495–512.

3   Ibid.

4   'The Battle for the Gas Fields', June 2009. Television programme for TV3 by Gerry Gregg reviewed by Emmanuel Kehoe in the *Sunday Business Post*, 6 July 2009.

5   Lorna Siggins and Mary Fitzgerald, 'Eco-spy infiltrated Irish protests' in *The Irish Times*, 15 January 2011.

6   Lorna Siggins, *Once Upon a Time in the West: The Corrib Gas Controversy* (London: Transworld Ireland, 2010), and Risteard Ó Domhnaill, 'The Pipe', a documentary film for TG4 in 2010.

7   O'Rourke, 'Landscape Planning and Community Participation'.

8   Ed Vulliamy, 'Shell's Battle for the Heart of Ireland' in the *Observer* magazine, 29 May 2011.

9   Mark Garavan (ed.), *Our Story: The Rossport Five* (Knocknaquirk, Wicklow: Small World Media, 2006).

10   Paul Caprani, pers. com.

11   O'Rourke, 'Landscape Planning and Community Participation'.

12   Ibid., p 494.

13   Ibid., p. 492.

14   Ibid., p. 491.

15   Ibid., p. 491.

16   Jesmond Harding, *Discovering Irish Butterflies and their Habitats* (Privately published, 2008).

17   Simon Bourke, 'Media and Heritage in Ireland: Representations of Heritage in Irish Newspapers and the Praxis of Determination', PhD dissertation, Dublin City University, 2009.

18   Peace, 'A Sense of Place, A Place of Senses'.

19   Ibid.

20   Ibid., p. 495.

21   Lord Killanin and Michael V. Duignan, *The Shell Guide to Ireland* (London: Ebury Press, 1967).

22   Heritage Council, *Valuing Ireland's Heritage* (Kilkenny: Heritage Council, 2007).

23   Bourke, 'Media and Heritage in Ireland'.

24   Press release, Heritage Council, 13 December 2011.

25   Michel Peillon, 'State and Society in the Republic of Ireland: A Comparative Study', *Administration*, vol. 35, no. 2 (1987), pp. 190–212.

26   Peter P. Ekeh, 'Colonialism and the Publics in Africa', *Comparative Studies in Society and History*, vol.171 (1975), pp. 91–112.

27   Derick W. Brinkerhoff and Arthur A. Goldsmith, *Clientelism, Patrimonialism and Democratic Governance: An Overview and Framework for Assessment and Programming* (Washington, DC: U.S. Agency for International Development), Office of Democracy and Governance, DocID/Order No: PN-ACR-426, December 2002. <http://www.dec.org/pdf_docs/PNACR426.pdf

28   O'Rourke, 'Landscape Planning and Community Participation', p. 487.

29   Garret Fitzgerald, 'Ireland's lack of civic morality grounded in our history', *The Irish Times* 9 April, 2011.

30   Lee Komito, 'Irish Clientelism: A Reappraisal', *Economic and Social Review*, vol. 15, no. 3 (April 1984), pp. 173–194.

31   James Wickham, Gridlock: *Dublin's Transport Crisis and the Future of the City* (Dublin: TASC/New Island, 2006), p. 55.

32   Anne Lucey, 'Councillors vent anger at curbs on building', *The Irish Times*, 20 February 2001.

33   Frank Convery, Paper presented at the Burren Law School, Ballyvaughan, May 2004.

34   The Tribunal of Enquiry into Certain Planning Matters and Payments, http://www.planningtribunal.ie. [accessed 25 July 2012].

35   Frank McDonald and James Nix, *Chaos at the Crossroads* (Kinsale: Gandon Books, 2005), pp. 216–17.

36   Philip O'Sullivan and Katherine Shepherd, *Irish Planning Law and Practice* (Hayward Heath: Bloomsbury Professional, 2009).

37   See for instance 'An Taisce labelled secret society by councillor', *The Irish Times*, 17 May 2011.

38   Irish Planning Institute, *A Census of the Planning Profession in Ireland* (Dublin: Irish Planning Institute, 2007). Given the recent history of the development

sector, the 2007 census probably represents a high-water mark of the profession in Ireland, at least in numerical terms.

39 Much of the thinking about professions in this section is based on Donald A. Schön, *The Reflective Practitioner: How professionals Think in Action* (Aldershot: Ashgate Publishing, 1983). Schön describes planning as a 'minor profession' as defined by Nathan Glazer, who distinguishes between the traditional, 'learned professions' (divinity, medicine and the law) and the professions that emerged in the 20th Century, organised on the same lines as the older professions (Nathan Glazer, 'The Schools of the Minor Professions' in Minerva, no. 3 (1974), pp. 346–64).

40 Michael Bannon, *Planning: The Irish Experience 1920–1988* (Dublin: Wolfhound Press, 1989), Chapter 5.

41 Ibid., Chapter 6.

42 Richard Forman, *Urban Regions: Ecology and Planning Beyond the City* (Cambridge: Cambridge University Press, 2008).

43 John O'Connor, speech at the annual conference of the Irish Planning Institute, Galway, 2011.

44 An Taisce, *State of the Nation: A Review of Ireland's Planning System 2000–2011* (Dublin: An Taisce, 2012), p. 22.

45 Gerry Crilly, 'Sustainable planning is cure for growth delusion', *The Irish Times*, 19 July 2010.

46 An Bord Pleanála, *2008 Annual Report* (Dublin: An Bord Pleanála).

47 The Rossport Five are five local landowners jailed for contempt by the High Court in June 2005 for not obeying a court order to stop disrupting the construction of the Shell gas pipeline. See Mark Garavan *et al.*, op.cit.

48 Garavan (ed.), *Our Story*.

Chapter 6

1 T.J. Baker and L.M. O'Brien, 'The Irish Housing System: A Critical Overview', *Broadsheet*, no. 17 (Dublin: Economic Social and Research Institute, 1979).

2 E.E Davis and M. Fine-Davis, 'Predictors of Satisfaction with Housing and Neighbourhood: A Nationwide Survey in the Republic of Ireland', *Social Indicators Research*, no. 9 (1981), pp. 477–94.

3 *The Irish Times*, week beginning Monday 21 June, 2010.

4 Lorna Siggins, *Once Upon a Time in the West: The Corrib Gas Controversy* (London: Transworld Ireland, 2010) pp. 33–4.

5 The report by the inspector, Kevin Moore, is available on An Bord Pleanála's website (www.pleanala.ie) under file reference PL16.126073

6 Editorial and letters in Irish Times, 15th June 2011.

7 The inspector's report and board directions are available on An Bord Pleanála's website (www.pleanala.ie) under file reference PL22. 237958

8   Feasta, Submission to the All Party Oireachtas Committee on the Constitution Concerning Property Rights, 2003.

9   Hugh Brody, *The Other Side of Eden* (London: Faber & Faber, 2001), p. 353.

10   Brian Lalor (ed.), *The Encyclopedia of Ireland* (Dublin: Gill & Macmillan, 2003).

11   Thomas Bartlett, *Ireland: A History* (Cambridge: Cambridge University Press, 2010).

12   Ibid.

13   Ibid., p. 328.

14   Ann and Malcolm MacEwen, *National Parks: Conservation or Cosmetics?* (London: George Allen & Unwin, 1982), p. 278.

15   Alannah Hopkin, *Eating Scenery: West Cork, The People and The Place* (Cork: The Collins Press, 2008), Chapter 5; Frank McDonald and James Nix, *Chaos at the Crossroads* (Dublin: Gandon Books, 2005) Chapter 5.

16   Éamon Galligan, 'Judicial Review of Planning Decisions', Planning law seminar for the Irish Planning Institute, December 2003.

17   Hopkin, *Eating Scenery*.

18   Brendan McGrath, 'Suburban development in Ireland, 1960–80', *Planning Perspectives*, vol. 7 (1992), pp. 27–46.

19   Fintan O'Toole, *Ship of Fools: How Stupidity and Corruption Sank the Celtic Tiger* (London: Faber & Faber, 2010), p. 107.

20   Nicholas Taylor, *The Village in the City* (London: Temple Smith, 1983), p. 206.

21   Eileen O'Rourke, 'Iveragh's Uplands: Farming and Society', in John Crowley and John Sheehan (eds), *The Iveragh Peninsula: A Cultural Atlas of the Ring of Kerry* (Cork: Cork University Press, 2009).

22   John G. O'Dwyer 'Farming on the edge', in *The Irish Times*, 10 October, 2009.

23   Ibid.

Chapter 7

1   Department of the Environment and Local Government, Ghost Estates Survey, 2010 (Dublin: Department of the Environment and Local Government, 2011); Department of the Environment and Local Government, 2006 Census of Population (Dublin: Department of the Environment and Local Government, 2007).

2   Seamus Heaney, 'The Sense of Place' in *Preoccupations: Selected Prose 1968–1978* (London: Faber & Faber, 1980).

3   P.J. Duffy, 'The Changing Rural Landscape 1750–1850: The Pictorial Evidence' in Gillespie Raymond and Brian P. Kennedy (eds), *Ireland: Art into History* (Dublin: Town House, 1994), p. 36.

4   Quoted by Fintan O'Toole, *The Ex-Isle of Erin* (Dublin: New Island Books, 1997), p. 101.

5   Speech in Dáil Éireann, 7 March 1939.

6   Daniel Dixon, Dorothea Lange's Ireland (London: Elliot & Clark, 1996), p. 16.

7   Pádraig Standún, 'The Aran Islands Today: A Personal View' in John Waddell, J.W. O'Connell and Anne Korff (eds), The Book of Aran (Kinvara: Tír Eolas, 1994).

8   John Feehan, Farming in Ireland: History Heritage and Environment (Dublin: UCD Press, 2003), Chapter 5.

9   Kevin Whelan, 'Settlement Patterns in the West of Ireland in the pre-Famine Period' in T. Collins (ed.), Decoding the Landscape (Galway: Social Sciences Research Centre, UCG, 1994).

10 Dominic Stevens, Rural (Leitrim: Mermaid Turbulence, 2007).

11 Central Statistics Office censi of population.

12 David Blayney Brown, Romanticism (London: Phaedon Press, 2001).

13 Mr and Mrs S.C. Hall, Ireland: Its Scenery and Character, (3 vols.) vol. III (London: How & Parsons, 1841), p. 392.

14 John O'Donoghue, Divine Beauty: The Invisible Embrace (London: Bantam, 2003), p. 45.

15 Kieran R. Hickey, 'A Geographical Perspective on the Decline and Extermination of the Irish Wolf Canis Lupis: An Initial Assessment' Irish Geography, vol. 33, no. 2 (2000), pp. 185–98.

16 Roy Foster, Luck and the Irish: A Brief History of Change from 1970 (Oxford: Oxford University Press, 2008), p. 161.

17 Kevin Hourihan, 'Urban Change in the Republic of Ireland' Cities, no. 6, (1989), pp. 209–25.

18 F.H.A. Aalen, 'Public Housing in Ireland 1880–1921', Planning Perspectives vol. 2 (1987), pp. 175–193.

19 Speech to the Conservative Group for Europe in April 1993 quoting George Orwell's essay 'The Lion and the Unicorn'.

20 Brendan McGrath, 'Suburban Development in Ireland, 1960–1980', Planning Perspectives, vol. 7 (1992), pp. 27–46.

21 A.T. Humphreys, New Dubliners. Urbanization and the Irish Family (London: Routledge & Kegan Paul, 1966).

22 Eileen O'Rourke, 'Landscape Planning and Community Participation: Local Lessons from Mullaghmore, The Burren National Park, Ireland', Landscape Research, vol. 30, no. 4 (2005), pp. 483–500.

23 F.H.A. Aalen, 'The Irish Rural Landscape: Synthesis of Habitat and History' in F.H.A. Aalen, Kevin Whelan and Matthew Stout (eds), Atlas of the Irish Rural Landscape (Cork: Cork University Press, 1997), p. 30.

24 Thomas J Whyte, The Story of Woodstock in Inistioge (Dublin: Cappagh Press, 2007).

25 Kilkenny County Council, Woodstock Local Area Plan 2008.

26 Foster, Luck and the Irish, p. 88.

27   Frank McDonald and James Nix, *Chaos at the Crossroads* (Kinsale: Gandon Books, 2005).

28   Fintan O'Toole, *Ship of Fools: How Stupidity and Corruption Sank the Celtic Tiger* (London: Faber & Faber, 2009), Chapter 5.

29   Edwin McGreal, 'Anglo Avenger's Achill Antics' in Mayo News, 29 November 2011.

Chapter 8

1   Paul Clements, *Burren Country* (Cork: Collins, 2011), p. 232.

2   Tim Robinson, 'Introduction' in J.M. Synge, *The Aran Islands* (London: Penguin Books, 1992).

3   The philosophical discussion of beauty and art appreciation in this chapter is primarily based on John Armstrong, *The Secret Power of Beauty: Why Happiness is in the Eye of the Beholder* (London: Allen Lane, 2004).

4   Lady Chatterton, 'Rambles in the South of Ireland during the Year 1838', London, vol. 16 (1839).

5   Armstrong, *The Secret Power of Beauty*.

6   Tim Robinson, *Stones of Aran: Labyrinth* (Dublin: Lilliput Press, 1995), p. 122.

7   Alice Roberts, *Evolution: The Human Story* (London: Dorling Kindersley, 2011).

8   Ibid., p. 140.

9   Edward O. Wilson, *Biophilia* (Cambridge, MA: Harvard University Press, 1984), p. 112.

10   John Feehan, 'Urban Nature and Human Nature', Paper presented at 'Natura 2000 and Biodiversity in the City' conference organised by the Urban Institute Ireland in Loughlinstown Dublin on 12 September, 2002.

11   Judith H. Heerwagen and Gordon H. Orians, 'Humans, Habitats and Aesthetics' in Stephen R. Kellert and Edward O. Wilson (eds), *The Biophilia Hypothesis* (Washington: Island Press, 1993), pp. 138–172.

12   Ibid., p.150.

13   Ibid.

14   F.H.A Aalen, Kevin Whelan and Matthew Stout (eds), *Atlas of the Irish Rural Landscape* (Cork University Press, 1997), p. 202.

15   Heerwagen and Orians, 'Humans, Habitats and Aesthetics', pp. 153–5.

16   Ibid., p. 155.

17   Simon Carswell, *Anglo Republic: Inside the bank that broke Ireland* (Dublin: Penguin Ireland, 2011), p. 85.

18   Ibid.

19   Ian Russell,'Romantic notions simplify the debate', *The Irish Times*, 28 July 2007.

20   Meath County Council. Manager's Report of submissions re Tara-Skyrne Landscape Conservation Area, . http:/www.meath.ie/LocalAuthorities/Planning/TaraSkryne LandscapeProject [accessed on 25 July 2012].

21   Area 16 on the 1994 Bord Failte map is labelled 'Glenties'. Given its location and relative scenic character, I am assuming that this is a mistake and the identified scenic area refers to the Lough Eske area, north of Donegal town.

Chapter 9

1   Roy Foster, *Luck and the Irish: A Brief History of Change from 1970* (Oxford: Oxford University Press, 2008), p. 30.

2   Department of Communications, Marine and Natural Resources, *Health Effects of Electromagnetic Fields* (Dublin: Department of Communications, Marine and Natural Rescources, 2007).

3   Radiological Protection Institute of Ireland and Health Service Executive, *Radon Gas in Ireland* (Dublin: Radiological Protection Institute of Ireland and HSE, 2010).

4   Inge Buckley, 'Wind Energy in Ireland: The Present Situation', in Richard Douthwaite (ed.), *Before the Wells Run Dry: Ireland's Transition to Renewable Energy* (Dublin: Feasta, 2003)

5   www.IWEA.com [accessed 25 July 2012].

6   Richard Barker, 'Coming Down from the Mountains, Landscape Challenges Arising from Recent Trends in Wind Farm Development', paper presented to wind energy conference of the Sustainable Energy Authority of Ireland, September, 2011.

7   Aengus Parsons, Jackie Hunt and Brendan McGrath, *Review of the Implications for Heritage of the Expansion of the Wind Energy Industry in Ireland*, report for the Heritage Council (Kilkenny: Heritage Council, 2002).

8   Tim Robinson, *Connemara: Listening to the Wind* (Dublin: Penguin Ireland, 2006), p. 128.

9   Frank Mitchell and Michael Ryan, *Reading the Irish Landscape* (Dublin: Town House, 2007), p. 355.

10   Department of the Environment and Local Government, *Wind Energy Guidelines for Planning Authorities*, (Dublin: Department of the Environment and Local Government, 1996).

11   Mayo County Council, *County Development Plan, 2003*, Landscape Sensitivity Matrix in Appendix X.

12   Cork, Donegal, Galway, Kerry and Mayo County Councils have current development plans that were adopted in 2009. The Clare plan was adopted in 2011.

13   Paul Clements, *Burren Country* (Cork: The Collins Press, 2011), p. 90.

14   Galway County Council, *SEA for Draft County Galway Wind Energy Strategy, 2011*, p. 10.

15   Galway County Development Plan (2009–2015), Mayo County Development Plan (2008–2014) and Donegal County Development Plan (2006–2112), The Galway Wind Energy Strategy 2012.

16   Sylvia White, 'Towers multiply and environment is gone with the wind' (from the *Los Angeles Times*), quoted by Robert Righter in Martin J Pasqualetti, Paul Gipe and Robert W Righter (eds.), *Wind Power in View: Energy Landscapes in a Crowded World* (San Diego: Academic Press, 2002), p. 20.

17   Gordon G. Brittan Jr., 'The Wind in One's Sails; A Philosophy', in Martin J Pasqualetti, Paul Gipe and Robert W Righter (eds), *Wind Power in View: Energy Landscapes in a Crowded World* (San Diego: Academic Press, 2002), p. 20.

18   Western Development Commission (WDC), *To Catch the Wind. The Potential for Community Ownership of Wind Farms in Ireland* (Ballaghaderreen, Co. Roscommon: WDC, 2004).

19   Ibid.

20   Frode Birk Nielsen, 'A Formula for Success in Denmark', in Martin J Pasqualetti, Paul Gipe and Robert W Righter (eds), *Wind Power in View: Energy Landscapes in a Crowded World* (San Diego: Academic Press, 2002).

21   Ibid., p. 26.

22   Wikipedia, www.en.wikipedia.org/wiki/Astronaut on 22 August 2012.

23   James Lovelock, *Gaia: A New Look at Life on Earth*, (Oxford: Oxford University Press, 1979).

24   Michael Viney 'Wind turbines, rural Ireland and my backyard', *The Irish Times*, 28 June 2011.

25   Paul Selman, 'What Do We Mean by Sustainable Landscape?' *Sustainability: Practice and Policy*, vol. 4, no.2 (Fall/Winter 2008), pp. 23–8.

26   Environmental Protection Agency (EPA), *Bogland: Sustainable Management of Peatlands in Ireland*, a STRIVE report by UCD (Wexford: EPA, 2011), p. 44.

27   Ibid.

28   Michael Viney, *A Living Island. Ireland's Responsibility to Nature* (Dublin: Comhar, 2003).

29   The Board's decision can be viewed on An Bord Pleanála's website (www.pleanala.ie) under file reference PL 07.238734.

30   Mayo County Council, Renewable Energy Strategy for County Mayo 2011–2020

31   Robert Lloyd Praeger, *The Way That I Went* (Cork: The Collins Press, 1997 edition), p. 206.

32   Quoted by Edward Dowden, *The Life of Percy Bysshe Shelley, 7th Impression* (London: Routledge and Kegan Paul, 1951) p. 192.

Chapter 10

1   *Irish Times* Magazine, 17 February 2001.

2   Gordon Deegan, 'Lecturer warns of collapse of Irish Agriculture', *The Irish Times* 4 May 2004.

3   Martin Mansergh, 'What ordinary people want still counts for something', *The Irish Times*, 13 March 2004.

4   Gerry Sheeran, letter to *The Irish Times*, 9 March 2010.

5   Ibid.

6   Roy Foster, *Luck and the Irish: A Brief History of Change from 1970* (Oxford: Oxford University Press, 2008), p. 26.

7   John Cleland, 'Rural Planning Policy in Northern Ireland', paper presented at the Irish Planning Institute national conference in 2001.

8   An Taisce, *State of the Nation: A Review of Ireland's Planning System 2000–2011* (Dublin: An Taisce, 2012), p. 36.

9   James Killen, 'Communications' in FHA. Aalen, Kevin Whelan and Matthew Stout. (eds), *Atlas of the Irish Rural Landscape, First Edition* (Cork: Cork University Press, 1997).

10 Fintan O'Toole, *Ship of Fools: How Stupidity and Corruption Sank the Irish Tiger* (London: Faber & Faber, 2010), Chapter 5.

11 Conor Skehan, 'New Planning Perspectives on the Assessment and Protection of Landscapes', *Pleanáil*, vol. 16 (2002), p. 42.

12 Cork County Council, *Cork Rural Design Guide, 2003*.

13 Gordon Deegan, 'Planners vie with Taliban for Notoriety', *Clare Champion*, 20 December, 2002.

14 Fergal McCabe, 'How We Wrecked Rural Ireland in the Latter Part of the 20th Century', *Pleanáil*, vol. 15 (2001), p. 64.

15 Jack Fitzsimons, *Bungalow Bashing* (Meath: Kells Publishing, 1990), p. 161.

16 Irish Rural Dwellers Association (IRDA), *Positive Planning for Rural Houses* (IRDA, 2004).

17 Ethel Crowley, *Land Matters. Power Struggles in Rural Ireland* (Dublin: The Lilliput Press, 2006), pp. 154–5.

18 Pete McCarthy, *McCarthy's Bar: A Journey of Discovery in Ireland* (London: Hodder & Stoughton, 2000).

19 Tim Robinson, *Connemara, A Little Gaelic Kingdom* (Dublin: Penguin Ireland, 2011), pp. 310–14.

20 Ibid., p. 311.

21 Ibid., p. 311.

22 Michael Healy-Rae, 'Democracy in Planning' in Irish Rural Dwellers Association, *Positive Planning for Rural Houses*, p. 30.

23 Government of Ireland, *Sustainable Development: A Strategy for Ireland* (Dublin: Government Publications, 1997), p. 151.

24 Martin Mansergh, in *The Irish Times*, 13 March 2004.

25 Ibid.

26 Royal Institute of Architects of Ireland, Submission to Joint Oireachtas Committee on rural housing, 2003.

27 Irish Rural Dwellers Association, 'Introduction', in *Positive Planning for Rural Houses*.

28   Nuala O'Faolain, 'Another Fine Mess', *Irish Times* Magazine, 12 May 2001.

29   Mid-West Regional Authority, *Mid-West Regional Guidelines 2010–2020* (Nenagh: Mid-West Regional Authority, 2010) p. 72.

30   Ibid., p. 27.

31   Clare County Council, *Clare County Development Plan, 1988*, p. 14.

32   Clare County Council, *Ennis and Environs Development Plan, 2008*, p. 28.

33   Donegal County Council, *Donegal County Development Plan, 2000*.

34   Donegal County Council, *Buncrana and Environs Development Plan, 2007.*

35   Robert Jennings and Stephaney Bissett, *A Study of New House Purchasers* (Dublin: Environmental Research Unit, 1989).

36   EPA, *Sustainable Rural Development: Managing Housing in the Countryside*, Mark Scott (ed.), STRIVE report 44 by UCD for the EPA (Wexford: EPA, 2010).

37   Jennings and Bissett, *A Study of New House Purchasers*, p. 112.

38   Craig Bullock, 'Economic and Social Cost of Rural Housing', in EPA, *Sustainable Rural Development: Managing Housing in the Countryside*, op.cit., Chapter 11, p. 32.

39   James Nix, 'Smarter Communities', paper presented by James Nix of the Irish Environmental Network to the Irish Planning Institute, 2010.

40   Bullock, 'Economic and Social cost of Rural Housing'.

41   An Taisce, *State of the Nation*, p. 26.

42   Adrian Phillips, *Management Guidelines for IUCN Category V Protected Areas* (Gland, Switzerland: IUCN, 2002).

Chapter 11

1   Terry O'Regan, *A Guide to Undertaking a Landscape Circle Study in Seven Easy Steps* (Dublin: Landscape Alliance, 2008).

2   Ibid., p.18.

3   Conor Newman, 'Landscapes 'Я' Us', Proceedings of the Irish National Landscape Conference 2009 (Kilkenny: Heritage Council), pp. 8–14.

4   Lewis Mumford, *The Culture of Cities* (New York: Harcourt Brace Jovanovich, 1970), p. 386.

5   Liam Lysaght, 'The Burren. The Case for a Different Kind of National Park', *Heritage Outlook* (Summer/Autumn 2005), pp. 8–12.

6   Ibid.

7   Ibid.

8   Burren LIFE was the first major farming for conservation project in Ireland. Running from 2004 to 2009 the project was a partnership of the National Parks and Wildlife Service (NPWS), Teagasc and Burren IFA with the financial support of the EU LIFE Nature fund.

9   Brendan Dunford, pers.com.

10   Michael Starrett, 'The Burren: A New Dawn?', *Burren Insight*, no. 3 (2011), p. 4.

11   Paul Clements, *Burren Country* (Cork: The Collins Press, 2011), pp. 234–6.

12   The United Nations Educational Scientific and Cultural Organisation is a specialised agency of the UN, responsible for international collaboration in the fields of education, science and culture. The UNESCO programme to protect world cultural and natural heritage sites started in 1972.

13   The commentary on Southern Oland is based on a presentation by Susanne Forslund, Kalmar County Administrative Board to the Burren Spring Conference 'The Burren: What is to be Done?' Ballyvaughan, 2011.

14   Jan Turtinen, 'Världsarvets villkor: Intressen, forhandlingar och bruk i internationell politik', doctoral thesis in Faculty of Humanities (Stockholm University, 2006), p. 189.

15   Anne and Malcolm MacEwen, National Parks: Conservation or Cosmetics? (London: George Allen & Unwin, 1982), p. 261.

16   In 2006, 9,000 people lived in the Clifden Rural Area as defined by the Central Statistics Office. This area is somewhat smaller (790 square kilometres) than the barony of Ballynahinch.

17   Loch Lomond and the Trossachs National Park Authority, *Annual Report and Accounts 2008–2009.*

18   Adrian Phillips, *Management Guidelines for IUCN Category V Protected Areas* (Gland, Switzerland: IUCN, 2002), p. 9.

19   Ibid.

20   Fáilte Ireland, *Feasibility Study to Identify Scenic Lands in Ireland*, report by MosArt (Dublin: Fáilte Ireland, 2007).

21   A. Runte, *National Parks, The American Experiment* (Lincoln, NE: University of Nebraska Press, 1979).

22   Ibid.

23   Ruth McAreavey, *Towards a Mourne National Park: Emergent Prospects and Pitfalls from Articulating Needs in a Local Context*, ISEP Working Paper 2 (Belfast: Queens University, 2002).

24   MacEwen and MacEwen, *National Parks: Conservation or Cosmetics?* (London: George Allen & Unwin, 1982), pp. 249–50.

25   Fingal County Council, Howth Special Amenity Area Order (1999).

26   The Bray Head SAAO reports are available on An Bord Pleanála's website (www.pleanala.ie) under file reference SX2001.

27   Department of the Environment, Heritage and Local Government (DEHLG), *The Monastic City of Clonmacnoise and its Cultural Landscape. Management Plan 2009–2014*, (Dublin: DEHLG, 2009).

28   Finian Coghlan, 'IFA protest potential UNESCO restrictions' in Athlone Advertiser, 31 July 2009

29   McAreavey, *Towards a Mourne National Park.*

30   Reported by Frank McDonald, in 'Rural housing advocate advises tourists to go to Scotland', in *The Irish Times*, 13 March 2004.

31   Fintan O'Toole, *Black Hole Green Card: The Disappearance of Ireland* (Dublin: New Ireland Books, 1994).

32   Fintan O'Toole, 'State needs to clean up its act' in *The Irish Times*, 19 June 2007.

33   Heritage Council, *Proposals for Ireland's Landscapes* (Kilkenny: Heritage Council, 2010).

34   Michel Peillon, 'State and Society in the Republic of Ireland: A Comparative Study', *Administration* (1987).

35   Jim Kelly of National Parks and Wildlife Service, presentation to Irish Planning Institute Autumn Conference, November 2009.

36   Gordon Deegan, 'Lecture warns of collapse of Irish Agriculture', a report of Conor Skehan's lecture at the Burren Law School, *The Irish Times*, 2 May 2004.

37   Irish Uplands Council, *Challenges, Changes and Opportunities in Irish Uplands*, Research project by Zena Hoctor for the Irish Uplands Council, 2009.

38   Pers. Comm., 2011.

39   Michael Viney, 'People in their Place', in *Burren Insight*, no. 3 (2011), pp. 4–5.

40   Starrett, 'The Burren: A New Dawn?'

41   Eileen O'Rourke, 'Landscape Planning and Community Participation: Local Lessons from Mullaghmore, the Burren National Park, Ireland', *Landscape Research*, vol. 30, no. 4 (2005), p. 496.

42   Han Lorzing, *The Nature of Landscape: A Personal Quest* (Rotterdam: 010 Publishers, 2001).

43   Ibid.

44   Ibid., p. 169.

45   Environmental Protection Agency, *Bogland: Sustainable Management of Peatlands in Ireland*. a STRIVE report by UCD for the EPA (Wexford: EPA, 2011).

46   Quoted in David Hickie, *Native Trees and Forests of Ireland* (Dublin: Gill & Macmillan, 2002).

47   Gordon Cherry, *National Parks and Recreation in the Countryside* (London: HMSO, 1975) cited in MacEwen and MacEwen, National Parks: Conservation or Cosmetics?, p. 7.

INDEX

Note: illustrations are indicated by page numbers in bold.